Himouto (干物妹)

A lazy little sister who never lifts a finger around the house.
"At home, Umaru is a himouto."
Origin: a portmanteau of imouto (little sister) and himono (a woman who is elegant and polished in public, but secretly a slob at home).

From Shueisha's *Imouto Dictionary.*

201
No Soliciting

HIMOUTO! UMARU-CHAN 1

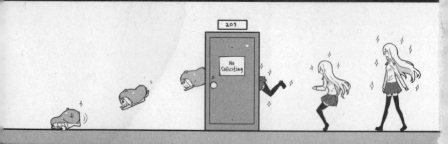

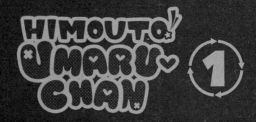

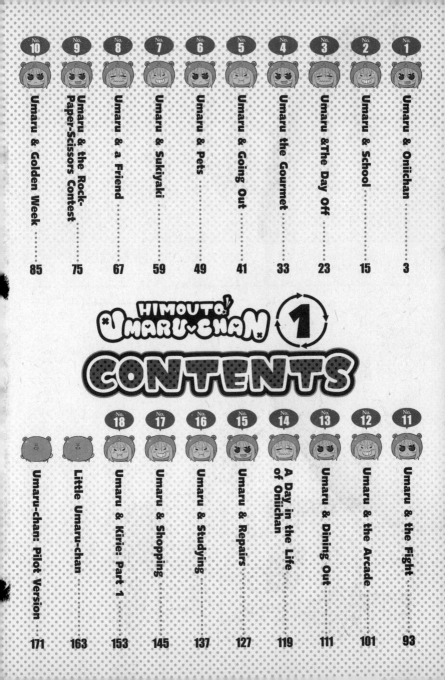

HIMOUTO! UMARU-CHAN ① CONTENTS

No. 1 Umaru & Oniichan

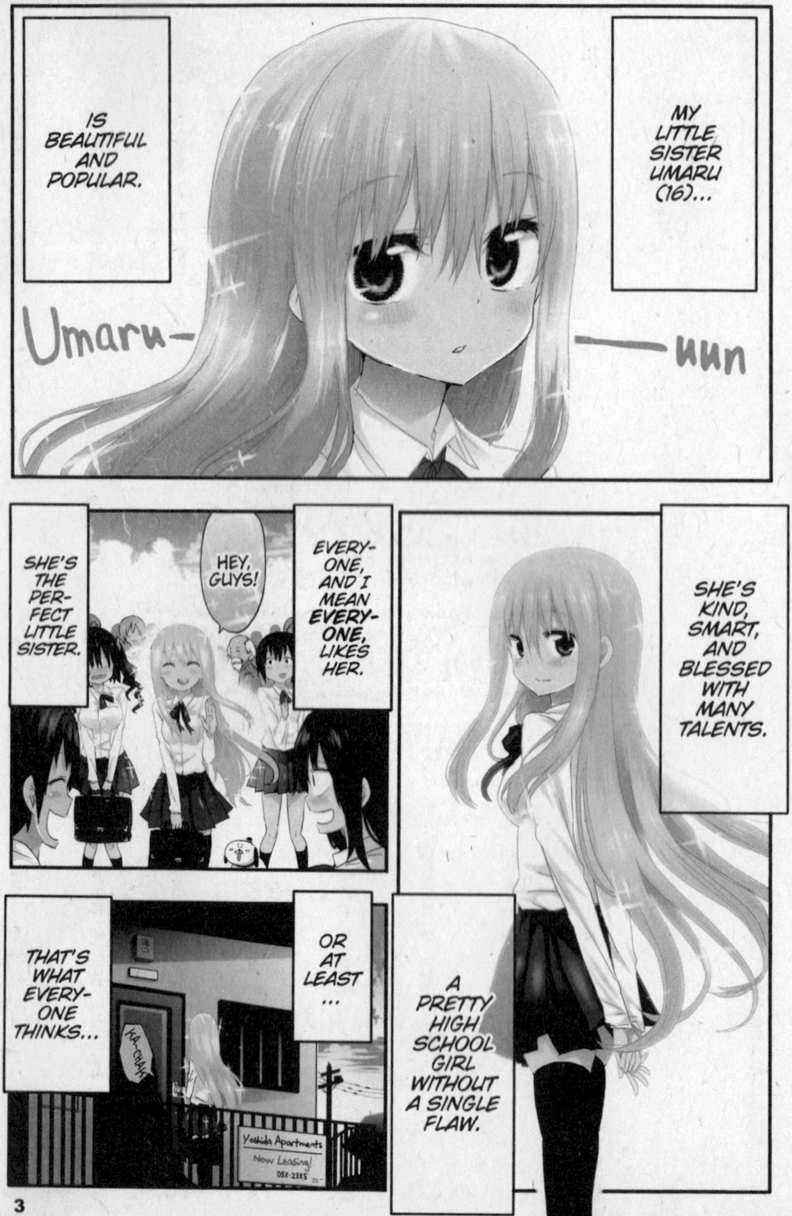
MY LITTLE SISTER UMARU (16)...
IS BEAUTIFUL AND POPULAR.
Umaru- —uun
SHE'S KIND, SMART, AND BLESSED WITH MANY TALENTS.
A PRETTY HIGH SCHOOL GIRL WITHOUT A SINGLE FLAW.
EVERY-ONE, AND I MEAN EVERY-ONE, LIKES HER.
HEY, GUYS!
SHE'S THE PER-FECT LITTLE SISTER.
OR AT LEAST...
THAT'S WHAT EVERY-ONE THINKS...
KA-CHAK
Yoshida Apartments
Now Leasing!
05X-23X5

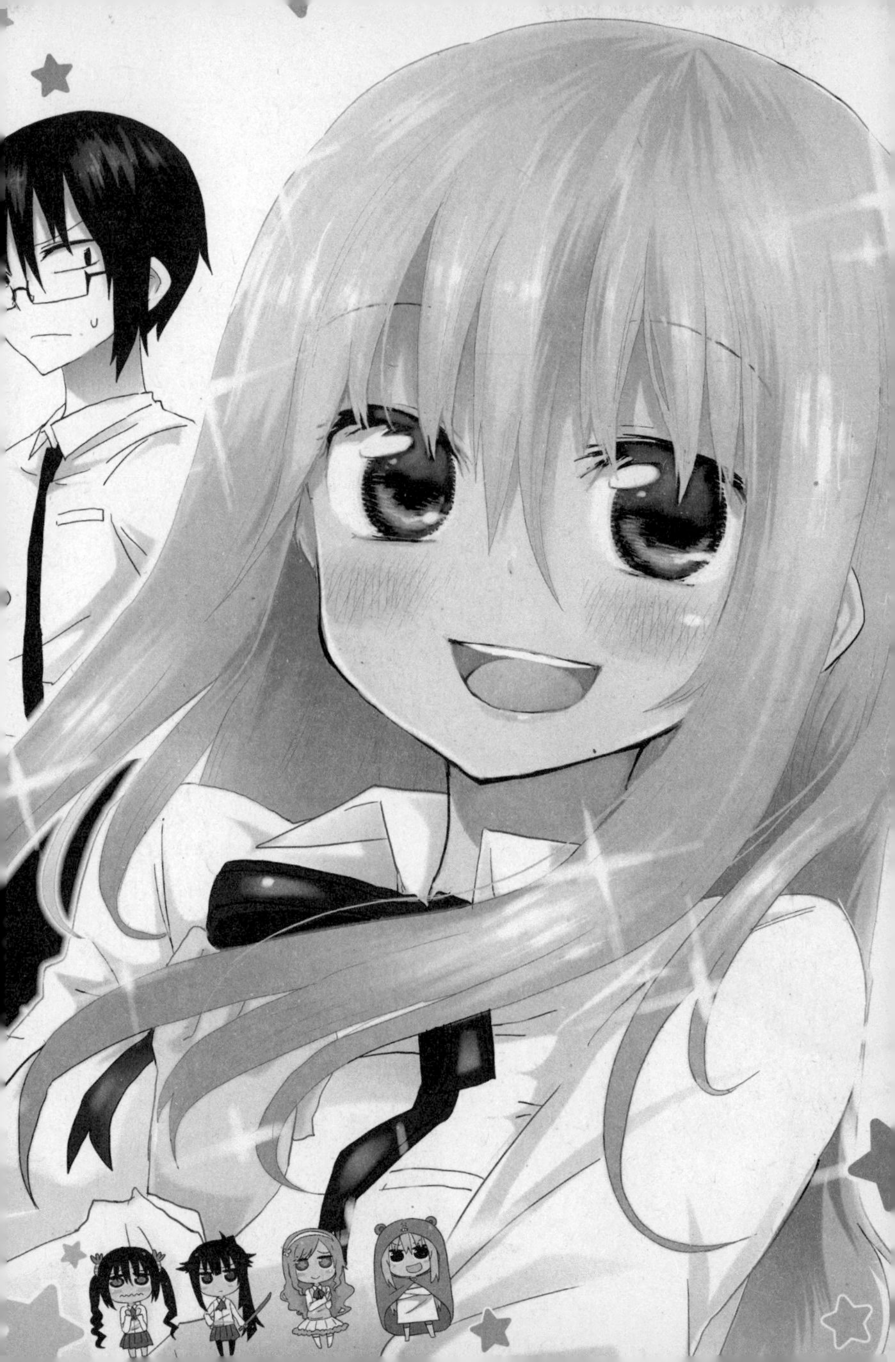

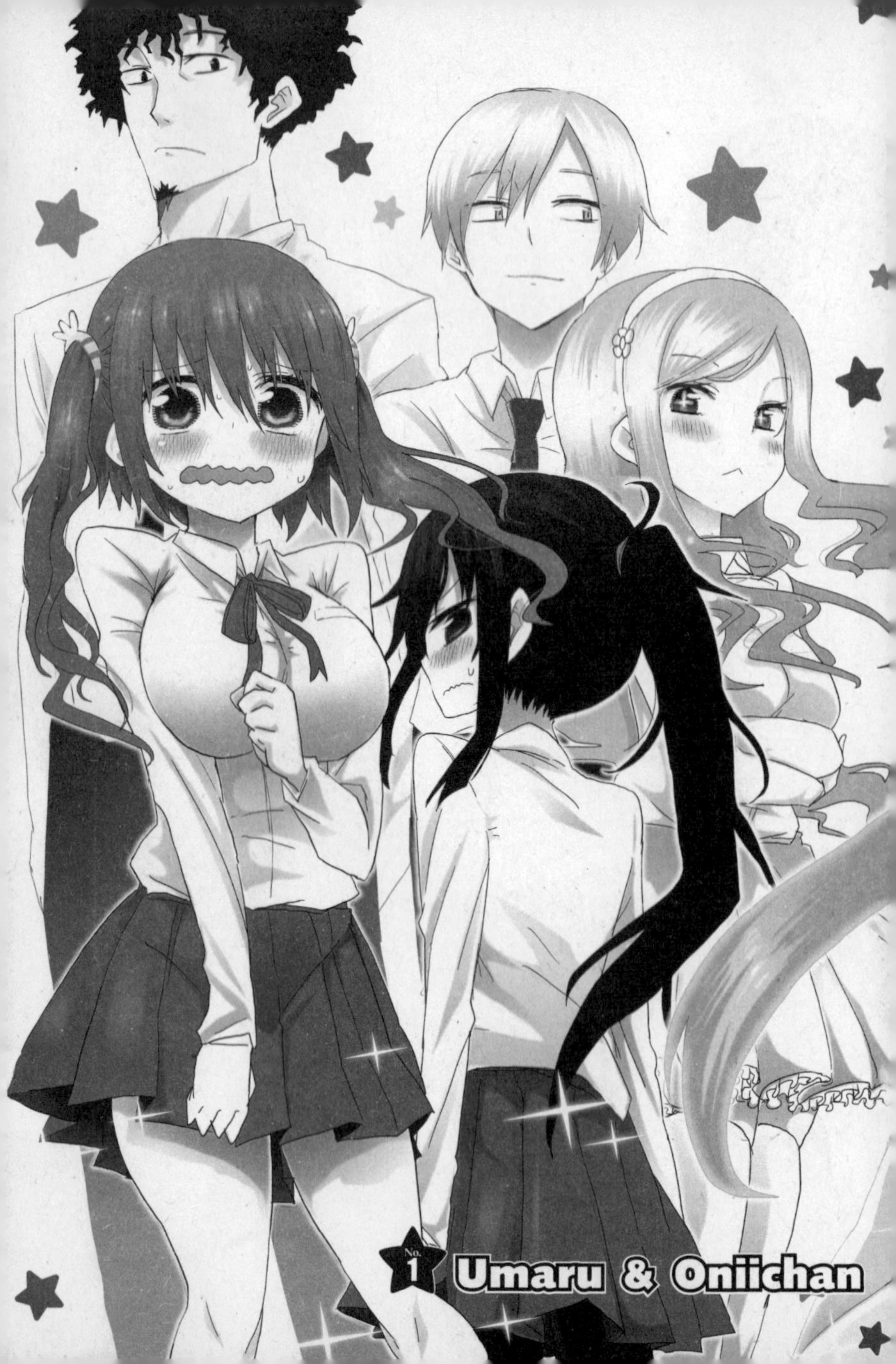
No. 1 Umaru & Oniichan

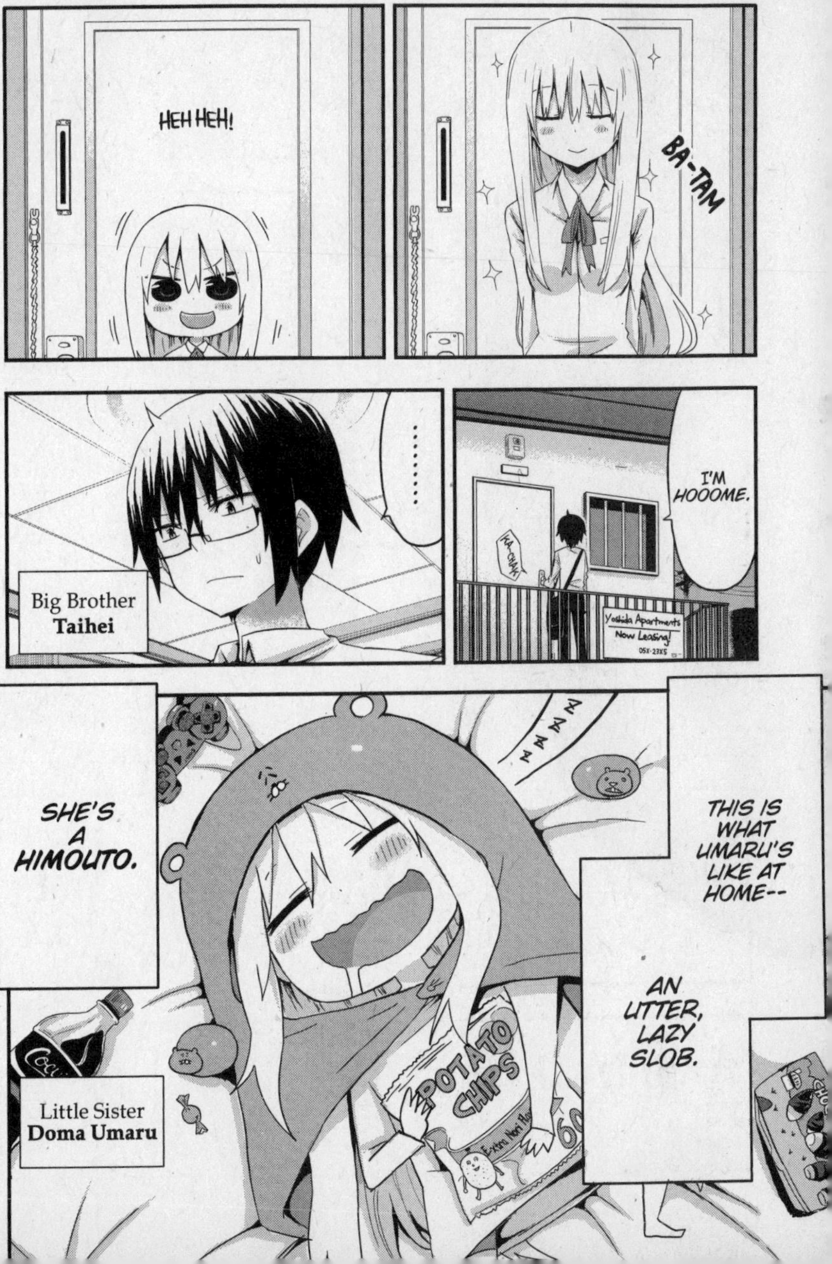

BA-TAM
HEH HEH!
I'M HOOOME.
KA-CHAK
Yoshida Apartments
Now Leasing!
......
Big Brother
Taihei
THIS IS WHAT UMARU'S LIKE AT HOME--
AN UTTER, LAZY SLOB.
SHE'S A HIMOUTO.
ZZZZ
POTATO CHIPS
Little Sister
Doma Umaru

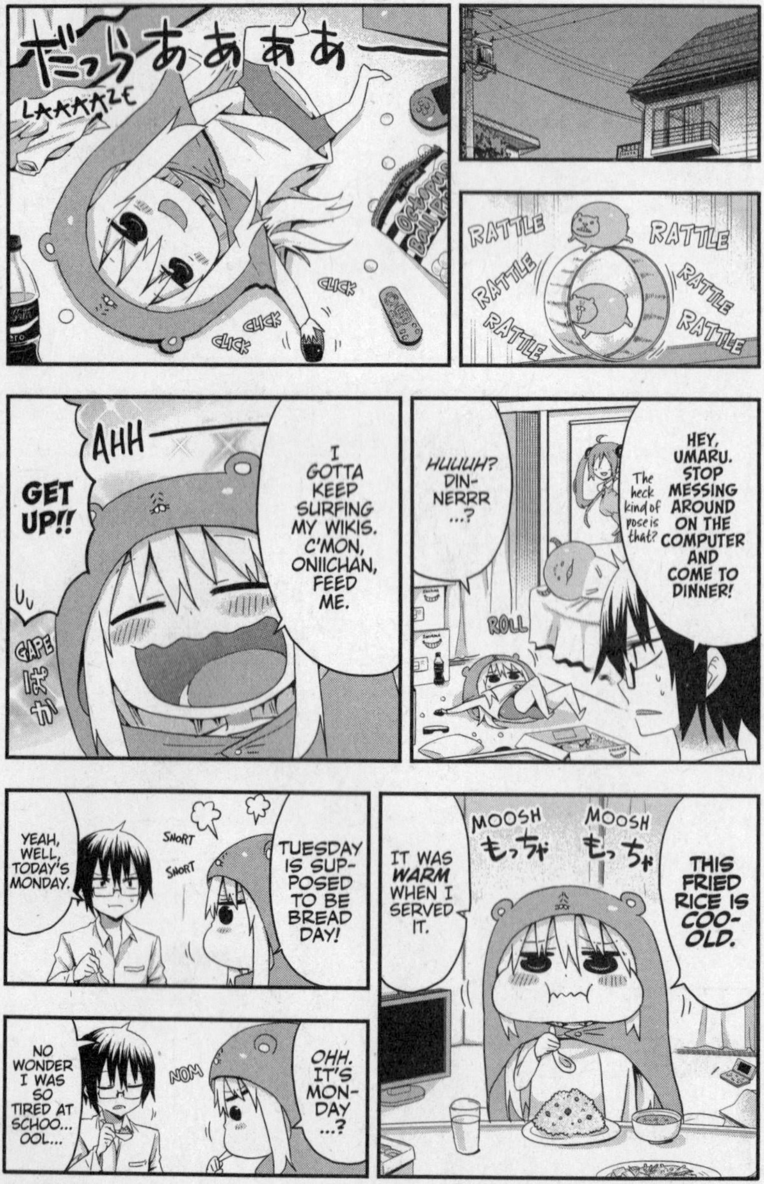
RATTLE RATTLE RATTLE RATTLE RATTLE RATTLE
だっらああああ
LAAAAZE
CLICK CLICK CLICK
HEY, UMARU. STOP MESSING AROUND ON THE COMPUTER AND COME TO DINNER!
The heck kind of pose is that?
HUUUH? DIN-NERRR ...?
ROLL
AHH
GET UP!!
I GOTTA KEEP SURFING MY WIKIS. C'MON, ONIICHAN, FEED ME.
Uu
GAPE
ぱか
THIS FRIED RICE IS COO-OLD.
MOOSH もっちゃ
MOOSH もっちゃ
IT WAS WARM WHEN I SERVED IT.
TUESDAY IS SUP-POSED TO BE BREAD DAY!
SNORT
SNORT
YEAH, WELL, TODAY'S MONDAY.
OHH. IT'S MON-DAY ...?
NOM
NO WONDER I WAS SO TIRED AT SCHOO... OOL...

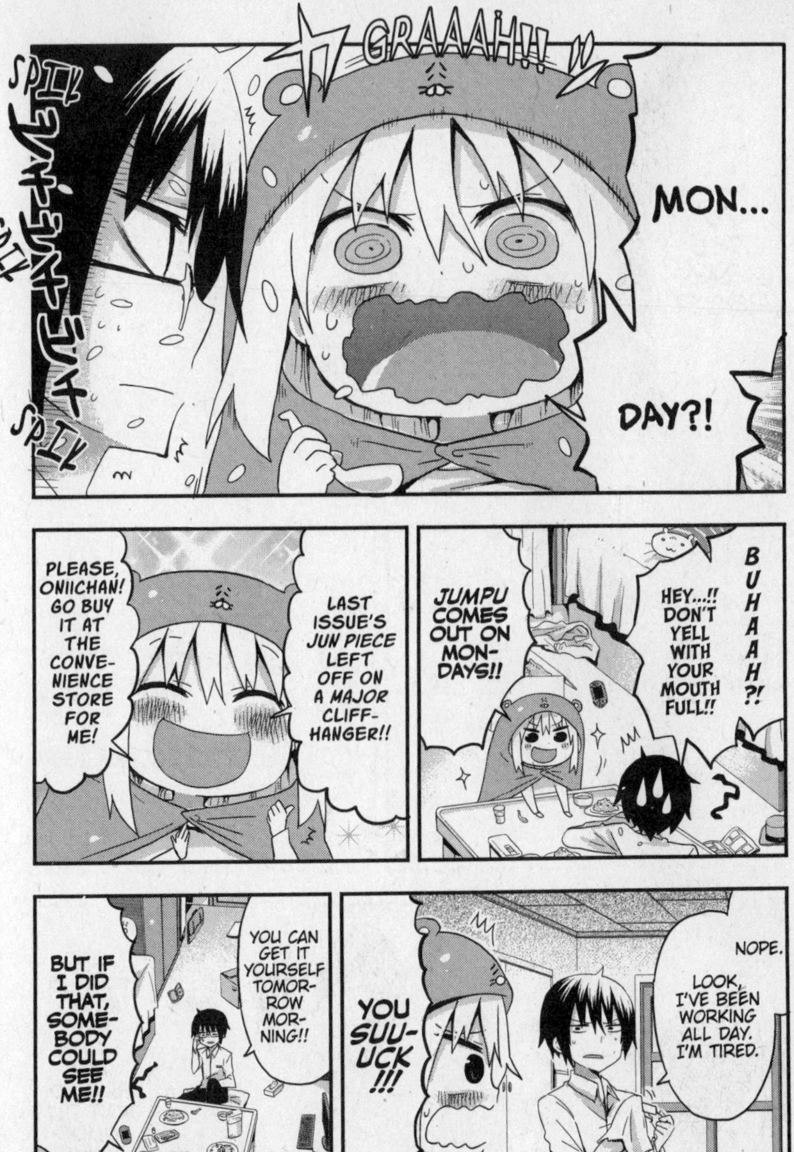
GRAAAH!!!
MON...
DAY?!
SPIT
SPIT
SPIT
BUHAAAH?!
HEY...!! DON'T YELL WITH YOUR MOUTH FULL!!
JUMPU COMES OUT ON MONDAYS!!
LAST ISSUE'S JUN PIECE LEFT OFF ON A MAJOR CLIFFHANGER!!
PLEASE, ONIICHAN! GO BUY IT AT THE CONVENIENCE STORE FOR ME!
NOPE.
LOOK, I'VE BEEN WORKING ALL DAY. I'M TIRED.
YOU SUUUCK!!!
YOU CAN GET IT YOURSELF TOMORROW MORNING!!
BUT IF I DID THAT, SOMEBODY COULD SEE ME!!

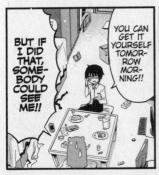

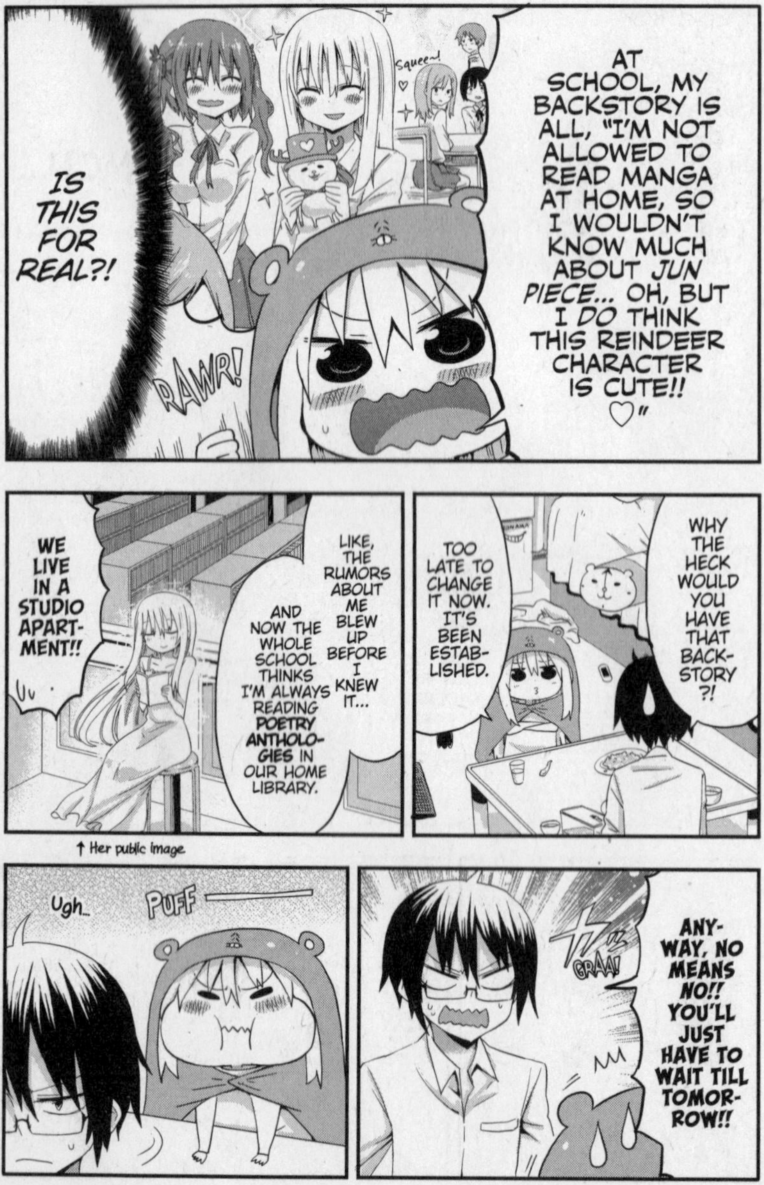
AT SCHOOL, MY BACKSTORY IS ALL, "I'M NOT ALLOWED TO READ MANGA AT HOME, SO I WOULDN'T KNOW MUCH ABOUT *JUN PIECE*... OH, BUT I *DO* THINK THIS REINDEER CHARACTER IS CUTE!! ♡"
Squee~!
IS THIS FOR REAL?!
RAWR!
WHY THE HECK WOULD YOU HAVE THAT BACK-STORY?!
TOO LATE TO CHANGE IT NOW. IT'S BEEN ESTAB-LISHED.
LIKE, THE RUMORS ABOUT ME BLEW UP BEFORE I KNEW IT...
AND NOW THE WHOLE SCHOOL THINKS I'M ALWAYS READING **POETRY ANTHOLOGIES** IN OUR HOME LIBRARY.
WE LIVE IN A STUDIO APART-MENT!!
Uu
↑ Her public image
ANY-WAY, NO MEANS *NO!!* YOU'LL JUST HAVE TO WAIT TILL TOMOR-ROW!!
GRAA!
PUFF
Ugh..

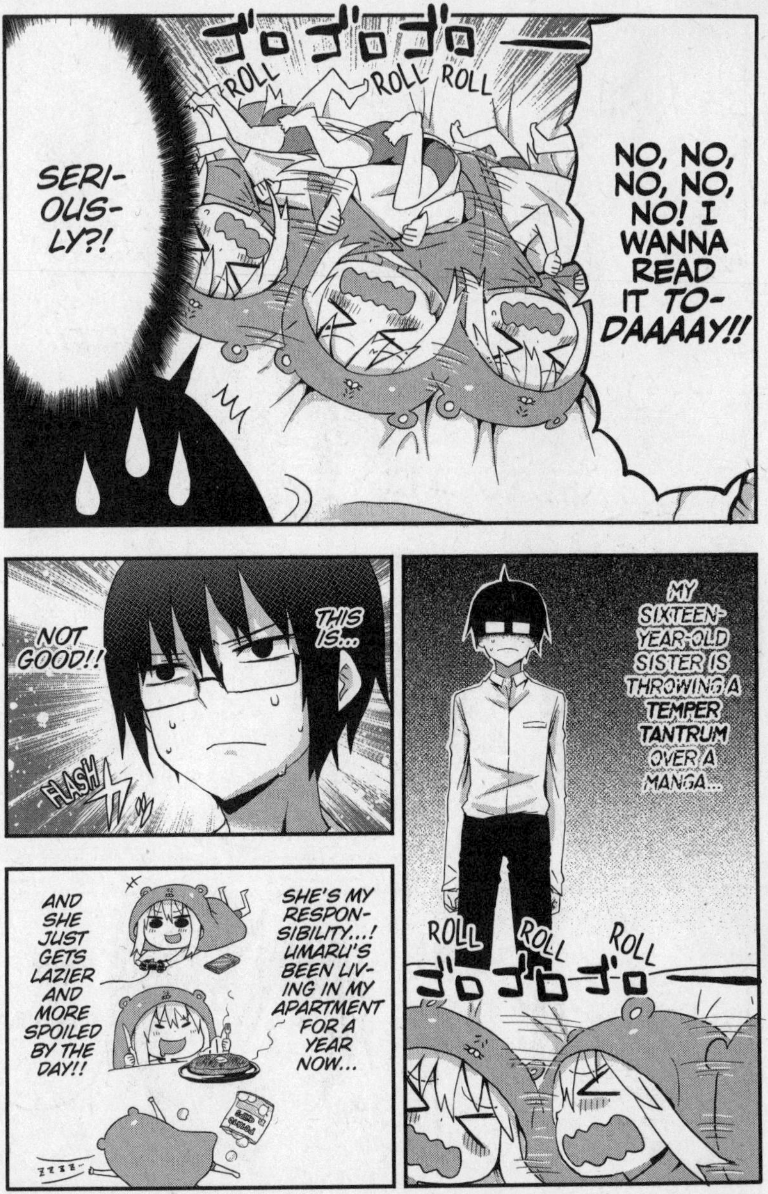
ゴロゴロゴロ
ROLL ROLL ROLL
NO, NO, NO, NO, NO! I WANNA READ IT *TO-DAAAAY!!*
SERI-OUSLY?!
MY SIXTEEN-YEAR-OLD SISTER IS THROWING A **TEMPER TANTRUM** OVER A MANGA...
ROLL ROLL ROLL
ゴロゴロゴロ
THIS IS...
NOT GOOD!!
FLASH
SHE'S MY RESPONSIBILITY...! UMARU'S BEEN LIVING IN MY APARTMENT FOR A YEAR NOW...
AND SHE JUST GETS LAZIER AND MORE SPOILED BY THE DAY!!

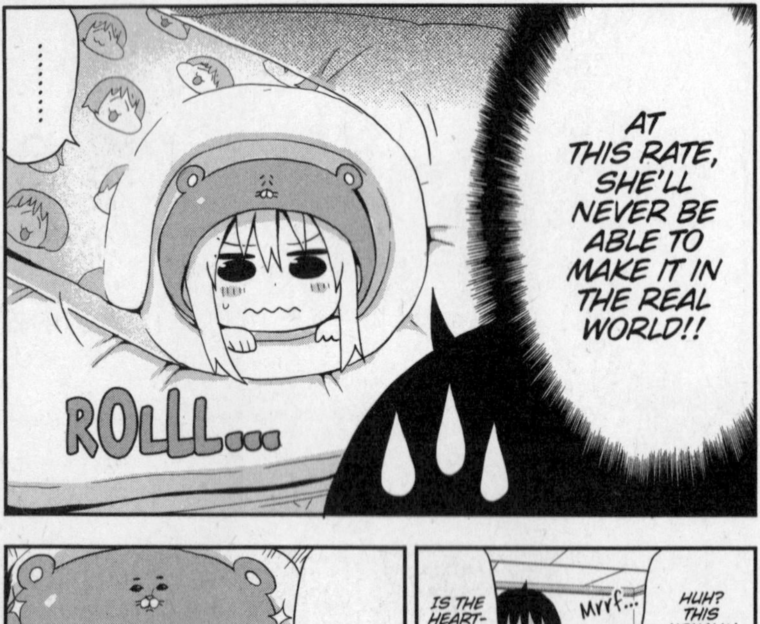
AT THIS RATE, SHE'LL NEVER BE ABLE TO MAKE IT IN THE REAL WORLD!!
......
ROLLL...
HUH? THIS USUALLY MAKES HIM FOLD FASTER THAN SUPER-MAN ON LAUNDRY DAY...
Mrrf...
IS THE HEART-BROKEN BABY SISTER ACT LOSING ITS PUNCH?
PLEASE, ONIICHAN? ♡
SHWIP

Outside Face

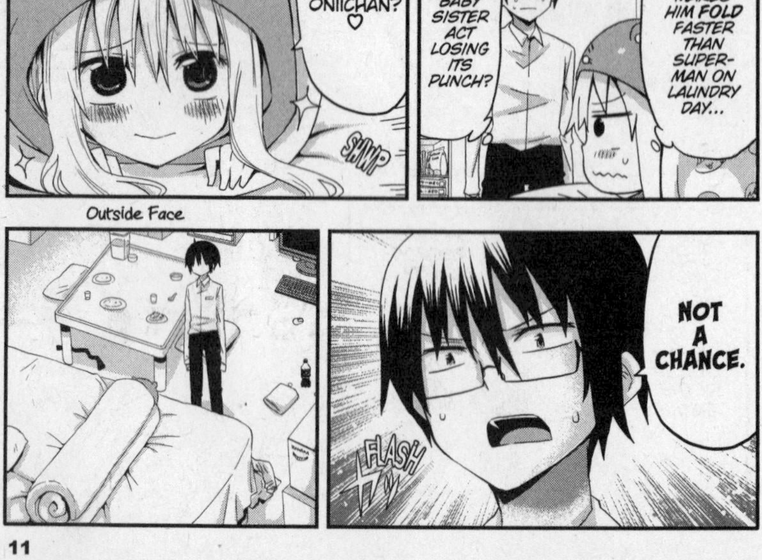
NOT A CHANCE.
FLASH

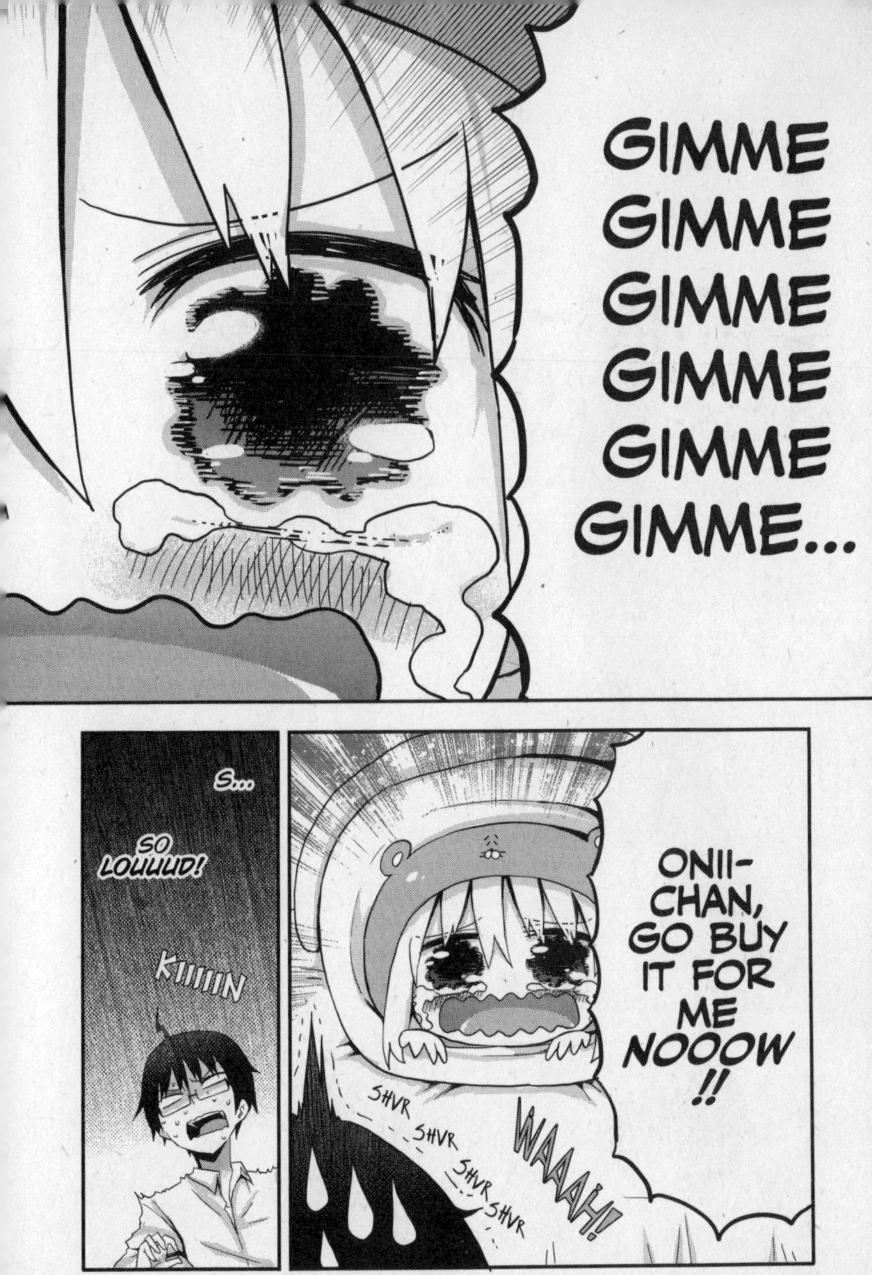
GIMME GIMME GIMME GIMME GIMME GIMME...
ONII-CHAN, GO BUY IT FOR ME NOOOW!!
WAAAH!
SHVR SHVR SHVR SHVR
S...
SO LOUUUD!
KIIIIIN

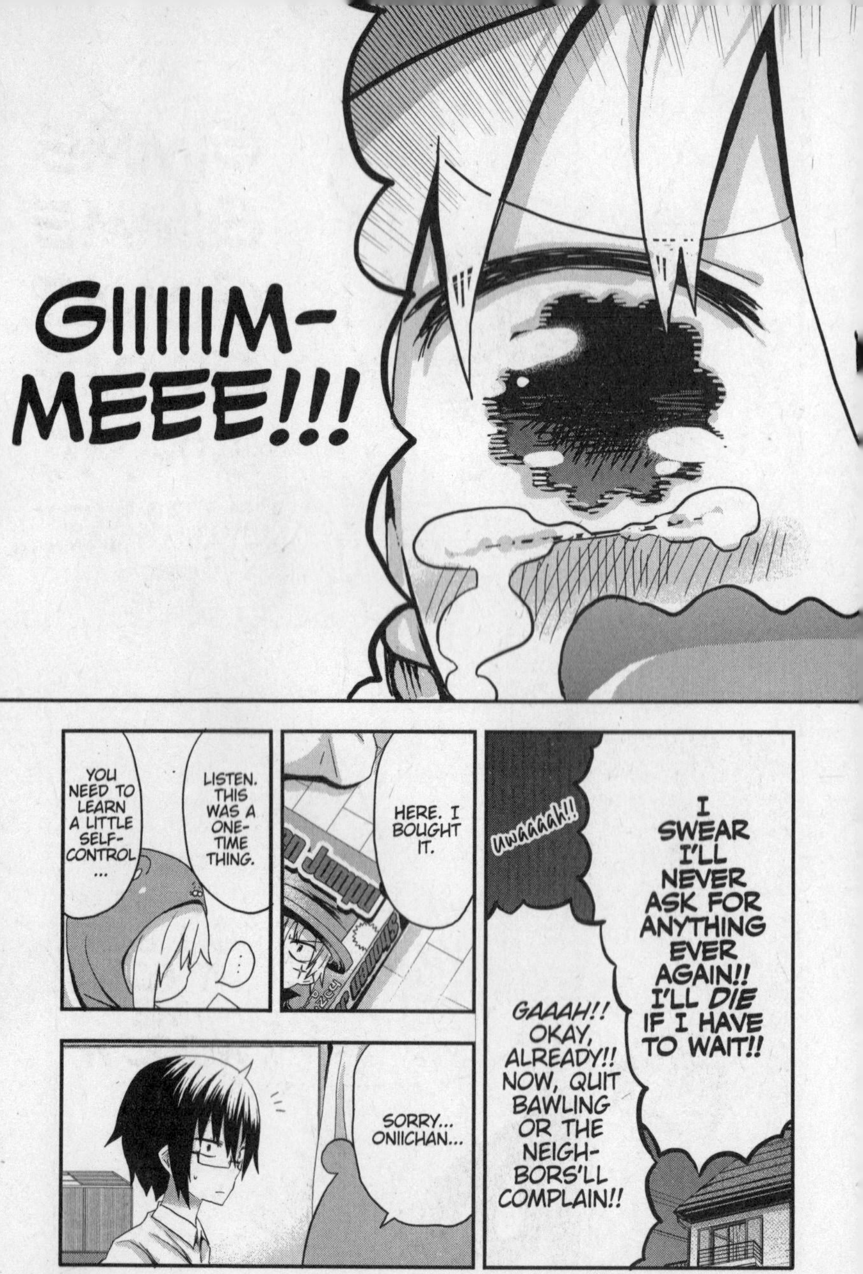
GIIIIIM-MEEE!!!
I SWEAR I'LL NEVER ASK FOR ANYTHING EVER AGAIN!! I'LL *DIE* IF I HAVE TO WAIT!!
Uwaaaaah!!
GAAAH!! OKAY, *ALREADY!!* NOW, QUIT BAWLING OR THE NEIGH-BORS'LL COMPLAIN!!
HERE. I BOUGHT IT.
LISTEN. THIS WAS A ONE-TIME THING.
YOU NEED TO LEARN A LITTLE SELF-CONTROL...
...
SORRY... ONIICHAN...

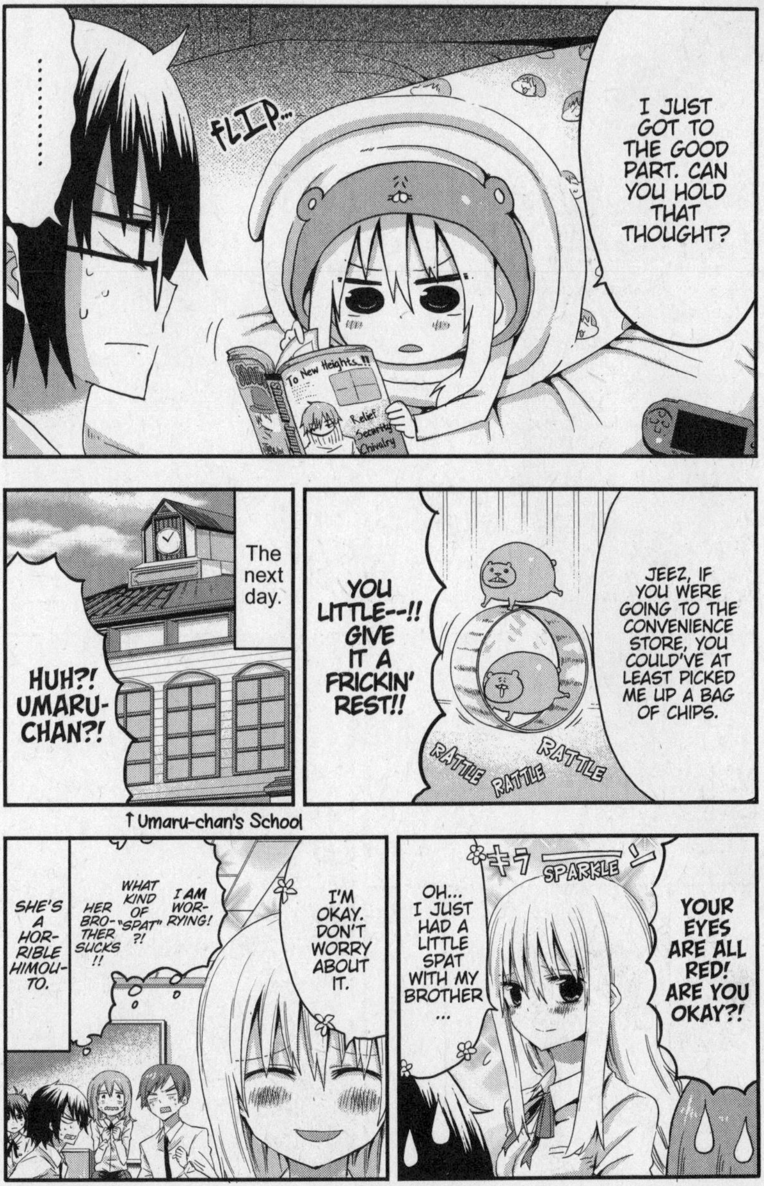
I JUST GOT TO THE GOOD PART. CAN YOU HOLD THAT THOUGHT?
FLIP...
To New Heights!!
Relief Security Chivalry
......
JEEZ, IF YOU WERE GOING TO THE CONVENIENCE STORE, YOU COULD'VE AT LEAST PICKED ME UP A BAG OF CHIPS.
RATTLE RATTLE RATTLE
YOU LITTLE--!! GIVE IT A FRICKIN' REST!!
The next day.
HUH?! UMARU-CHAN?!
↑Umaru-chan's School
キラーン SPARKLE
YOUR EYES ARE ALL RED! ARE YOU OKAY?!
OH... I JUST HAD A LITTLE SPAT WITH MY BROTHER ...
I'M OKAY. DON'T WORRY ABOUT IT.
I AM WORRYING!
WHAT KIND OF "SPAT"?!
HER BROTHER SUCKS!!
SHE'S A HORRIBLE HIMOUTO.

No. 2 Umaru & School

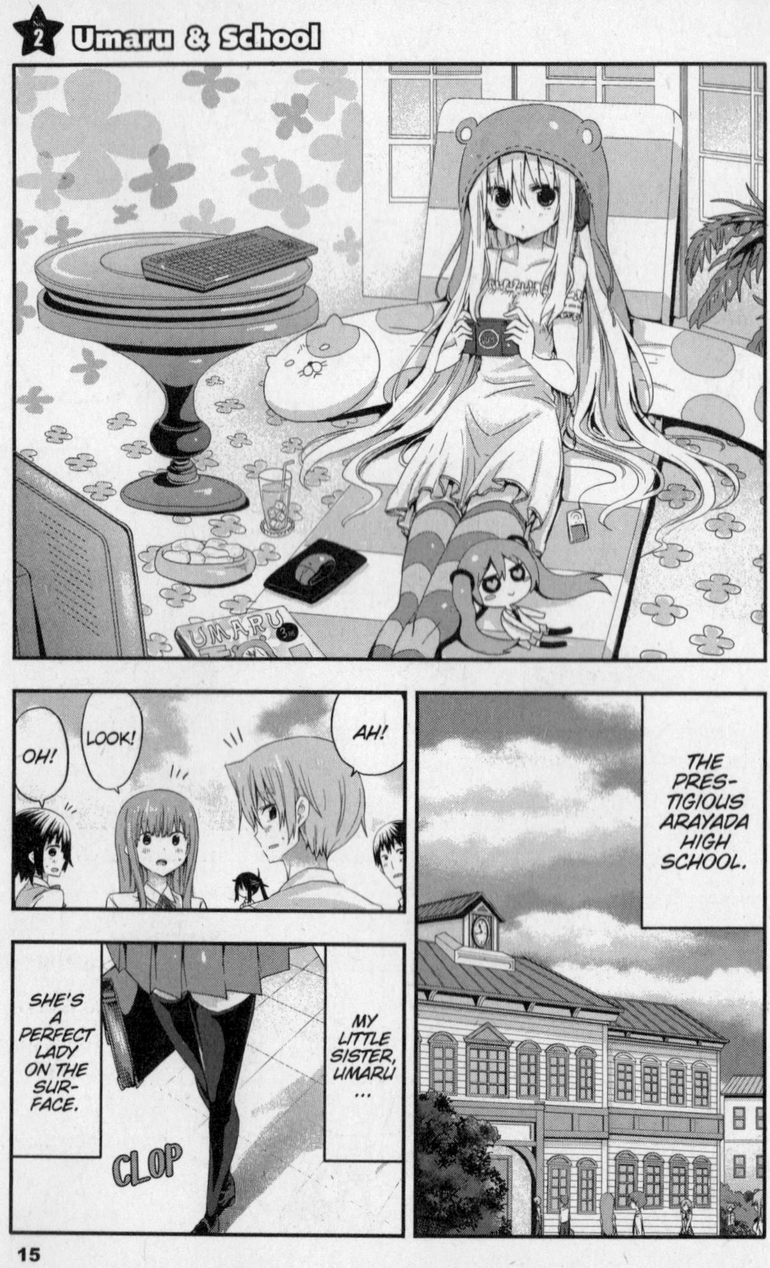
UMARU
THE PRESTIGIOUS ARAYADA HIGH SCHOOL.
AH!
LOOK!
OH!
MY LITTLE SISTER, UMARU ...
SHE'S A PERFECT LADY ON THE SURFACE.
CLOP

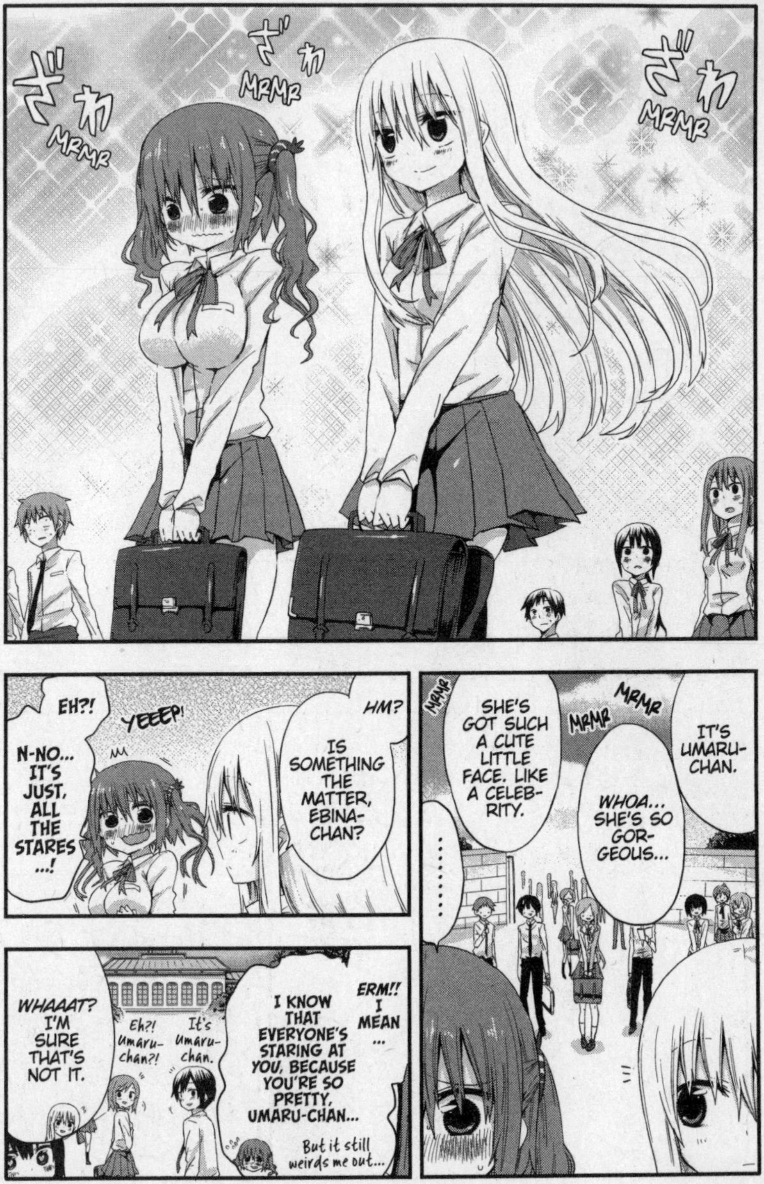
ざわ
MRMR
ざわ
MRMR
ざわ
MRMR
IT'S UMARU-CHAN.
MRMR
WHOA... SHE'S SO GORGEOUS...
MRMR
SHE'S GOT SUCH A CUTE LITTLE FACE. LIKE A CELEBRITY.
MRMR
......
HM?
IS SOMETHING THE MATTER, EBINA-CHAN?
YEEEP!
EH?!
N-NO... IT'S JUST, ALL THE STARES ...!
ERM!! I MEAN ...
I KNOW THAT EVERYONE'S STARING AT YOU, BECAUSE YOU'RE SO PRETTY, UMARU-CHAN...
But it still weirds me out...
It's Umaru-chan.
Eh?! Umaru-chan?!
WHAAAT? I'M SURE THAT'S NOT IT.

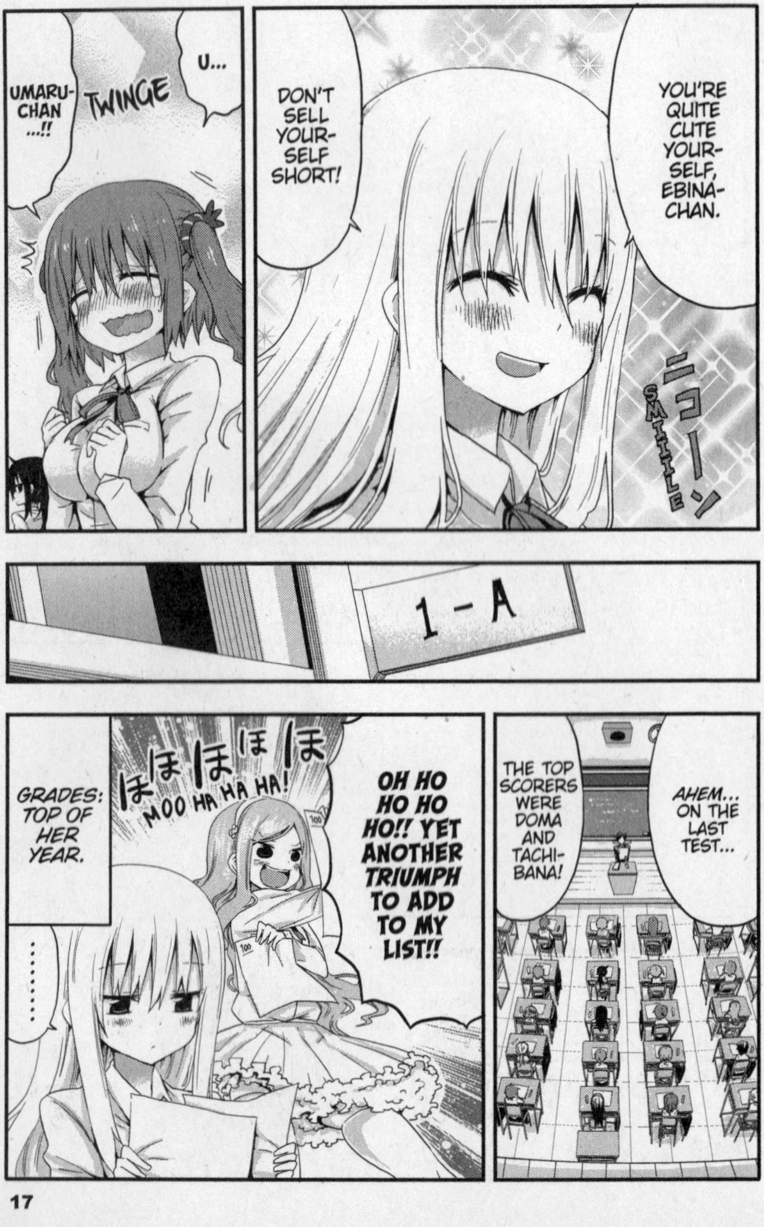
YOU'RE QUITE CUTE YOURSELF, EBINA-CHAN.
DON'T SELL YOURSELF SHORT!
ニコーッ
SMIIIILE
U...
TWINGE
UMARU-CHAN ...!!
1 - A
AHEM... ON THE LAST TEST...
THE TOP SCORERS WERE DOMA AND TACHIBANA!
ほほほほほ
MOO HA HA HA!
OH HO HO HO HO!! YET ANOTHER TRIUMPH TO ADD TO MY LIST!!
GRADES: TOP OF HER YEAR.
......

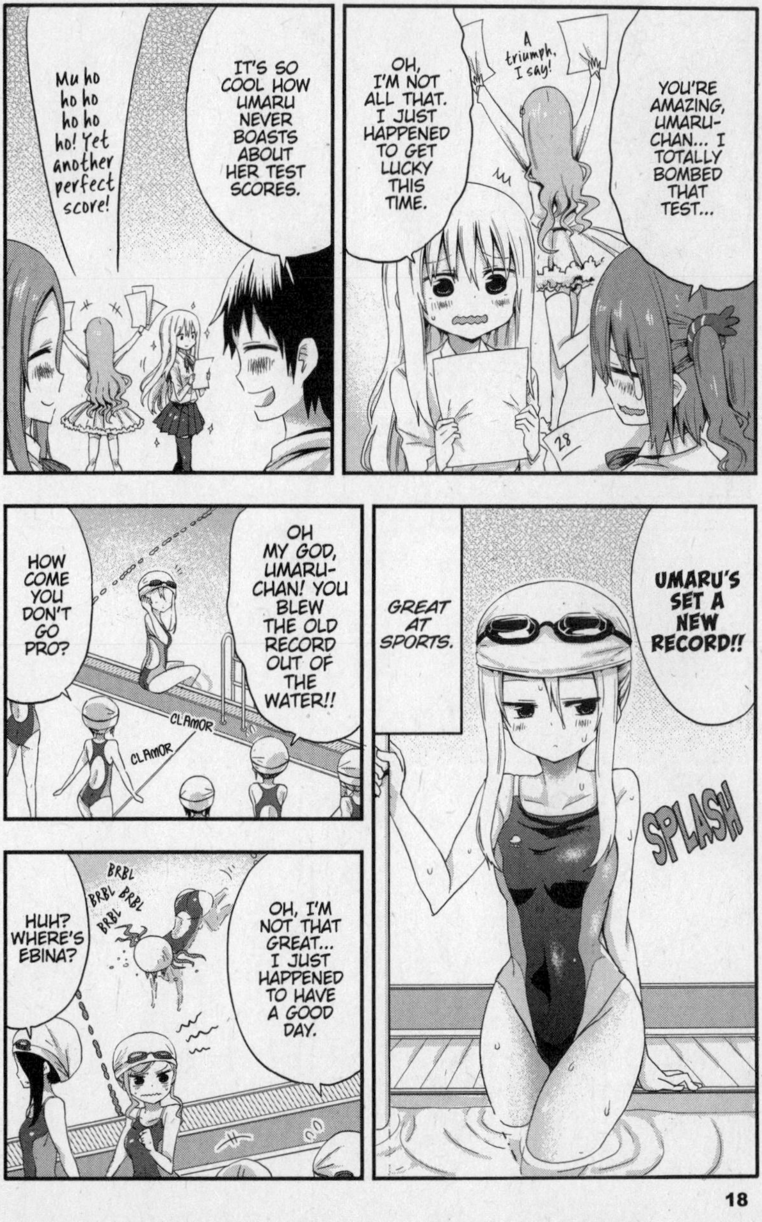

YOU'RE AMAZING, UMARU-CHAN... I TOTALLY BOMBED THAT TEST...
A triumph, I say!
OH, I'M NOT ALL THAT. I JUST HAPPENED TO GET LUCKY THIS TIME.
28
IT'S SO COOL HOW UMARU NEVER BOASTS ABOUT HER TEST SCORES.
Mu ho ho ho ho ho ho! Yet another perfect score!
UMARU'S SET A NEW RECORD!!
GREAT AT SPORTS.
SPLASH
OH MY GOD, UMARU-CHAN! YOU BLEW THE OLD RECORD OUT OF THE WATER!!
HOW COME YOU DON'T GO PRO?
CLAMOR
CLAMOR
OH, I'M NOT THAT GREAT... I JUST HAPPENED TO HAVE A GOOD DAY.
BRBL
BRBL BRBL
BRBL
HUH? WHERE'S EBINA?

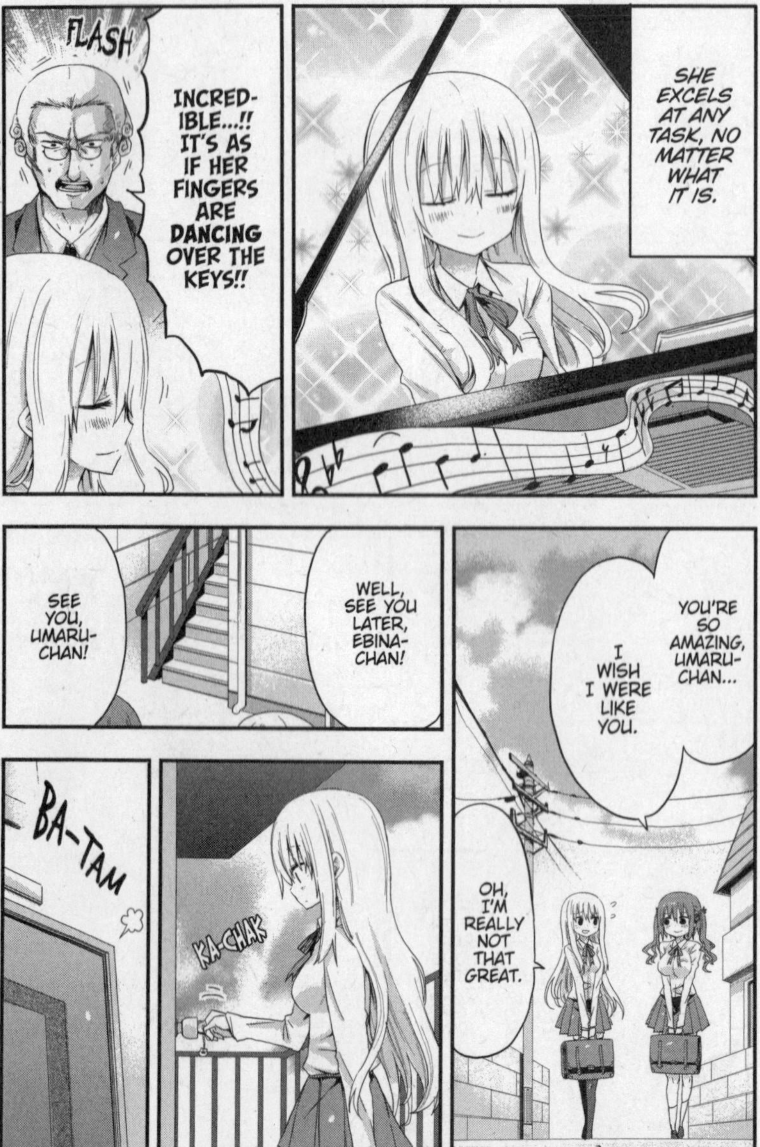
SHE EXCELS AT ANY TASK, NO MATTER WHAT IT IS.
FLASH
INCREDIBLE...!! IT'S AS IF HER FINGERS ARE DANCING OVER THE KEYS!!
Music Teacher
YOU'RE SO AMAZING, UMARU-CHAN...
I WISH I WERE LIKE YOU.
OH, I'M REALLY NOT THAT GREAT.
WELL, SEE YOU LATER, EBINA-CHAN!
SEE YOU, UMARU-CHAN!
KA-CHAK
BA-TAM

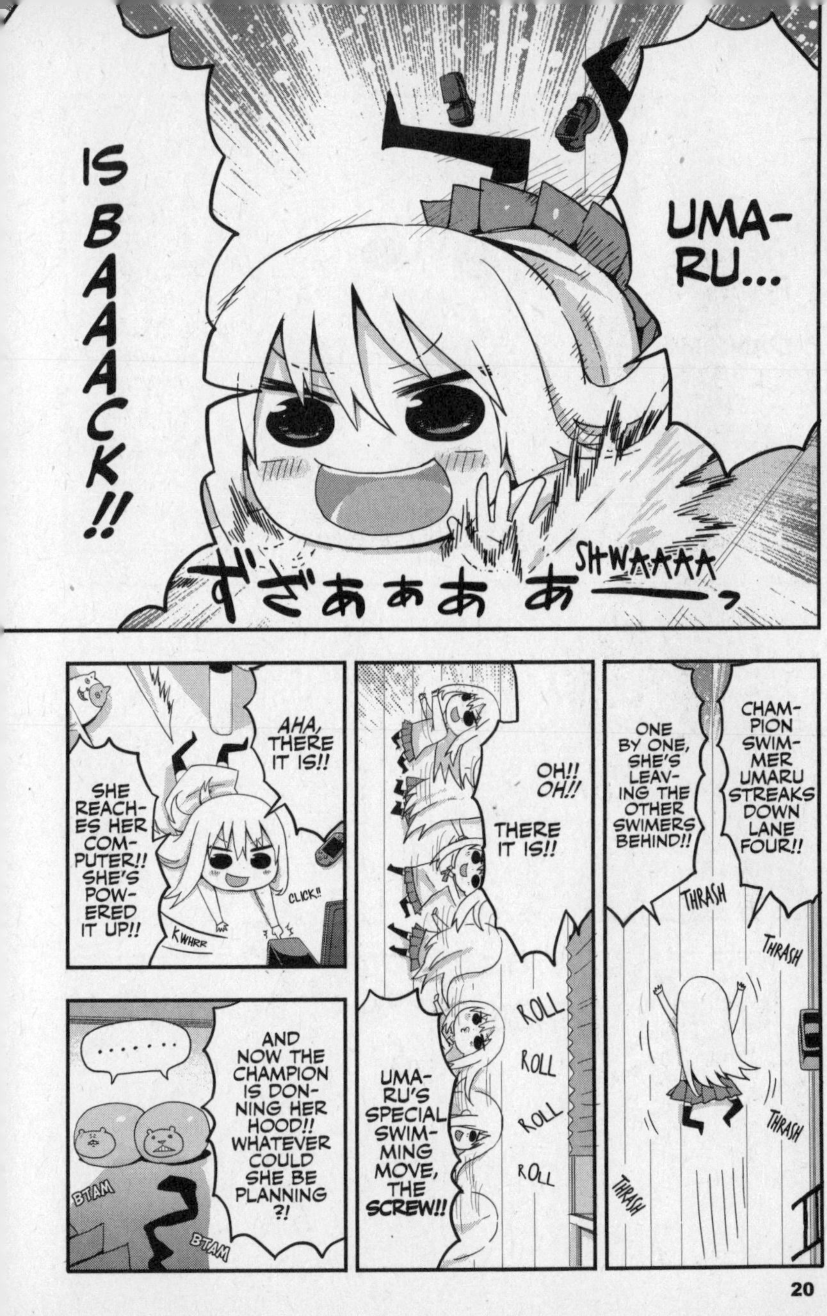
UMA-RU...
IS BAAAACK!!
ずざあああああーっ
SHWAAAA
CHAMPION SWIMMER UMARU STREAKS DOWN LANE FOUR!!
ONE BY ONE, SHE'S LEAVING THE OTHER SWIMERS BEHIND!!
THRASH
THRASH
THRASH
THRASH
OH!! OH!!
THERE IT IS!!
ROLL
ROLL
ROLL
ROLL
UMA-RU'S SPECIAL SWIMMING MOVE, THE SCREW!!
AHA, THERE IT IS!!
SHE REACHES HER COMPUTER!! SHE'S POWERED IT UP!!
CLICK!!
KWHRR
AND NOW THE CHAMPION IS DONNING HER HOOD!! WHATEVER COULD SHE BE PLANNING?!
....
BTAM
BTAM

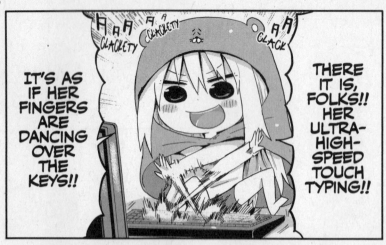

IT'S AS IF HER FINGERS ARE DANCING OVER THE KEYS!!

THERE IT IS, FOLKS!! HER ULTRA-HIGH-SPEED TOUCH TYPING!!

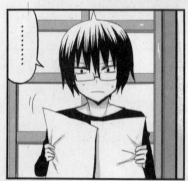

· · · · · · ·

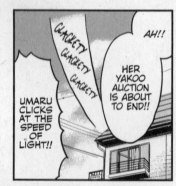

AH!!

HER YAKOO AUCTION IS ABOUT TO END!!

UMARU CLICKS AT THE SPEED OF LIGHT!!

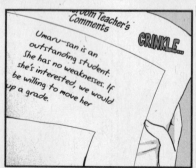

Homeroom Teacher's Comments

CRINKLE...

Umaru-san is an outstanding student. She has no weaknesses. If she's interested, we would be willing to move her up a grade.

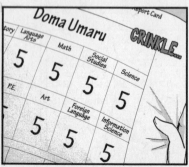

Report Card

Doma Umaru

CRINKLE...

History	Language Arts	Math	Social Studies	Science
	5	5	5	
P.E.			5	5
	Art	Foreign Language	Information Science	
	5	5	5	

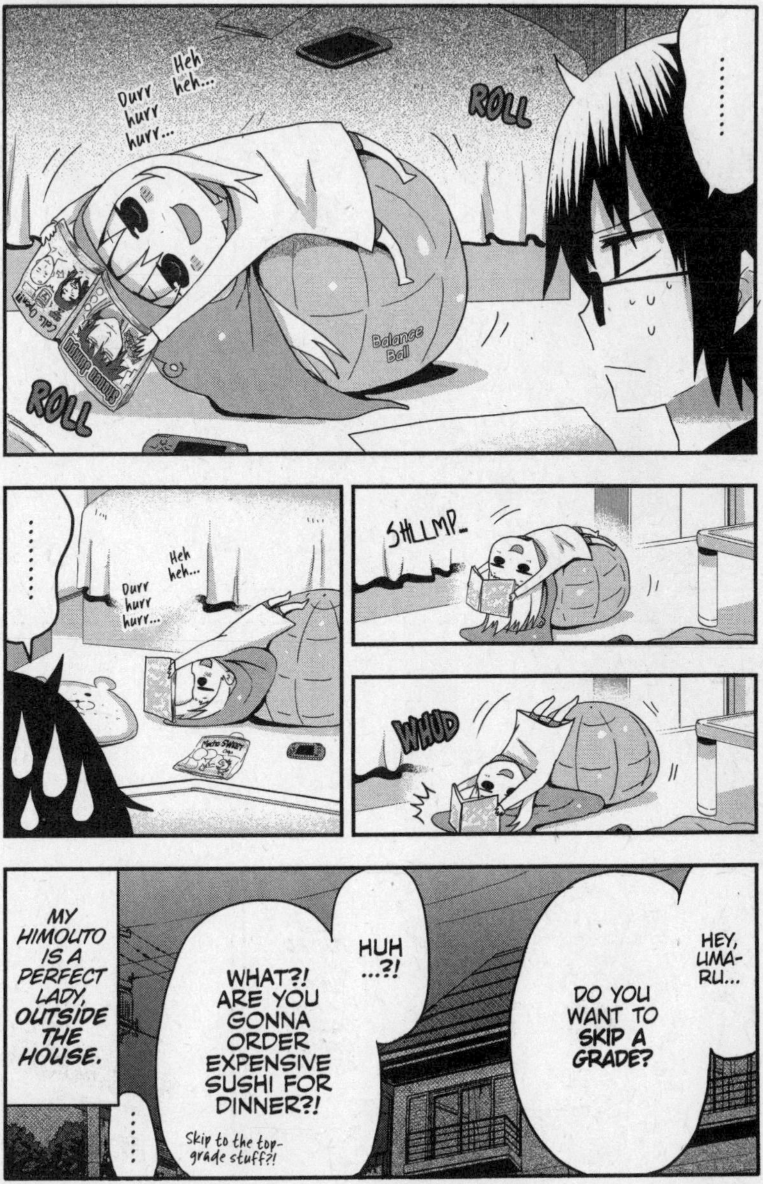
......
Heh heh...
Durr hurr hurr...
ROLL
Balance Ball
ROLL
SHLLMP...
WHUD
......
Heh heh...
Durr hurr hurr...
HEY, UMARU...
DO YOU WANT TO SKIP A GRADE?
HUH ...?!
WHAT?! ARE YOU GONNA ORDER EXPENSIVE SUSHI FOR DINNER?!
Skip to the top-grade stuff?!
......
MY HIMOUTO IS A PERFECT LADY, OUTSIDE THE HOUSE.

No. 3 Umaru & the Day Off

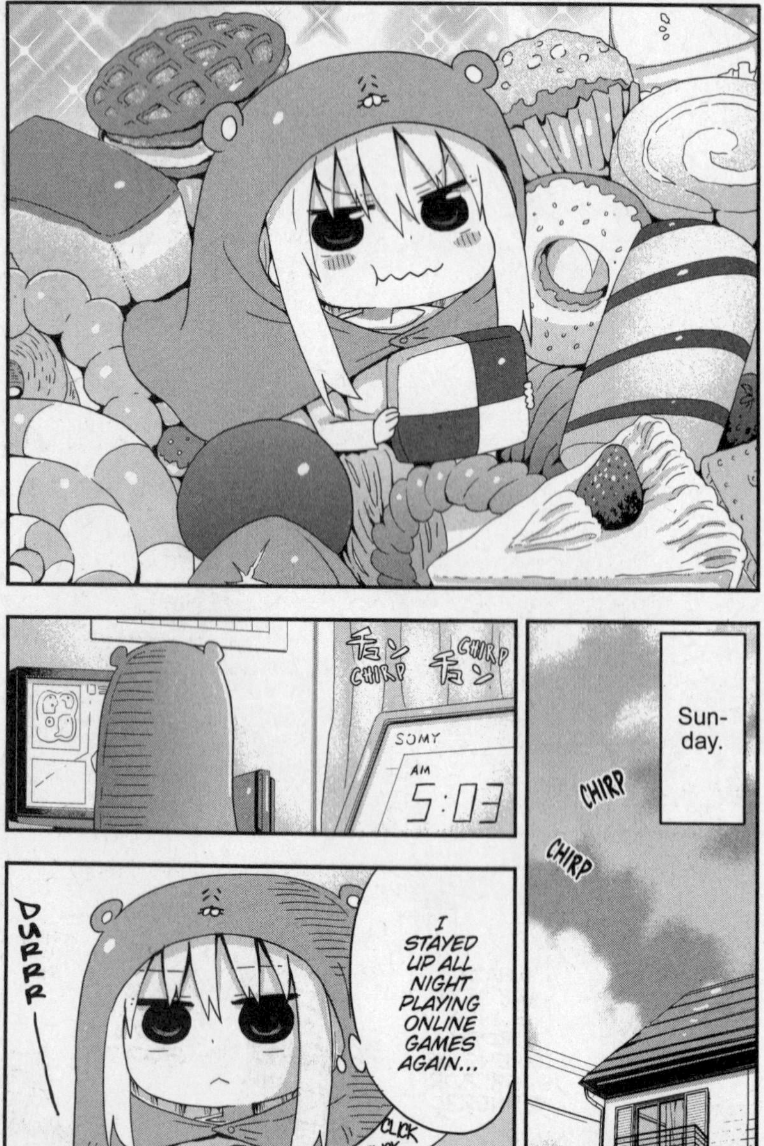
Sun-day.
CHIRP
CHIRP
チュン
CHIRP
チュン
CHIRP
SOMY
AM
5:03
I STAYED UP ALL NIGHT PLAYING ONLINE GAMES AGAIN...
DURRR—
CLICK
CLICK
CLICK

*Sunday morning anime/tokusatsu programming block.

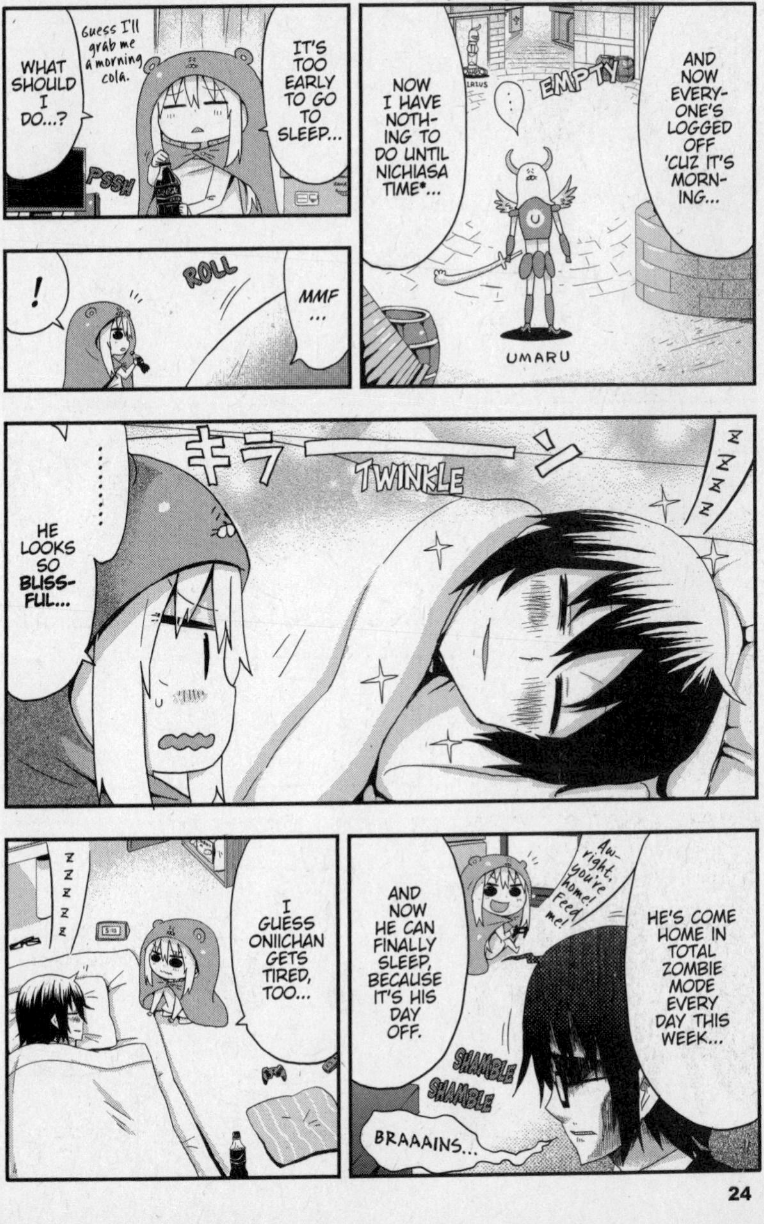
AND NOW EVERYONE'S LOGGED OFF 'CUZ IT'S MORNING...
EMPTY
NOW I HAVE NOTHING TO DO UNTIL NICHIASA TIME*...
...
UMARU
IT'S TOO EARLY TO GO TO SLEEP...
Guess I'll grab me a morning cola.
WHAT SHOULD I DO...?
PSSH
MMF...
ROLL
!
Z Z Z Z
TWINKLE
キラーン
......
HE LOOKS SO BLISSFUL...
HE'S COME HOME IN TOTAL ZOMBIE MODE EVERY DAY THIS WEEK...
Aw-right, you're home! Feed me!
AND NOW HE CAN FINALLY SLEEP, BECAUSE IT'S HIS DAY OFF.
SHAMBLE
SHAMBLE
BRAAAINS...
I GUESS ONIICHAN GETS TIRED, TOO...
Z Z Z Z Z

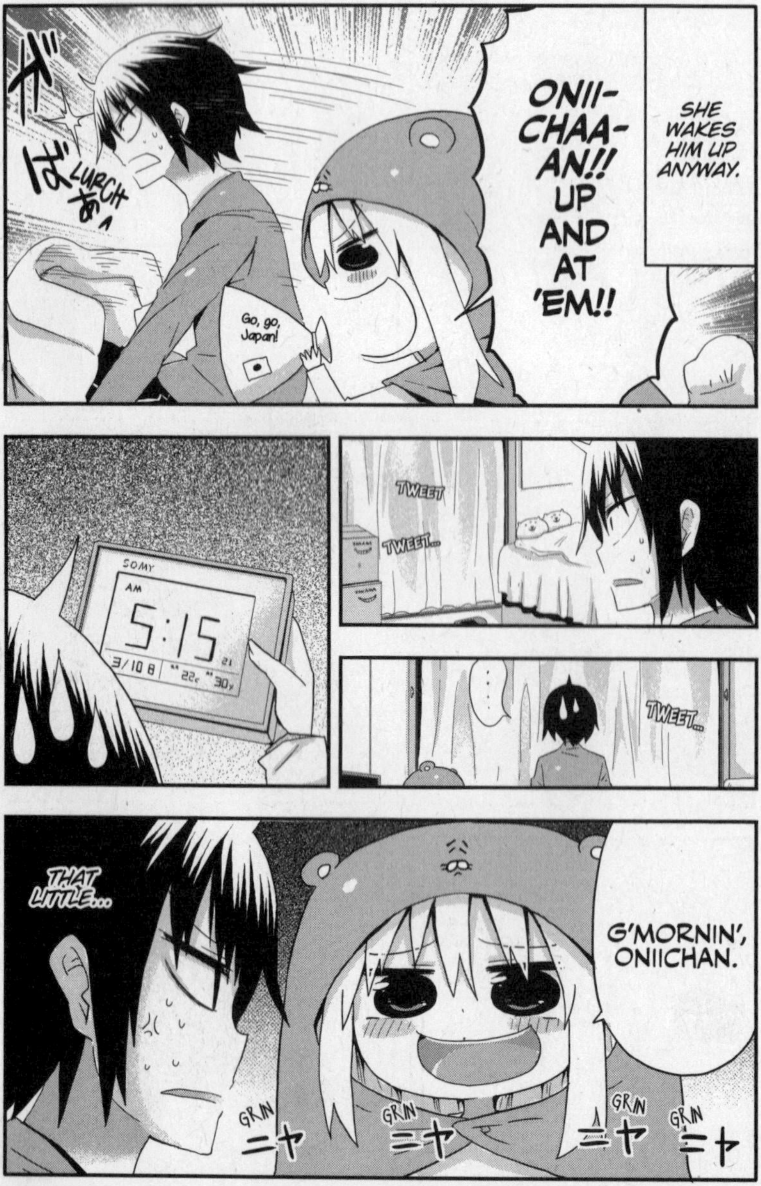
SHE WAKES HIM UP ANYWAY.
ONII-CHAA-AN!! UP AND AT 'EM!!
Go, go, Japan!
LURCH
TWEET
TWEET...
...
TWEET...
SOMY
AM
5:15
3/10
G'MORNIN', ONIICHAN.
THAT LITTLE...
GRIN
ニヤ
GRIN
ニヤ
GRIN
ニヤ
GRIN
ニヤ

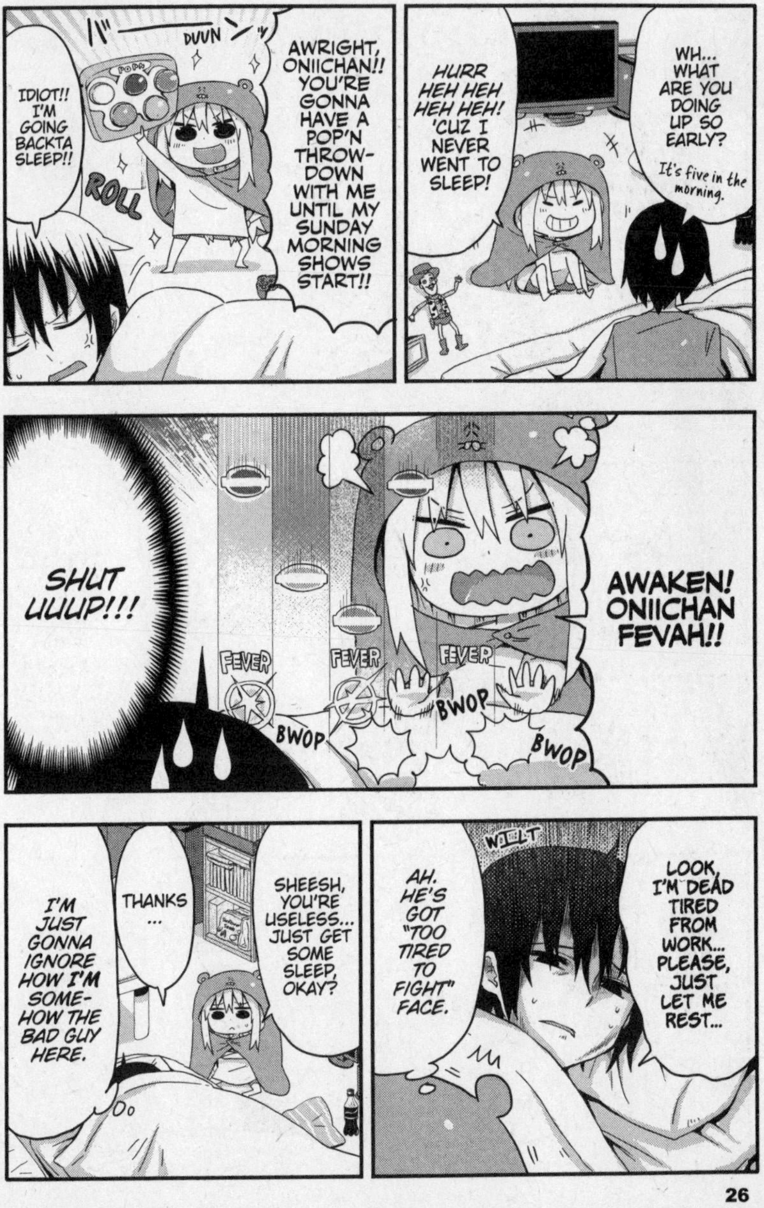
WH... WHAT ARE YOU DOING UP SO EARLY?
It's five in the morning.
HURR HEH HEH HEH HEH! 'CUZ I NEVER WENT TO SLEEP!
AWRIGHT, ONIICHAN!! YOU'RE GONNA HAVE A POP'N THROW-DOWN WITH ME UNTIL MY SUNDAY MORNING SHOWS START!!
DUUN
ROLL
IDIOT!! I'M GOING BACKTA SLEEP!!
AWAKEN! ONIICHAN FEVAH!!
FEVER
FEVER
FEVER
BWOP
BWOP
BWOP
SHUT UUUP!!!
WILT
LOOK, I'M DEAD TIRED FROM WORK... PLEASE, JUST LET ME REST...
AH. HE'S GOT "TOO TIRED TO FIGHT" FACE.
SHEESH, YOU'RE USELESS... JUST GET SOME SLEEP, OKAY?
THANKS ...
I'M JUST GONNA IGNORE HOW I'M SOME-HOW THE BAD GUY HERE.

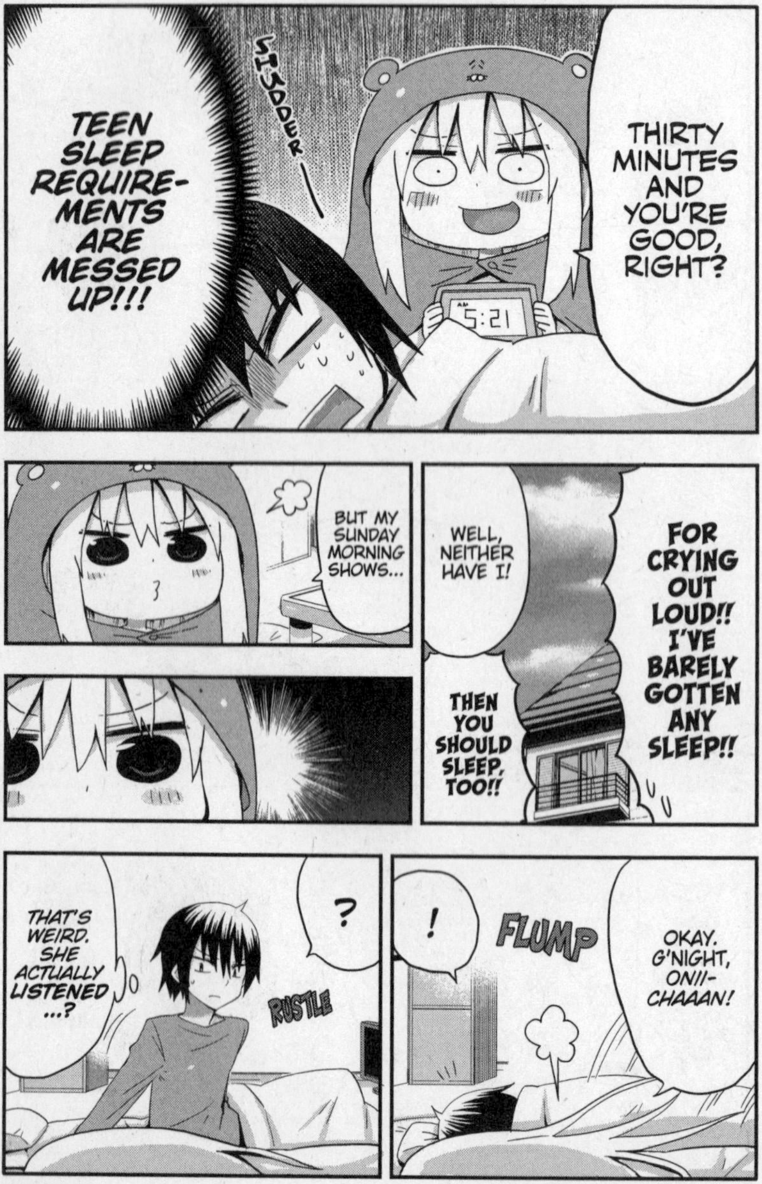
THIRTY MINUTES AND YOU'RE GOOD, RIGHT?
SHUDDER
AM 5:21
TEEN SLEEP REQUIRE-MENTS ARE MESSED UP!!!
FOR CRYING OUT LOUD!! I'VE BARELY GOTTEN ANY SLEEP!!
WELL, NEITHER HAVE I!
THEN YOU SHOULD SLEEP, TOO!!
BUT MY SUNDAY MORNING SHOWS...
OKAY. G'NIGHT, ONII-CHAAAN!
FLUMP
!
?
RUSTLE
THAT'S WEIRD. SHE ACTUALLY LISTENED ...?

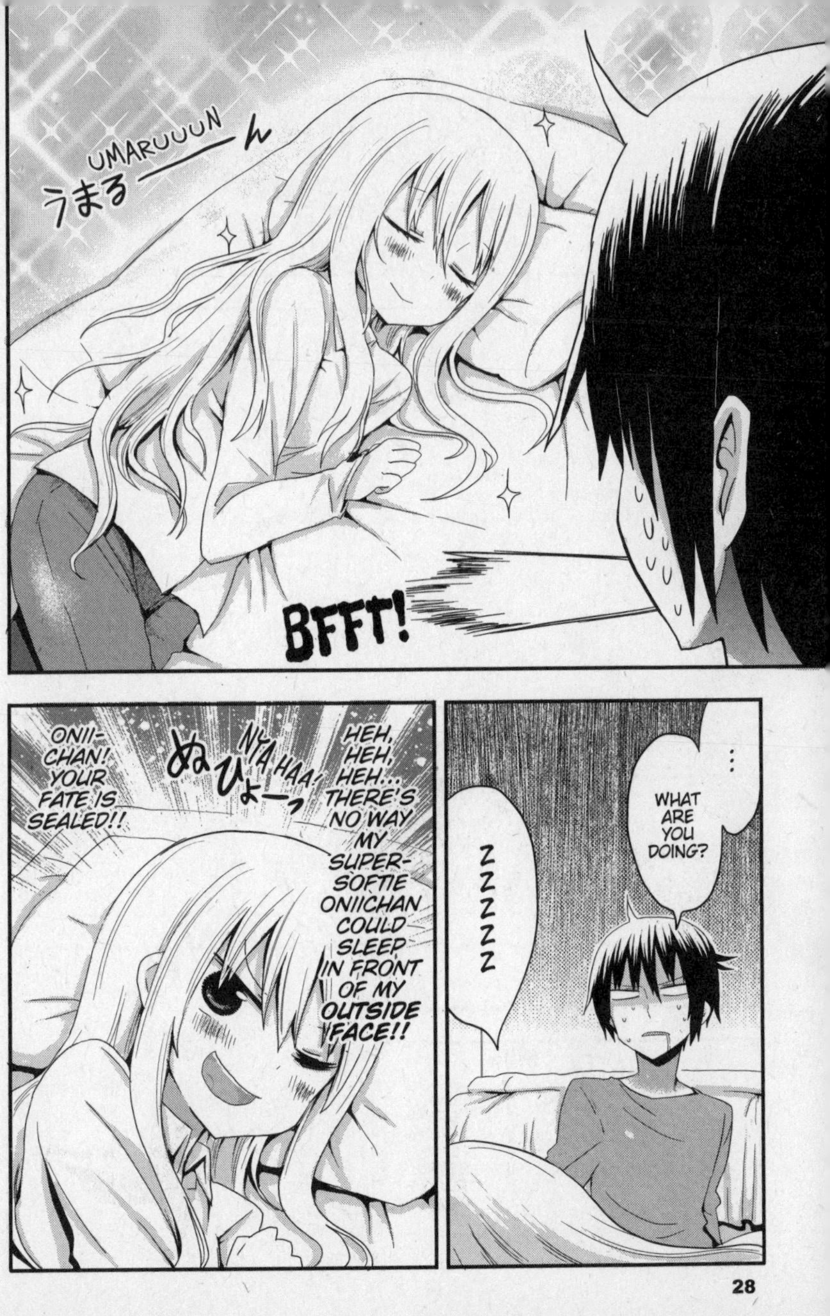
うまる――ん
UMARUUUN
BFFT!
...
WHAT ARE YOU DOING?
ZZZZZ
HEH, HEH, HEH... THERE'S NO WAY MY SUPER-SOFTIE ONIICHAN COULD SLEEP IN FRONT OF MY OUTSIDE FACE!!
ぬひょーっ
NYA HAA!
ONII-CHAN! YOUR FATE IS SEALED!!

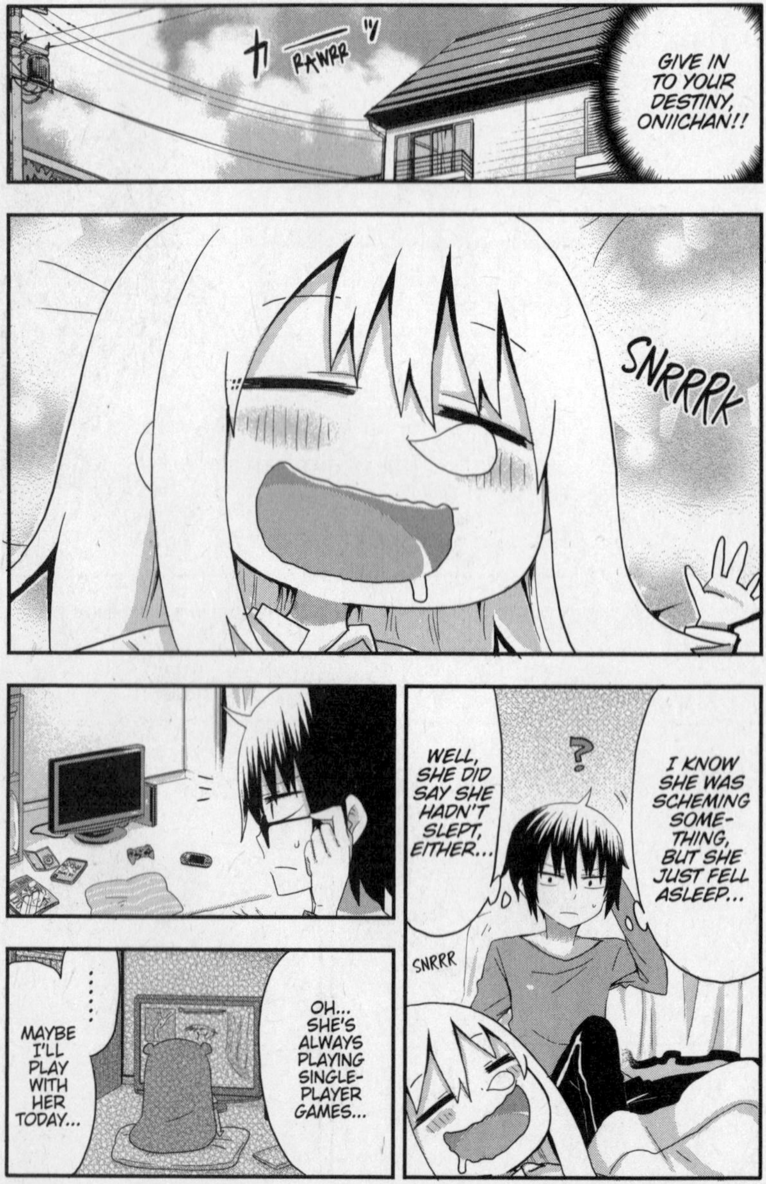

カ
RAWRR
ッ
GIVE IN TO YOUR DESTINY, ONIICHAN!!
SNRRRK
I KNOW SHE WAS SCHEMING SOME-THING, BUT SHE JUST FELL ASLEEP...
?
WELL, SHE DID SAY SHE HADN'T SLEPT, EITHER...
SNRRR
OH... SHE'S ALWAYS PLAYING SINGLE-PLAYER GAMES...
...... MAYBE I'LL PLAY WITH HER TODAY...

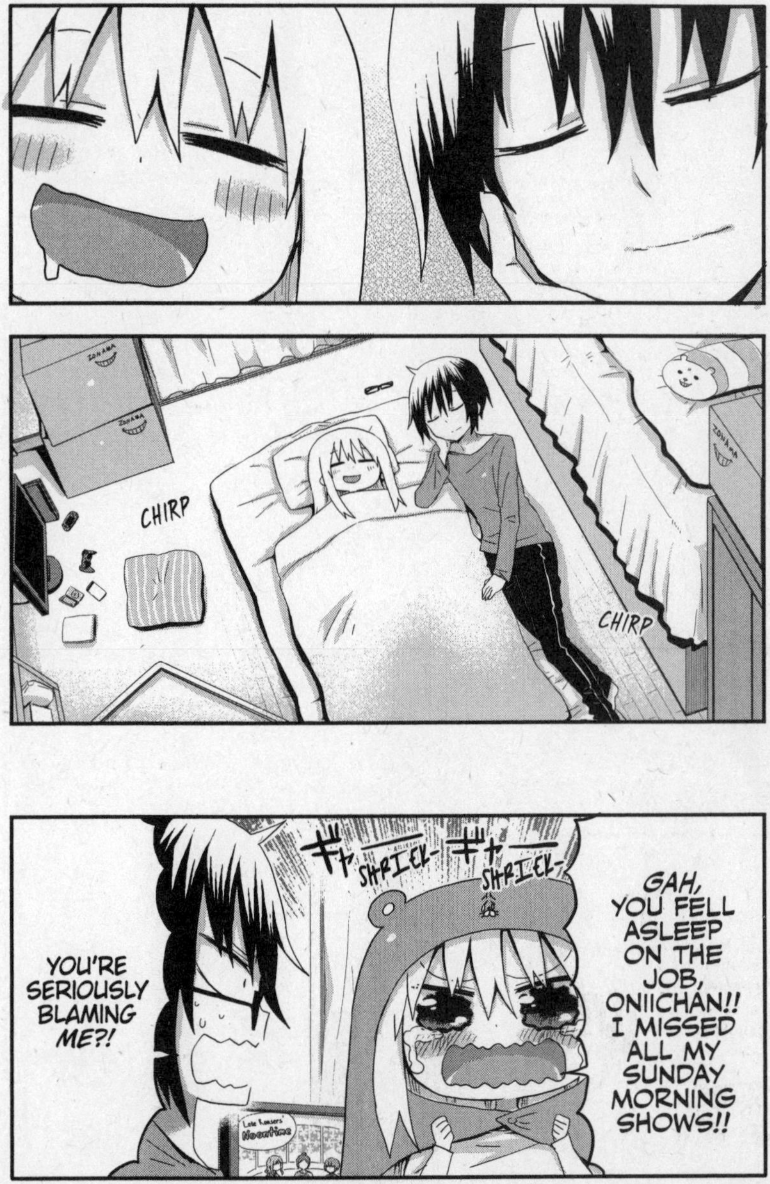
CHIRP
CHIRP
GAH, YOU FELL ASLEEP ON THE JOB, ONIICHAN!! I MISSED ALL MY SUNDAY MORNING SHOWS!!
ギャー SHRIEK
ギャー SHRIEK
YOU'RE SERIOUSLY BLAMING ME?!
Late Risers' Noontime

Evening

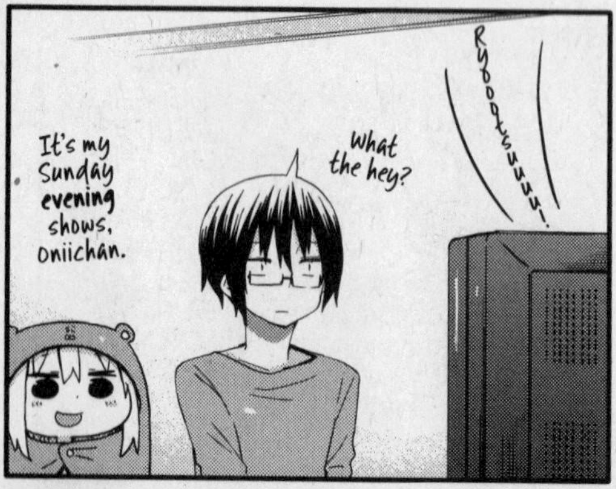
Ryooootsuuuu!
What the hey?
It's my Sunday evening shows, oniichan.

HIMOUTO! UMARU-CHAN

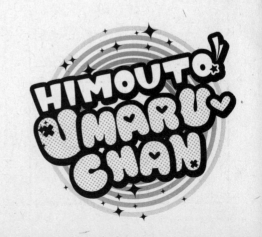

No. 4 Umaru the Gourmet

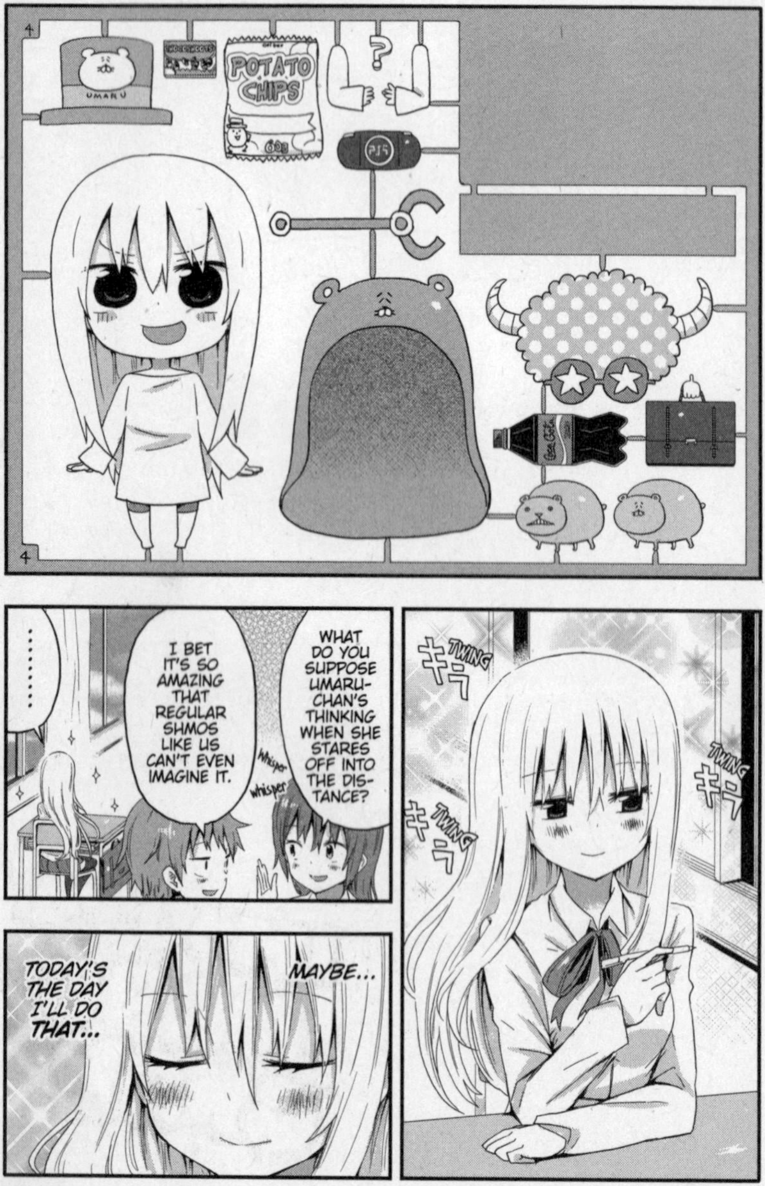

UMARU
POTATO CHIPS
TWING
TWING
TWING
WHAT DO YOU SUPPOSE UMARU-CHAN'S THINKING WHEN SHE STARES OFF INTO THE DISTANCE?
whisper
whisper
I BET IT'S SO AMAZING THAT REGULAR SHMOS LIKE US CAN'T EVEN IMAGINE IT.
......
MAYBE...
TODAY'S THE DAY I'LL DO THAT...

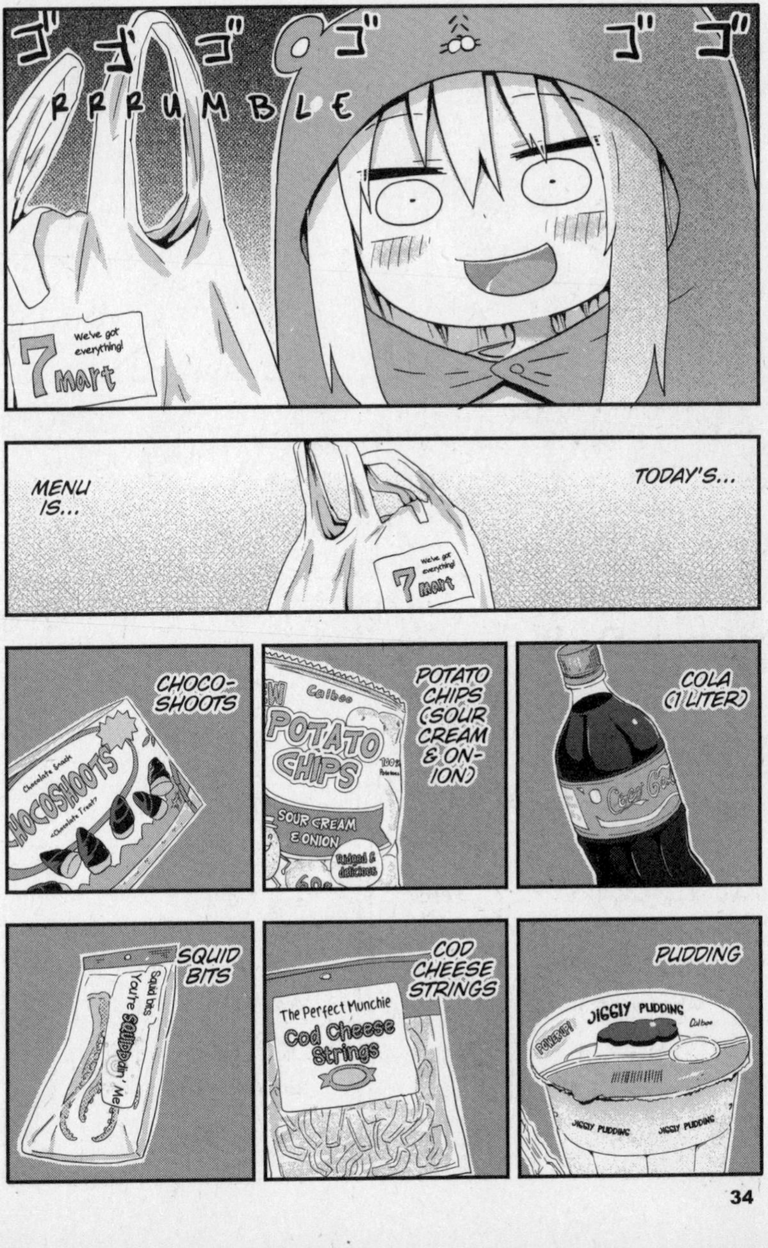
ゴゴ
ゴ
ゴゴゴ
RRRUMBLE
We've got everything!
7 mart
TODAY'S...
MENU IS...
We've got everything!
7 mart
COLA (1 LITER)
POTATO CHIPS (SOUR CREAM & ON-ION)
Calbee
POTATO CHIPS
SOUR CREAM & ONION
Ridged & delicious
CHOCO-SHOOTS
Chocolate Snack
CHOCOSHOOTS
<Chocolate Treat>
PUDDING
JIGGLY PUDDING
Calbee
POKEROP!
JIGGLY PUDDING
JIGGLY PUDDING
COD CHEESE STRINGS
The Perfect Munchie
Cod Cheese Strings
SQUID BITS
Squid Bits
You're SQUIDDin' Me

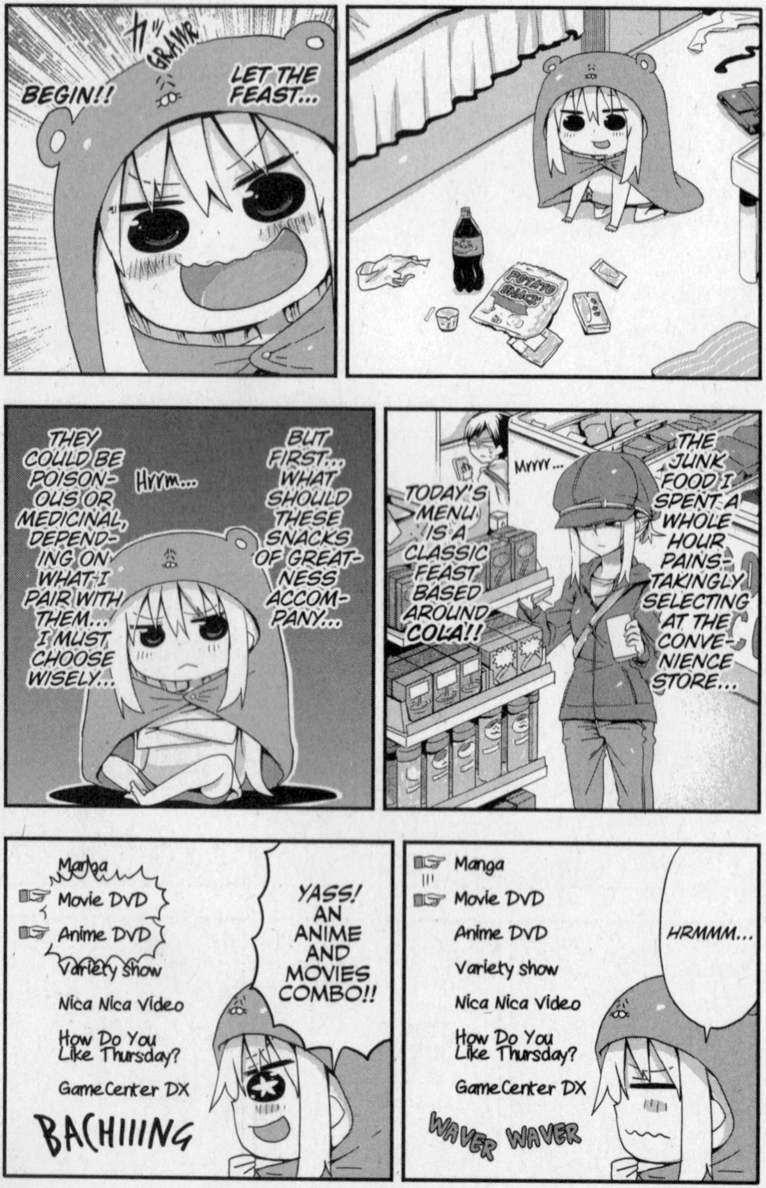
LET THE FEAST...
GRAWR
BEGIN!!
THE JUNK FOOD I SPENT A WHOLE HOUR PAINS-TAKINGLY SELECTING AT THE CONVE-NIENCE STORE...
Mrrrr...
TODAY'S MENU IS A CLASSIC FEAST BASED AROUND COLA!!
BUT FIRST... WHAT SHOULD THESE SNACKS OF GREAT-NESS ACCOM-PANY...
Hrrm...
THEY COULD BE POISON-OUS OR MEDICINAL, DEPEND-ING ON WHAT I PAIR WITH THEM... I MUST CHOOSE WISELY...
HRMMM...
Manga
Movie DVD
Anime DVD
Variety show
Nica Nica Video
How Do You Like Thursday?
GameCenter DX
WAVER WAVER
YASS! AN ANIME AND MOVIES COMBO!!
Manga
Movie DVD
Anime DVD
Variety show
Nica Nica Video
How Do You Like Thursday?
GameCenter DX
BACHIIING

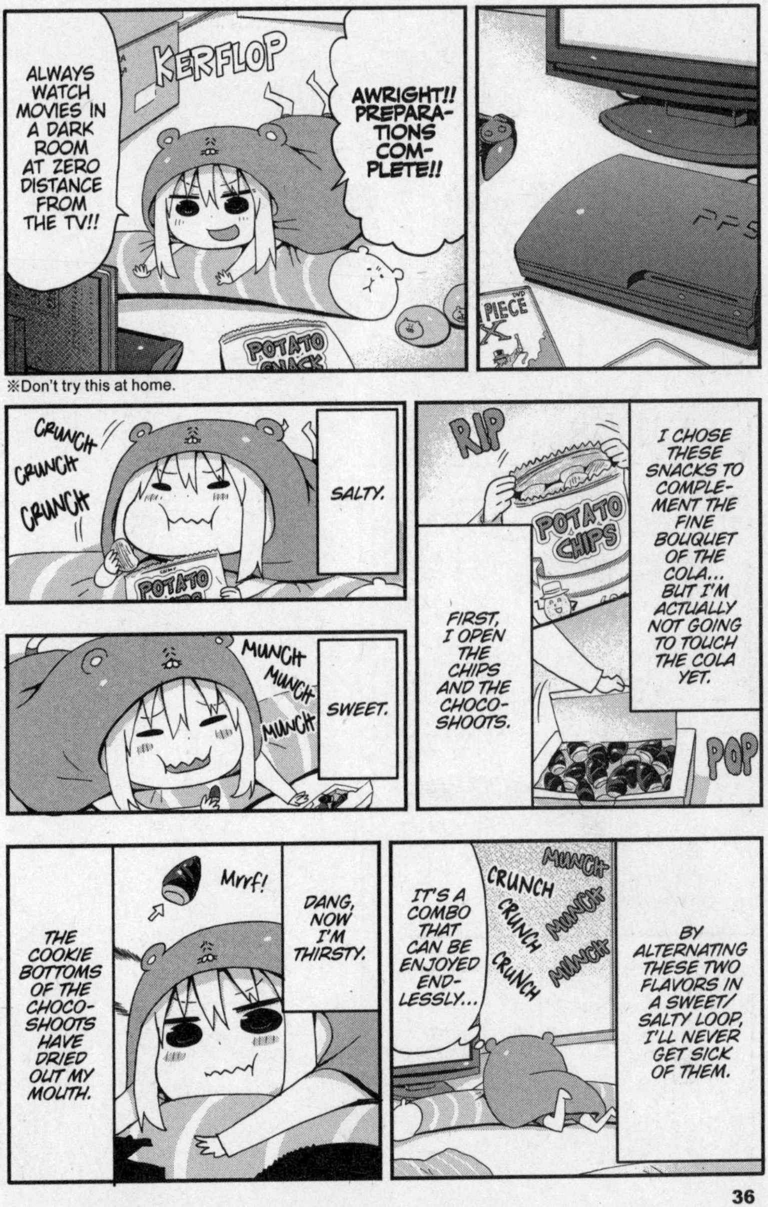
PIECE X
AWRIGHT!! PREPARATIONS COMPLETE!!
KERFLOP
ALWAYS WATCH MOVIES IN A DARK ROOM AT ZERO DISTANCE FROM THE TV!!
POTATO SNACK
※Don't try this at home.
RIP
I CHOSE THESE SNACKS TO COMPLEMENT THE FINE BOUQUET OF THE COLA... BUT I'M ACTUALLY NOT GOING TO TOUCH THE COLA YET.
POTATO CHIPS
FIRST, I OPEN THE CHIPS AND THE CHOCO-SHOOTS.
POP
SALTY.
CRUNCH
CRUNCH
CRUNCH
SWEET.
MUNCH
MUNCH
MUNCH
BY ALTERNATING THESE TWO FLAVORS IN A SWEET/ SALTY LOOP, I'LL NEVER GET SICK OF THEM.
MUNCH
MUNCH
MUNCH
CRUNCH
CRUNCH
CRUNCH
IT'S A COMBO THAT CAN BE ENJOYED ENDLESSLY...
DANG, NOW I'M THIRSTY.
Mrrf!
THE COOKIE BOTTOMS OF THE CHOCO-SHOOTS HAVE DRIED OUT MY MOUTH.

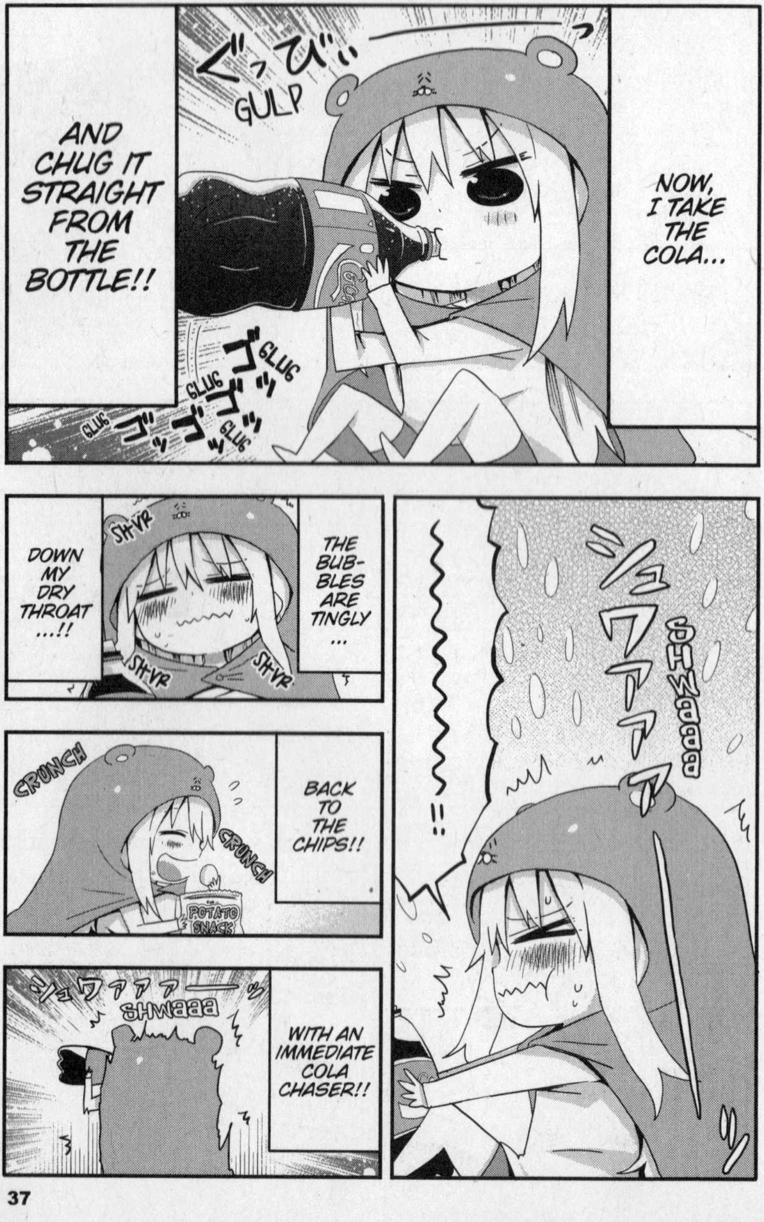
NOW, I TAKE THE COLA...
ぐっび
GULP
AND CHUG IT STRAIGHT FROM THE BOTTLE!!
ゴッ ゴッ ゴッ
GLUG GLUG GLUG GLUG
~~~~~~~~~~!!
シュワァァァ
SHWaaaa
THE BUB-BLES ARE TINGLY...
DOWN MY DRY THROAT...!!
SHVR SHVR SHVR
BACK TO THE CHIPS!!
CRUNCH CRUNCH
POTATO SNACK
WITH AN IMMEDIATE COLA CHASER!!
シュワァァァーッ
SHWaaa
~~~~~~~~~~

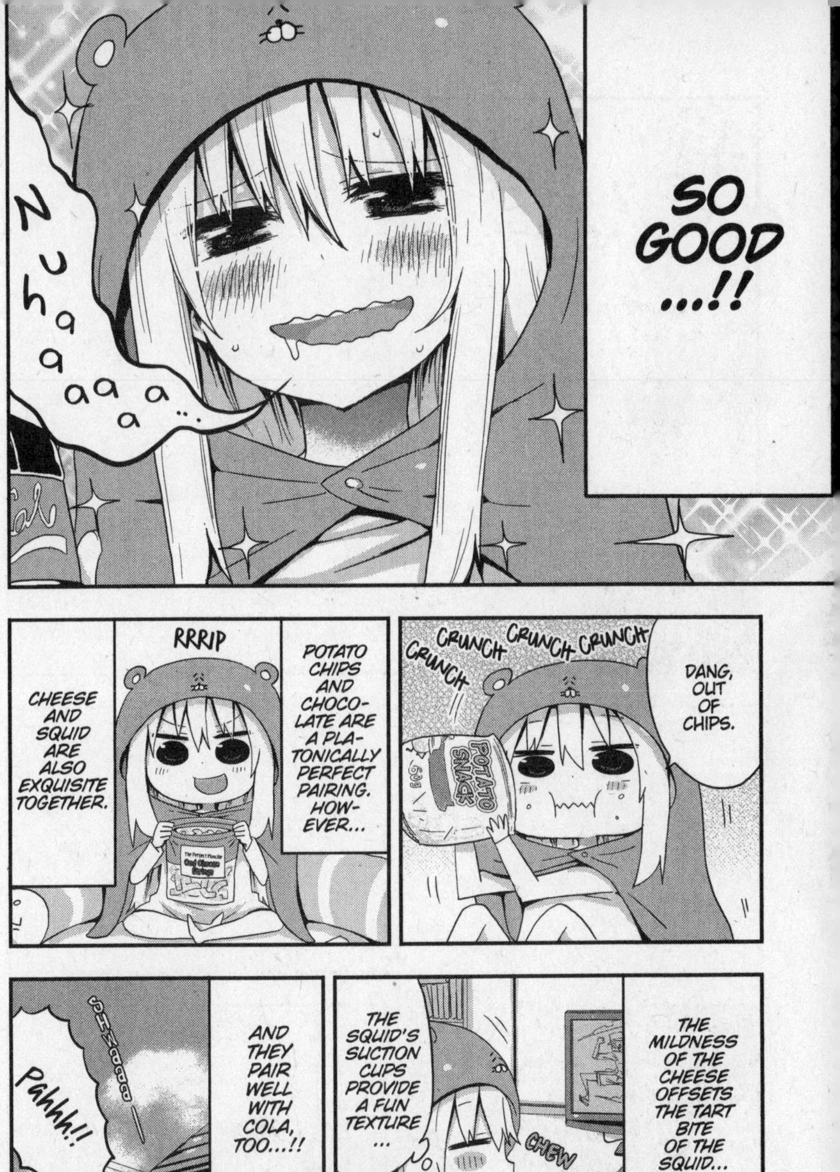

SO GOOD ...!!
Nuhaaaaaaa...
CRUNCH CRUNCH CRUNCH CRUNCH
DANG, OUT OF CHIPS.
POTATO SNACK
RRRIP
POTATO CHIPS AND CHOCOLATE ARE A PLATONICALLY PERFECT PAIRING. HOWEVER...
CHEESE AND SQUID ARE ALSO EXQUISITE TOGETHER.
THE MILDNESS OF THE CHEESE OFFSETS THE TART BITE OF THE SQUID...
THE SQUID'S SUCTION CUPS PROVIDE A FUN TEXTURE ...
CHEW
CHEW
AND THEY PAIR WELL WITH COLA, TOO...!!
Shwaaaaa—
Pahhh!!

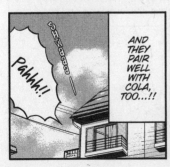

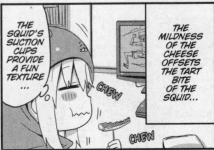

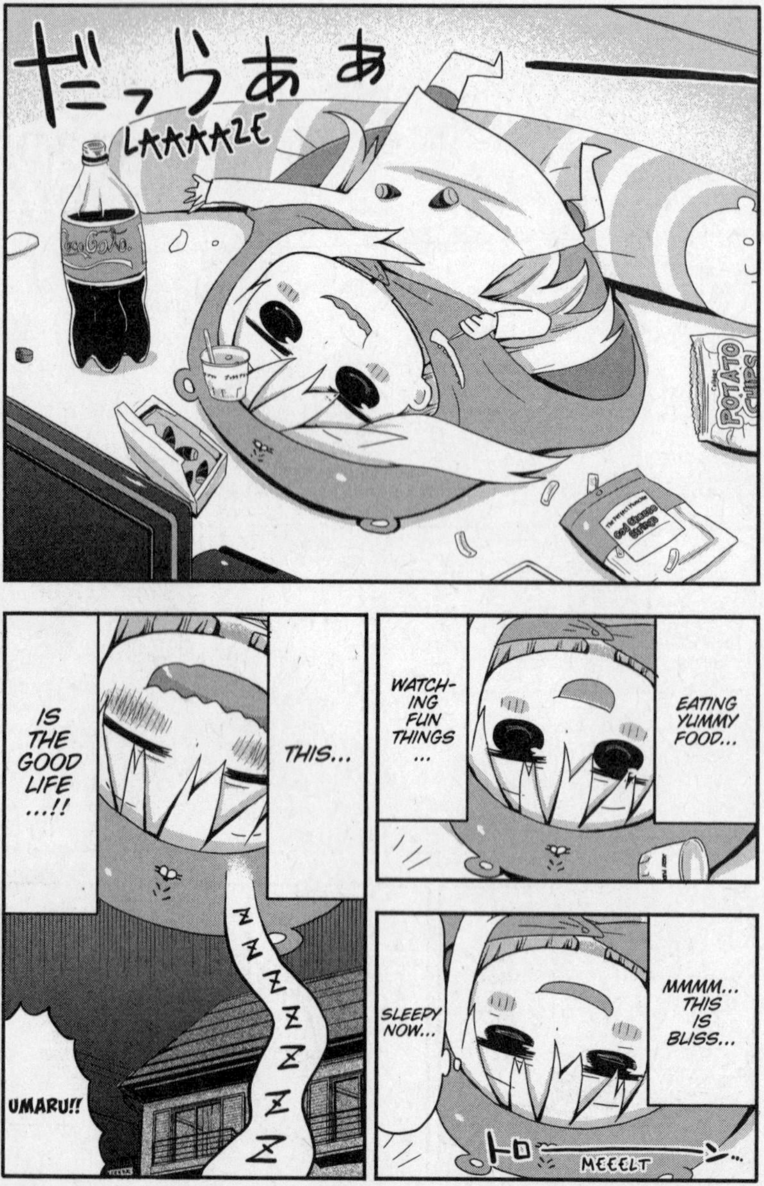
だっらあぁー
LAAAAZE
POTATO CHIPS
EATING YUMMY FOOD...
WATCHING FUN THINGS ...
MMMM... THIS IS BLISS...
SLEEPY NOW...
トロ
MEEELT
ン...
THIS...
IS THE GOOD LIFE ...!!
ZZZZZZZ
UMARU!!

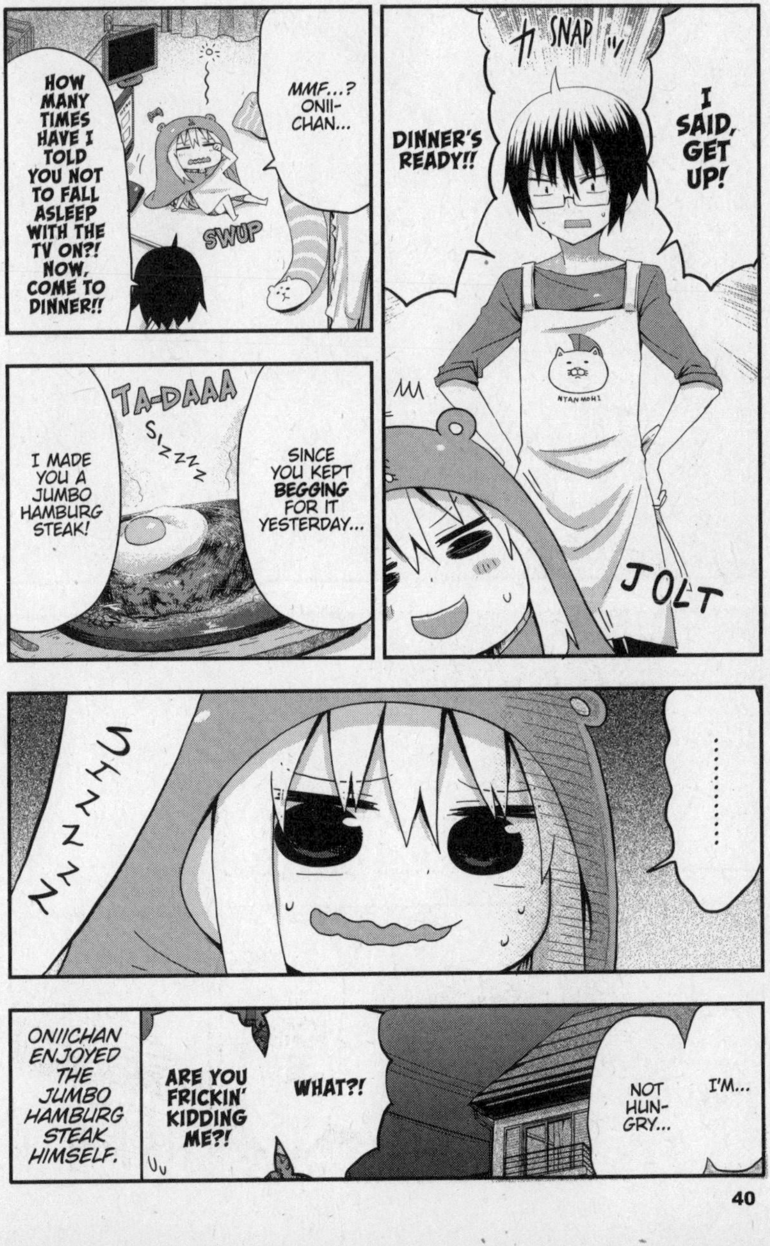
SNAP
I SAID, GET UP!
DINNER'S READY!!
JOLT
MMF...? ONII-CHAN...
HOW MANY TIMES HAVE I TOLD YOU NOT TO FALL ASLEEP WITH THE TV ON?! NOW, COME TO DINNER!!
SWUP
TA-DAAA
SIZZZZ
SINCE YOU KEPT BEGGING FOR IT YESTERDAY...
I MADE YOU A JUMBO HAMBURG STEAK!
....
I'M...
NOT HUNGRY...
WHAT?!
ARE YOU FRICKIN' KIDDING ME?!
ONIICHAN ENJOYED THE JUMBO HAMBURG STEAK HIMSELF.

No. 5 Umaru & Going Out

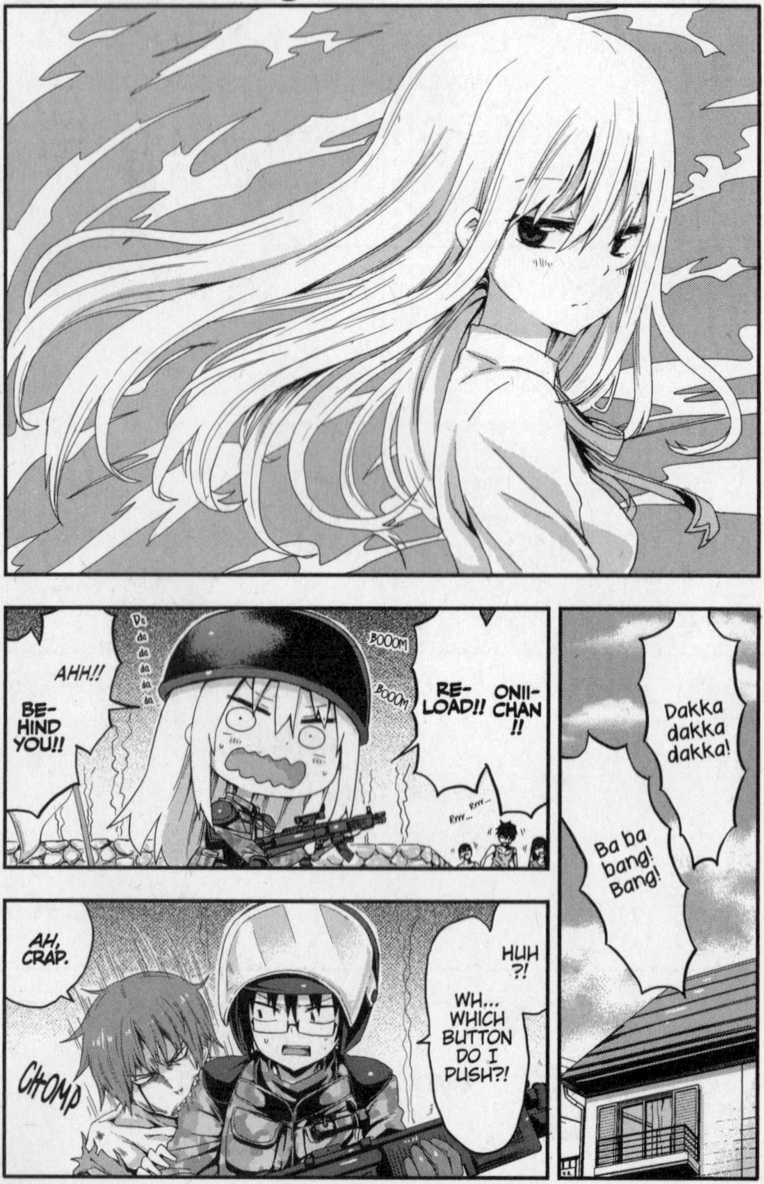
Dakka dakka dakka!
Ba ba bang! Bang!
ONII-CHAN!!
RE-LOAD!!
BOOOM
BOOOM
Da da da da da da
AHH!!
BE-HIND YOU!!
HUH?!
WH... WHICH BUTTON DO I PUSH?!
AH, CRAP.
CHOMP

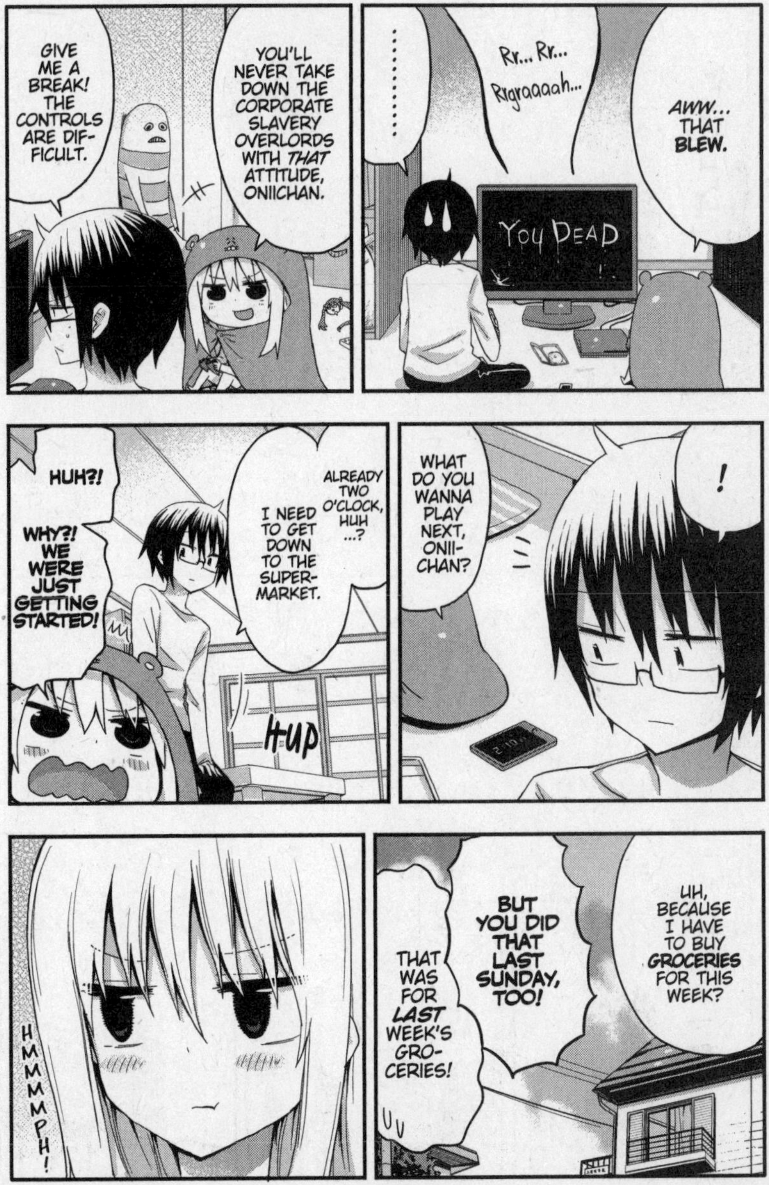
AWW... THAT BLEW.
Rr... Rr... Rrgraaaah...
......
YOU DEAD
YOU'LL NEVER TAKE DOWN THE CORPORATE SLAVERY OVERLORDS WITH THAT ATTITUDE, ONIICHAN.
GIVE ME A BREAK! THE CONTROLS ARE DIF-FICULT.
!
WHAT DO YOU WANNA PLAY NEXT, ONII-CHAN?
ALREADY TWO O'CLOCK, HUH ...?
I NEED TO GET DOWN TO THE SUPER-MARKET.
HUP
HUH?!
WHY?! WE WERE JUST GETTING STARTED!
UH, BECAUSE I HAVE TO BUY GROCERIES FOR THIS WEEK?
BUT YOU DID THAT LAST SUNDAY, TOO!
THAT WAS FOR LAST WEEK'S GRO-CERIES!
HMMMMPH!

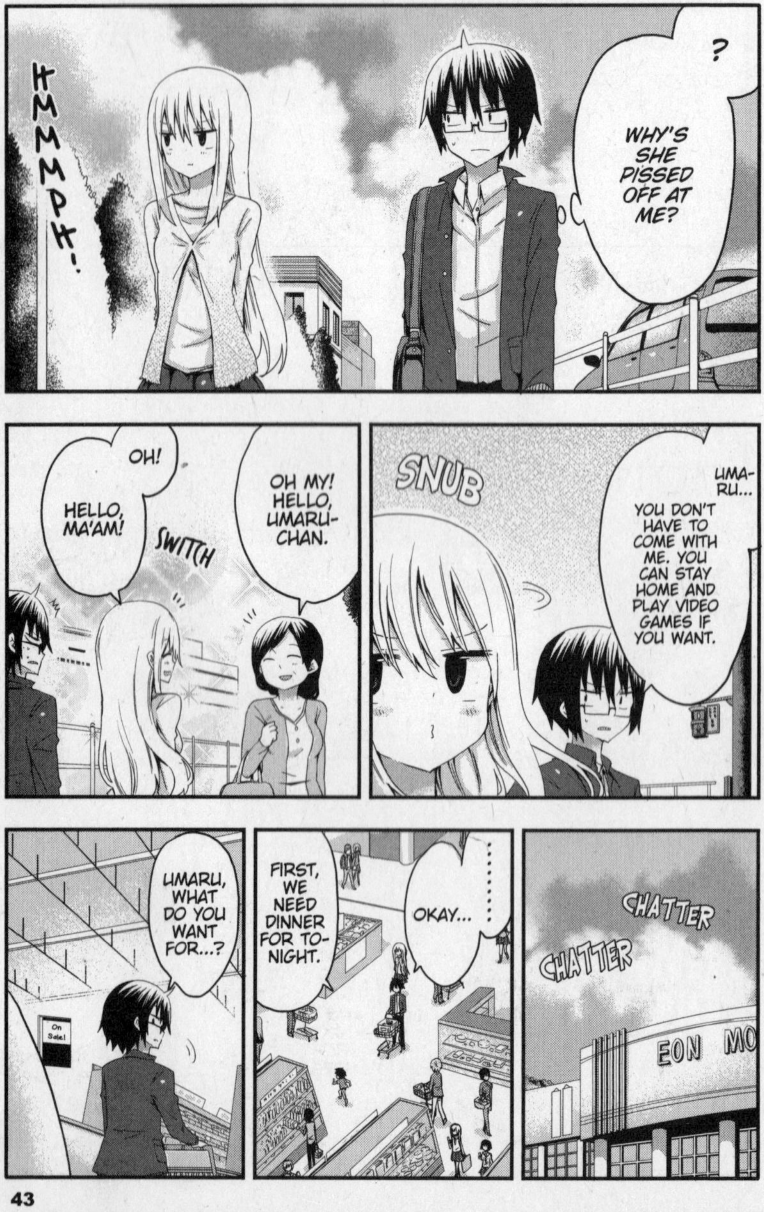
?
WHY'S SHE PISSED OFF AT ME?
HMMMPH!
UMARU... YOU DON'T HAVE TO COME WITH ME. YOU CAN STAY HOME AND PLAY VIDEO GAMES IF YOU WANT.
SNUB
OH MY! HELLO, UMARU-CHAN.
OH! HELLO, MA'AM!
SWITCH
CHATTER
CHATTER
EON MO
......
OKAY...
FIRST, WE NEED DINNER FOR TO-NIGHT.
UMARU, WHAT DO YOU WANT FOR...?
On Sale!

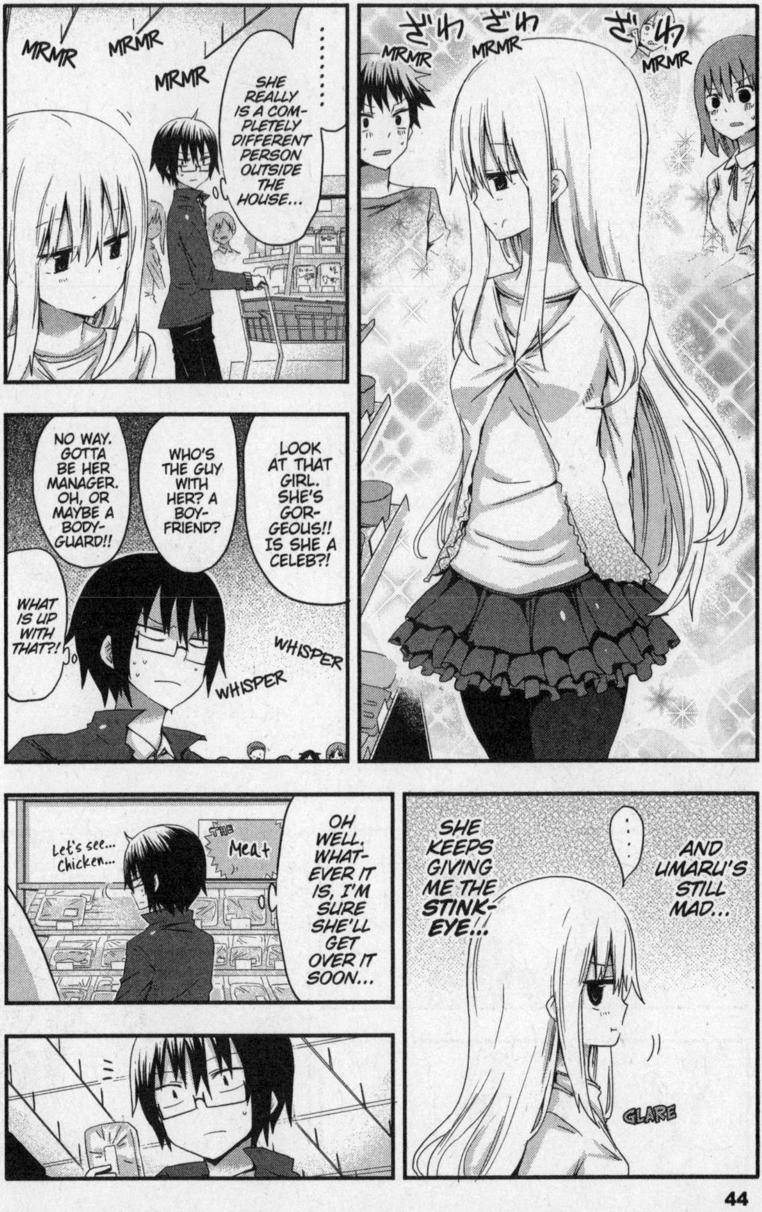
ざわ ざわ ざわ
MRMR
MRMR
MRMR
......
SHE REALLY IS A COMPLETELY DIFFERENT PERSON OUTSIDE THE HOUSE...
MRMR
MRMR
MRMR
LOOK AT THAT GIRL. SHE'S GORGEOUS!! IS SHE A CELEB?!
WHO'S THE GUY WITH HER? A BOYFRIEND?
NO WAY. GOTTA BE HER MANAGER. OH, OR MAYBE A BODYGUARD!!
WHAT IS UP WITH THAT?!
WHISPER
WHISPER
...
AND UMARU'S STILL MAD...
SHE KEEPS GIVING ME THE STINK-EYE...
GLARE
OH WELL. WHATEVER IT IS, I'M SURE SHE'LL GET OVER IT SOON...
THE Meat
Let's see... Chicken...

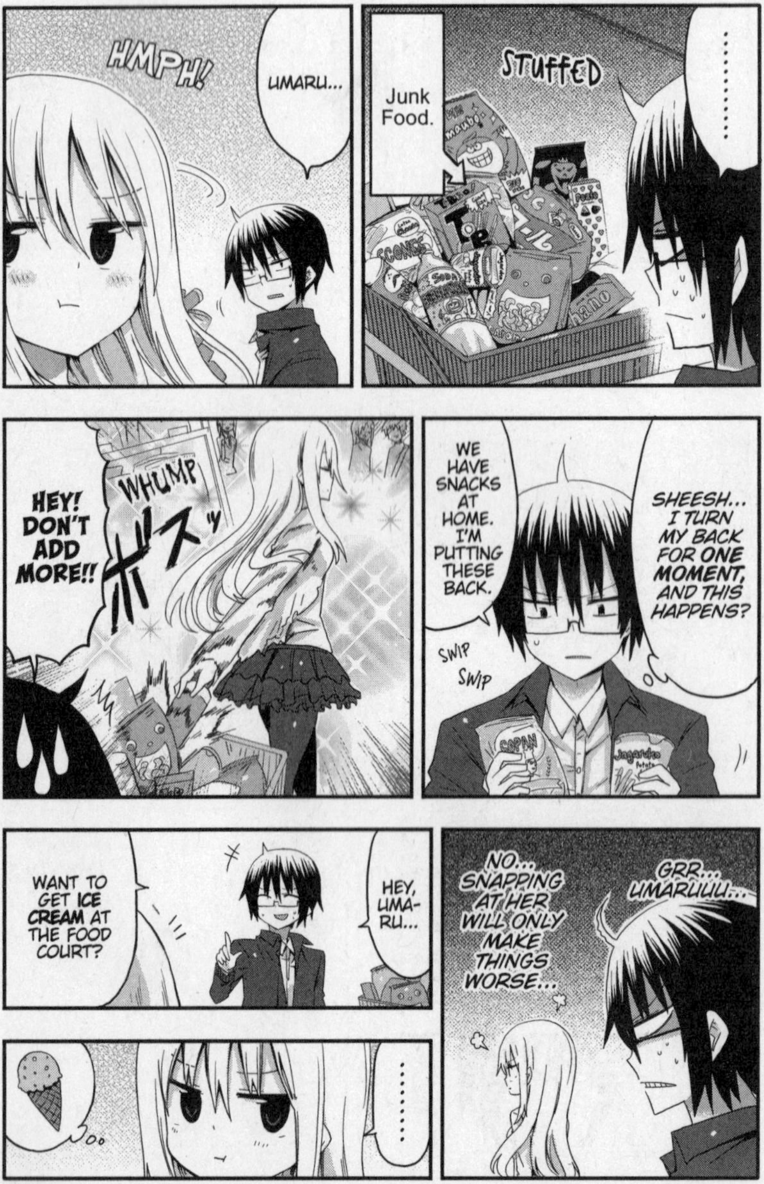

......
STUFFED
Junk Food.
UMARU...
HMPH!
SHEESH... I TURN MY BACK FOR ONE MOMENT, AND THIS HAPPENS?
WE HAVE SNACKS AT HOME. I'M PUTTING THESE BACK.
SWIP SWIP
WHUMP
ボスッ
HEY! DON'T ADD MORE!!
GRR... UMARUUU...
NO... SNAPPING AT HER WILL ONLY MAKE THINGS WORSE...
HEY, UMA-RU...
WANT TO GET ICE CREAM AT THE FOOD COURT?
......

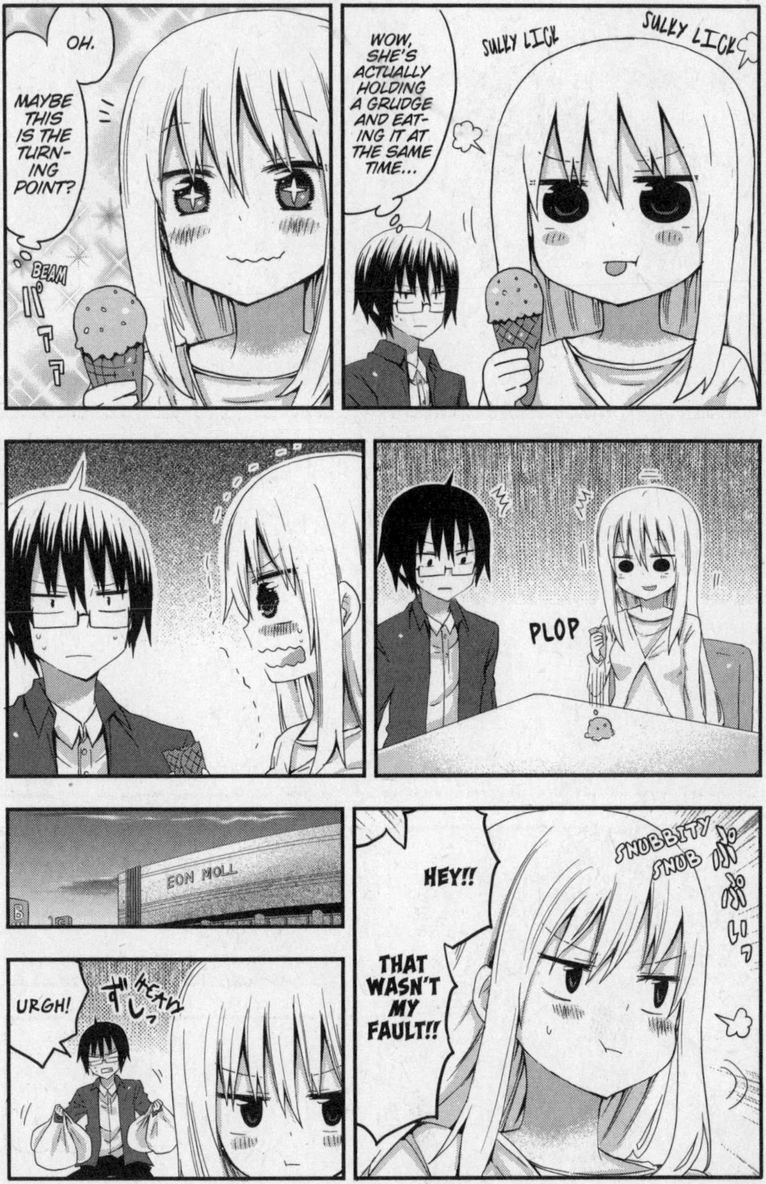

SULKY LICK
SULKY LICK
WOW, SHE'S ACTUALLY HOLDING A GRUDGE AND EATING IT AT THE SAME TIME...
OH.
MAYBE THIS IS THE TURNING POINT?
BEAM
PLOP
SNUBBITY SNOB
HEY!!
THAT WASN'T MY FAULT!!
EON MOLL
HEAVY
URGH!

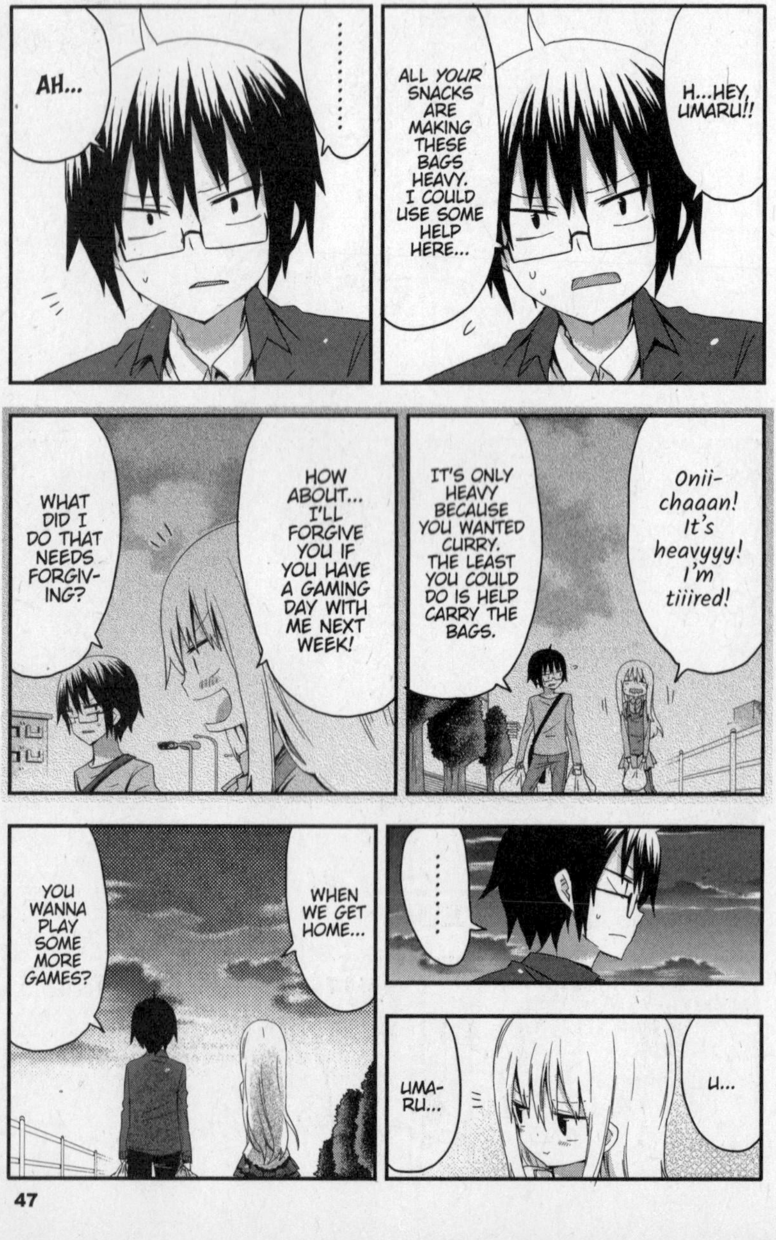
H...HEY, UMARU!!
ALL YOUR SNACKS ARE MAKING THESE BAGS HEAVY. I COULD USE SOME HELP HERE...
......
AH...
Onii-chaaan! It's heavyyy! I'm tiiired!
IT'S ONLY HEAVY BECAUSE YOU WANTED CURRY. THE LEAST YOU COULD DO IS HELP CARRY THE BAGS.
HOW ABOUT... I'LL FORGIVE YOU IF YOU HAVE A GAMING DAY WITH ME NEXT WEEK!
WHAT DID I DO THAT NEEDS FORGIVING?
......
U...
UMARU...
WHEN WE GET HOME...
YOU WANNA PLAY SOME MORE GAMES?

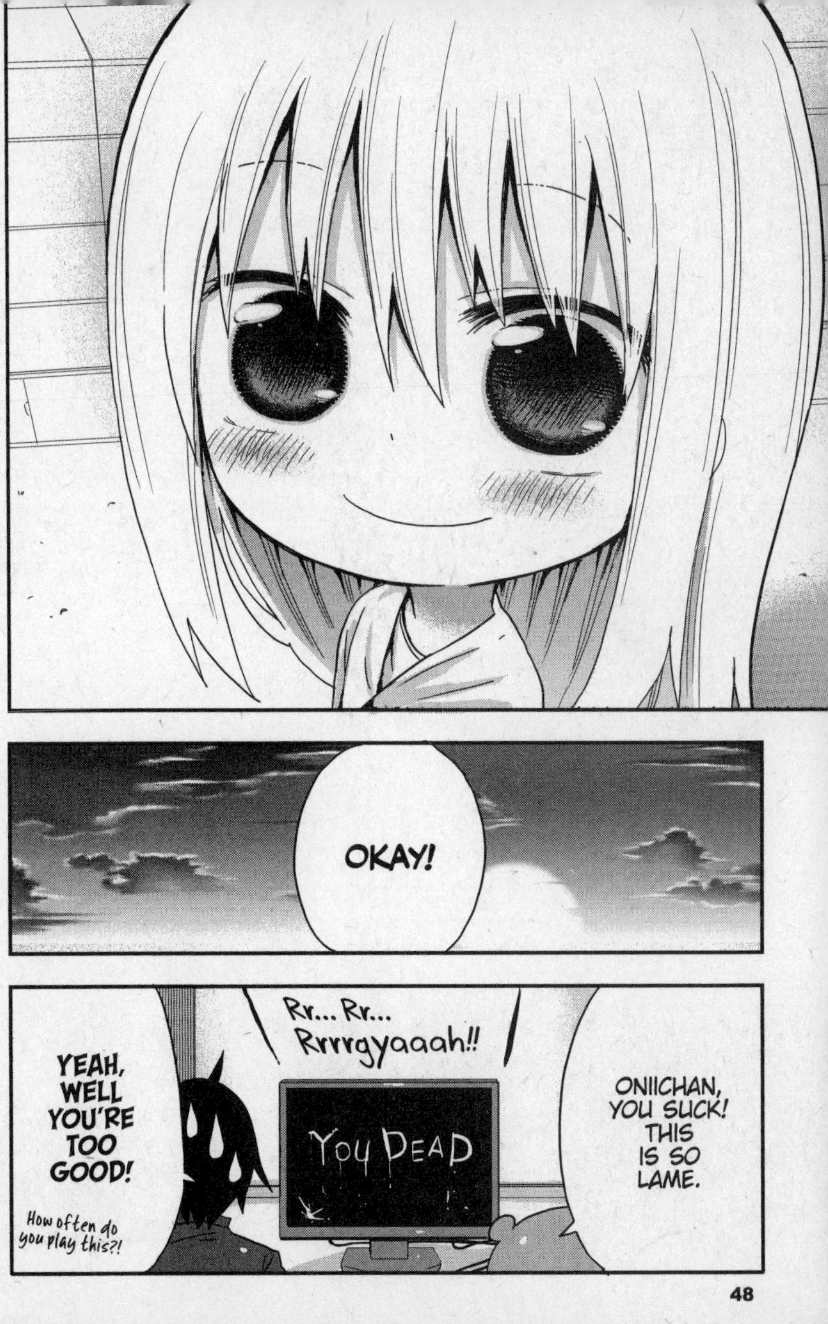
OKAY!
ONIICHAN, YOU SUCK! THIS IS SO LAME.
Rr... Rr... Rrrrgyaaah!!
YOU DEAD
YEAH, WELL YOU'RE TOO GOOD!
How often do you play this?!

No. 6 Umaru & Pets

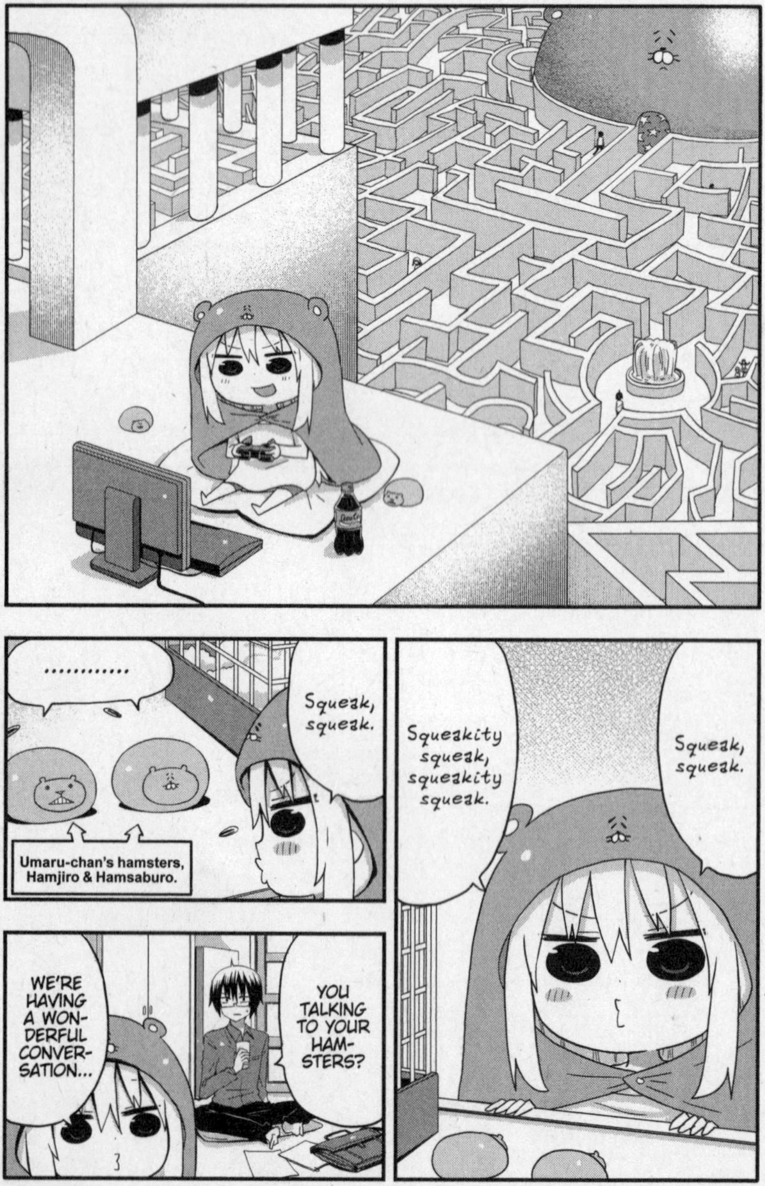

Squeak, squeak.
Squeakity squeak, squeakity squeak.
Squeak, squeak.
....
Umaru-chan's hamsters, Hamjiro & Hamsaburo.
YOU TALKING TO YOUR HAM-STERS?
WE'RE HAVING A WON-DERFUL CONVER-SATION...

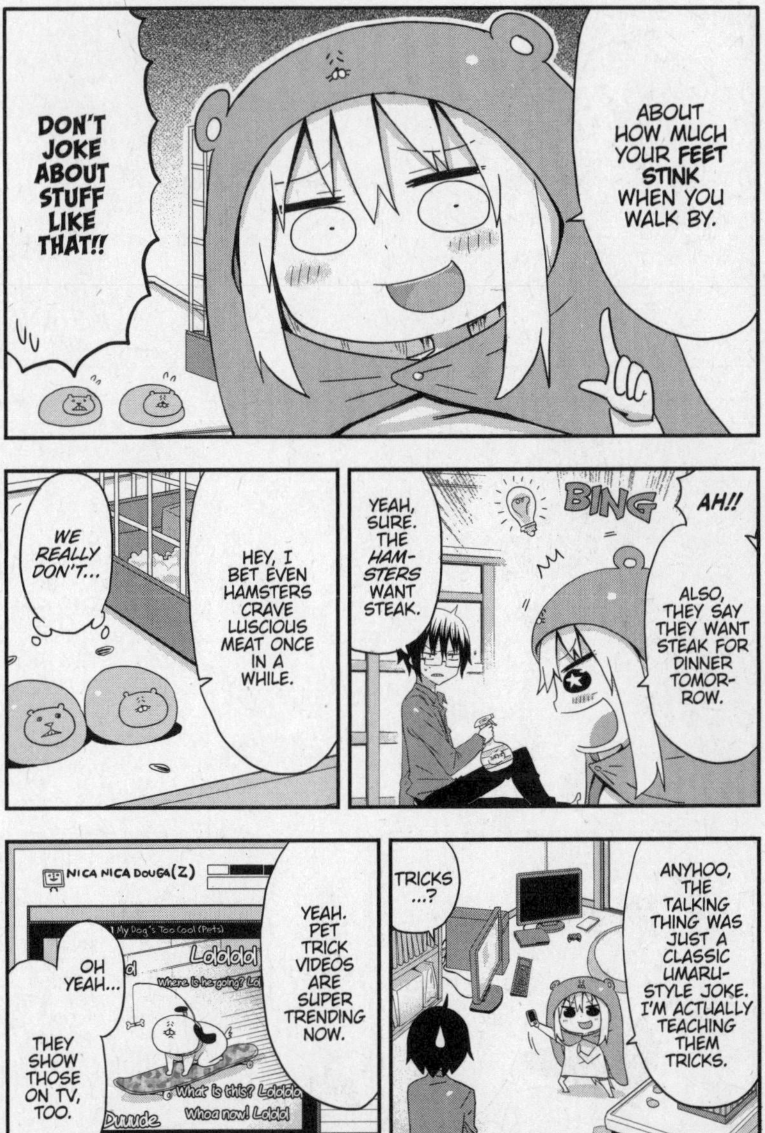
ABOUT HOW MUCH YOUR FEET STINK WHEN YOU WALK BY.
DON'T JOKE ABOUT STUFF LIKE THAT!!
AH!!
BING
ALSO, THEY SAY THEY WANT STEAK FOR DINNER TOMORROW.
YEAH, SURE. THE HAMSTERS WANT STEAK.
HEY, I BET EVEN HAMSTERS CRAVE LUSCIOUS MEAT ONCE IN A WHILE.
WE REALLY DON'T...
ANYHOO, THE TALKING THING WAS JUST A CLASSIC UMARU-STYLE JOKE. I'M ACTUALLY TEACHING THEM TRICKS.
TRICKS ...?
YEAH. PET TRICK VIDEOS ARE SUPER TRENDING NOW.
NICA NICA DOUGA(Z)
My Dog's Too Cool (Pets)
Lolololol
Where is he going? Lol
What is this? Lolololol
Whoa now! Lololol
Duuude
OH YEAH...
THEY SHOW THOSE ON TV, TOO.

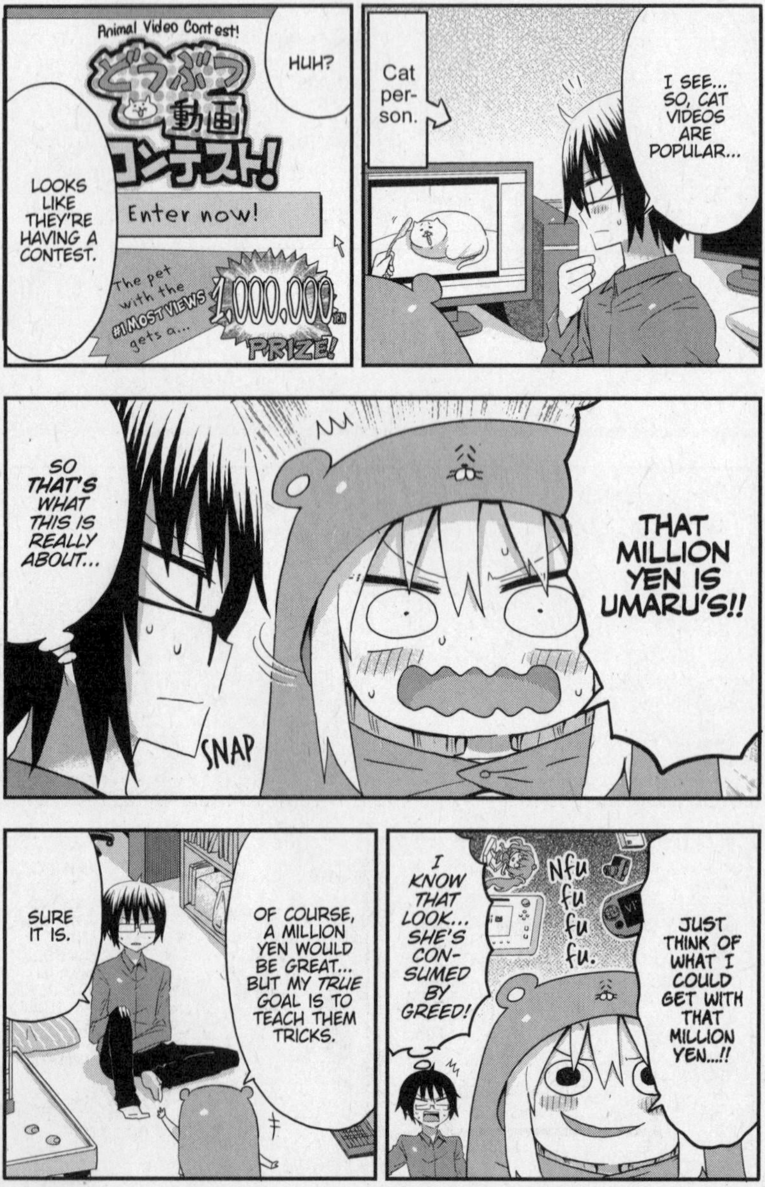
I SEE... SO, CAT VIDEOS ARE POPULAR...
Cat per-son.
HUH?
Animal Video Contest!
どうぶつ動画コンテスト!
Enter now!
LOOKS LIKE THEY'RE HAVING A CONTEST.
The pet with the #1 MOST VIEWS gets a... 1,000,000 YEN PRIZE!
THAT MILLION YEN IS UMARU'S!!
SO THAT'S WHAT THIS IS REALLY ABOUT...
SNAP
JUST THINK OF WHAT I COULD GET WITH THAT MILLION YEN...!!
Nfu fu fu fu.
I KNOW THAT LOOK... SHE'S CON-SUMED BY GREED!
OF COURSE, A MILLION YEN WOULD BE GREAT... BUT MY TRUE GOAL IS TO TEACH THEM TRICKS.
SURE IT IS.

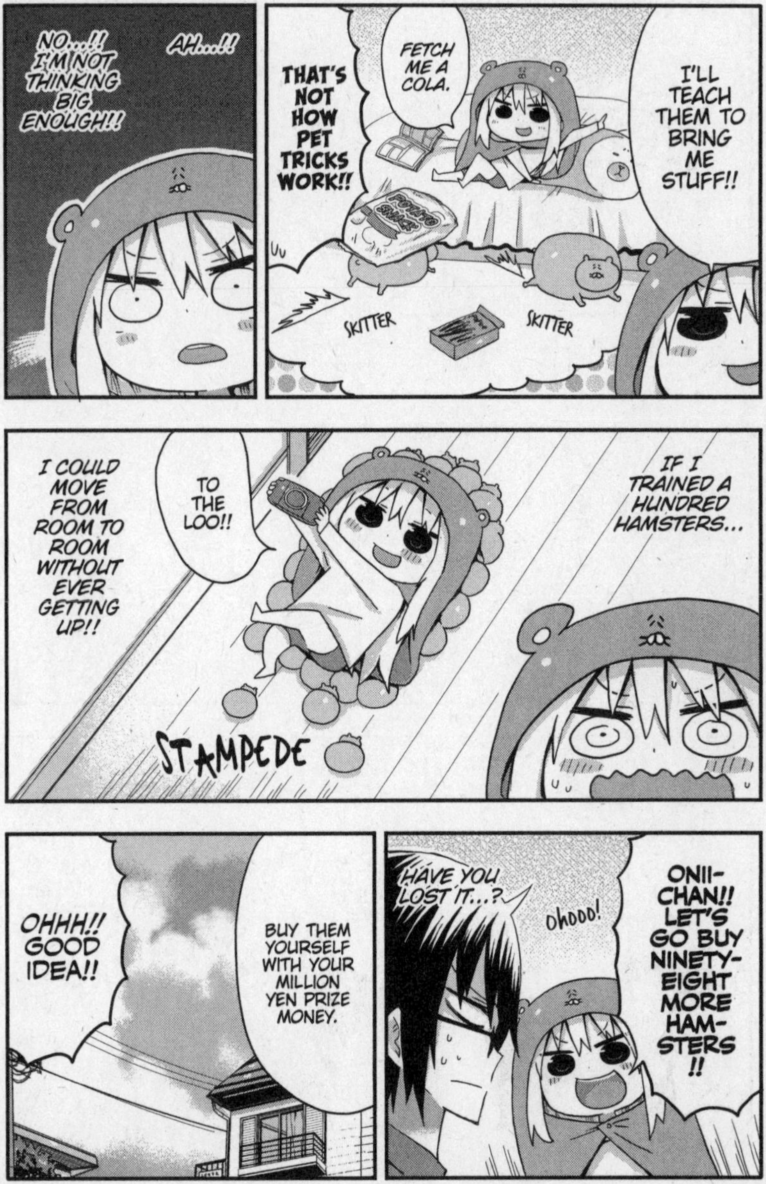
I'LL TEACH THEM TO BRING ME STUFF!!
FETCH ME A COLA.
THAT'S NOT HOW PET TRICKS WORK!!
SKITTER
SKITTER
AH...!!
NO...!! I'M NOT THINKING BIG ENOUGH!!
IF I TRAINED A HUNDRED HAMSTERS...
TO THE LOO!!
I COULD MOVE FROM ROOM TO ROOM WITHOUT EVER GETTING UP!!
STAMPEDE
ONII-CHAN!! LET'S GO BUY NINETY-EIGHT MORE HAMSTERS!!
Ohooo!
HAVE YOU LOST IT...?
BUY THEM YOURSELF WITH YOUR MILLION YEN PRIZE MONEY.
OHHH!! GOOD IDEA!!

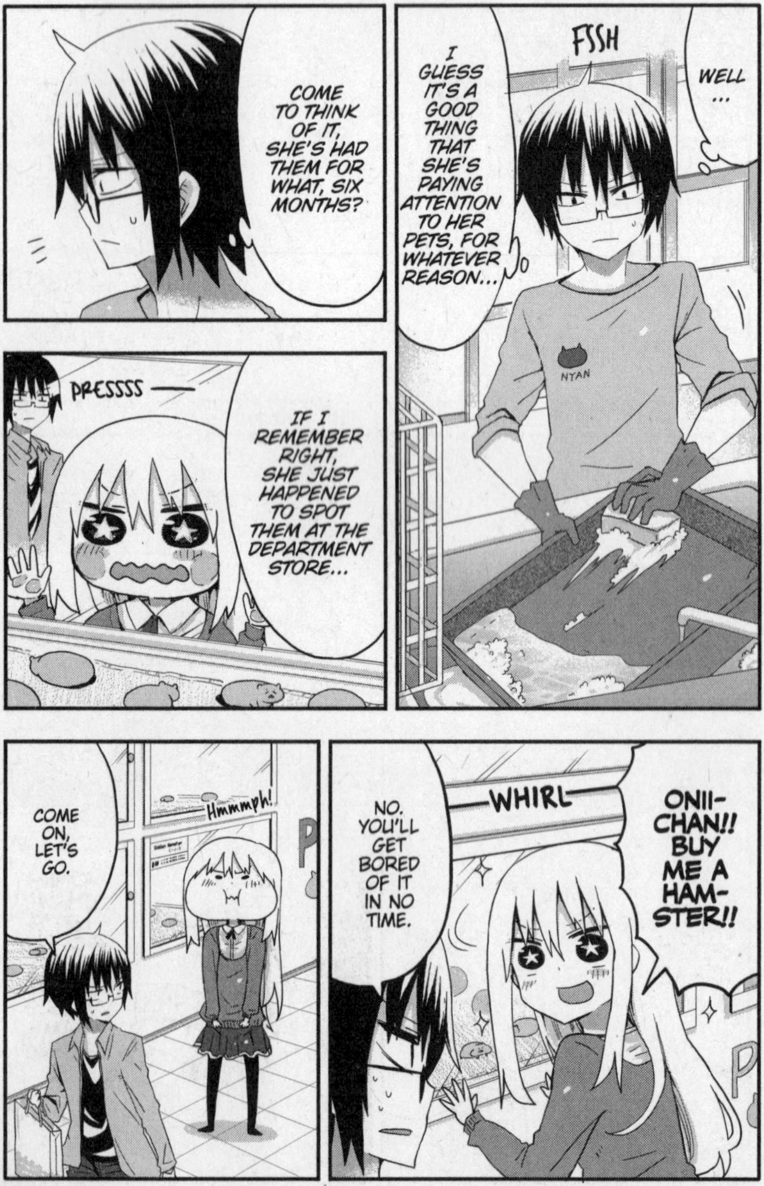
WELL ...
FSSH
I GUESS IT'S A GOOD THING THAT SHE'S PAYING ATTENTION TO HER PETS, FOR WHATEVER REASON...
COME TO THINK OF IT, SHE'S HAD THEM FOR WHAT, SIX MONTHS?
IF I REMEMBER RIGHT, SHE JUST HAPPENED TO SPOT THEM AT THE DEPARTMENT STORE...
PRESSSS —
NTAN
ONII-CHAN!! BUY ME A HAM-STER!!
WHIRL
NO. YOU'LL GET BORED OF IT IN NO TIME.
Hmmmph!
COME ON, LET'S GO.

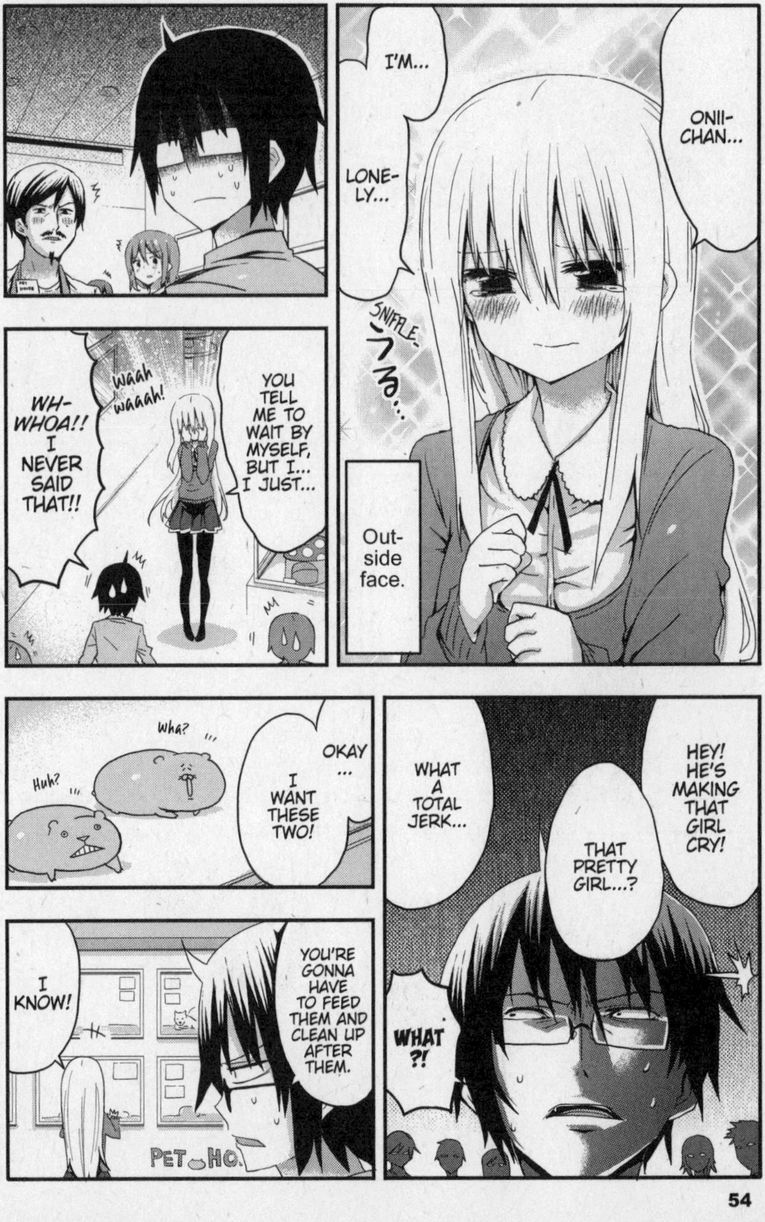
ONII-CHAN...
I'M...
LONELY...
SNIFFLE.
うる...
Out-side face.
YOU TELL ME TO WAIT BY MYSELF, BUT I... I JUST...
waah waaah!
WH-WHOA!! I NEVER SAID THAT!!
HEY! HE'S MAKING THAT GIRL CRY!
WHAT A TOTAL JERK...
THAT PRETTY GIRL...?
WHAT ?!
OKAY... I WANT THESE TWO!
Wha?
Huh?
YOU'RE GONNA HAVE TO FEED THEM AND CLEAN UP AFTER THEM.
I KNOW!
PET HO.

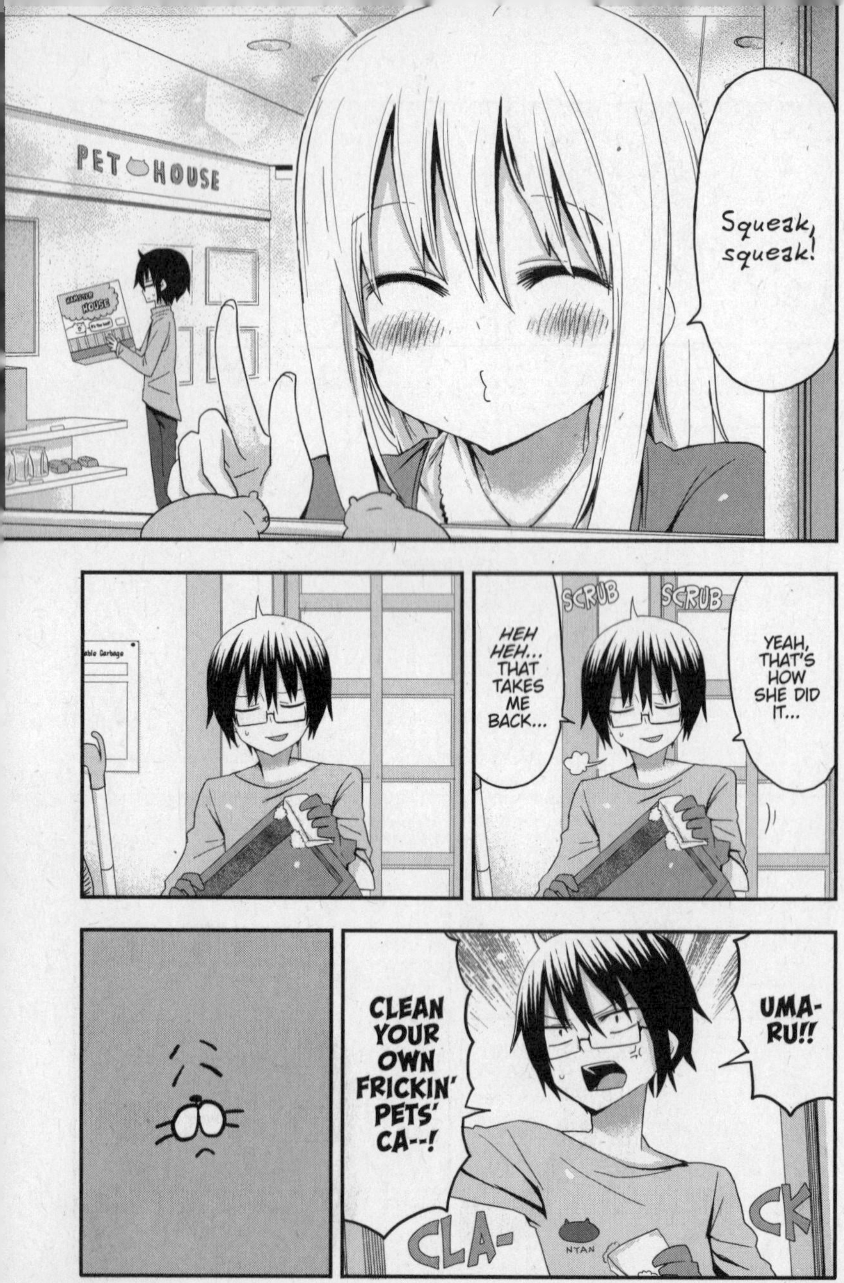

Squeak, squeak!
PET HOUSE
SCRUB SCRUB
YEAH, THAT'S HOW SHE DID IT...
HEH HEH... THAT TAKES ME BACK...
UMA-RU!!
CLEAN YOUR OWN FRICKIN' PETS' CA--!
CK
CLA-
NYAN

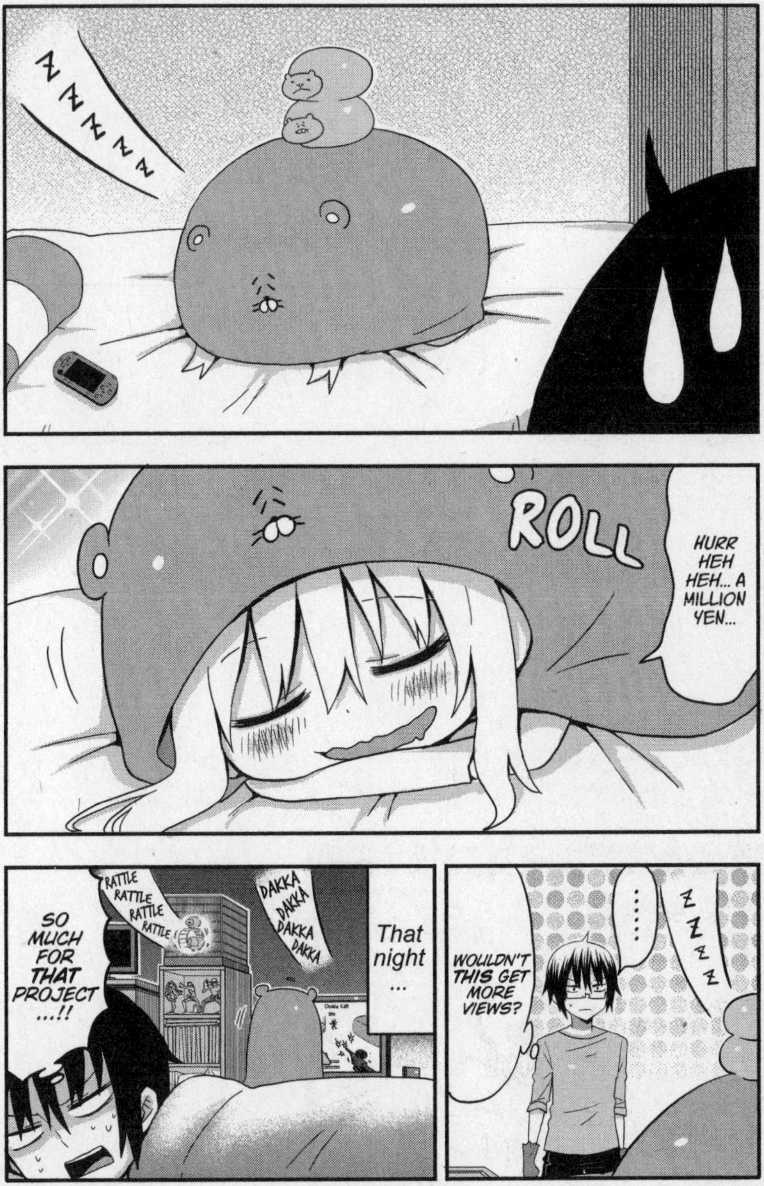

ZZZZZ
ROLL
HURR HEH HEH... A MILLION YEN...
ZZZZ
......
WOULDN'T THIS GET MORE VIEWS?
That night ...
DAKKA DAKKA DAKKA DAKKA
RATTLE RATTLE RATTLE RATTLE
SO MUCH FOR THAT PROJECT ...!!

The Winning Video

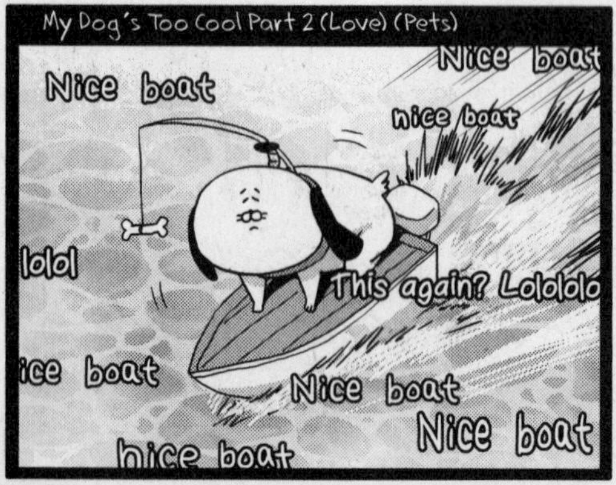
My Dog's Too Cool Part 2 (Love) (Pets)
Nice boat
Nice boat
nice boat
lolol
This again? Lolololo
ice boat
Nice boat
Nice boat
nice boat

HIMOUTO! UMARU-CHAN

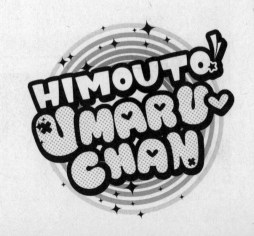

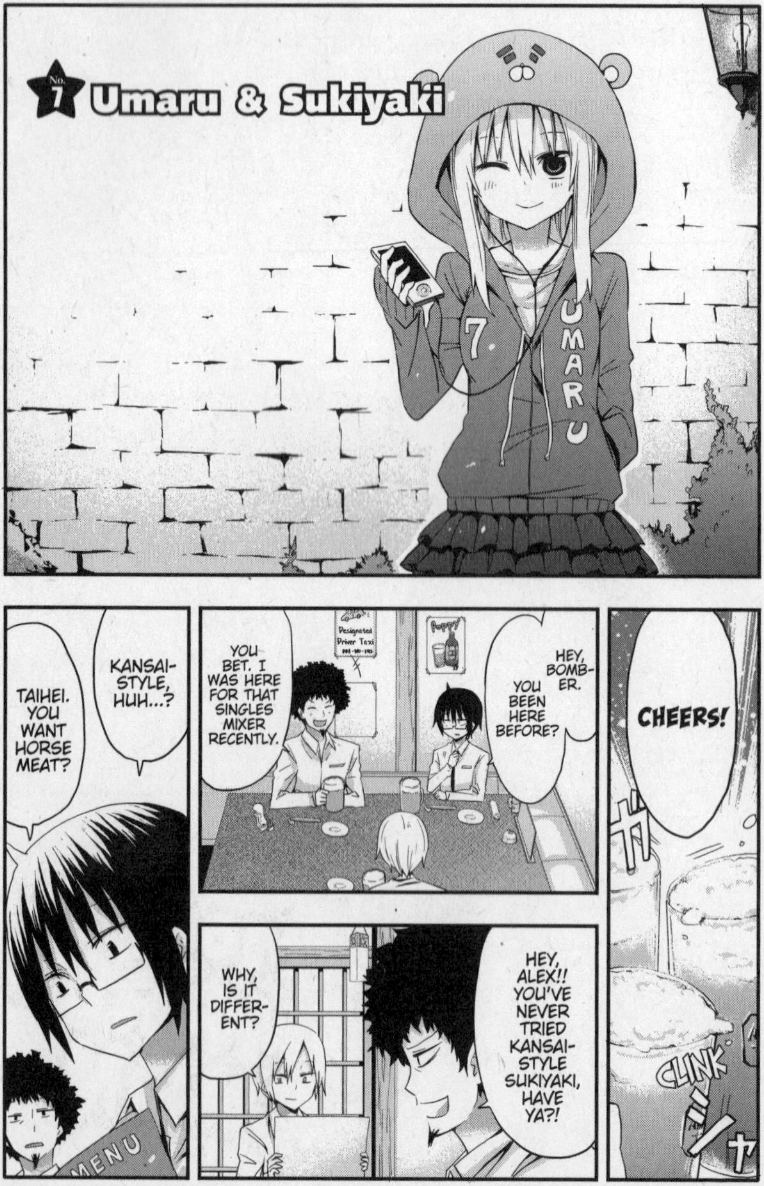
No. 7 Umaru & Sukiyaki
UMARU
CHEERS!
CLINK
Designated Driver Taxi
Poppy
HEY, BOMBER. YOU BEEN HERE BEFORE?
YOU BET. I WAS HERE FOR THAT SINGLES MIXER RECENTLY.
HEY, ALEX!! YOU'VE NEVER TRIED KANSAI-STYLE SUKIYAKI, HAVE YA?!
WHY, IS IT DIFFER-ENT?
KANSAI-STYLE, HUH...?
TAIHEI. YOU WANT HORSE MEAT?
MENU

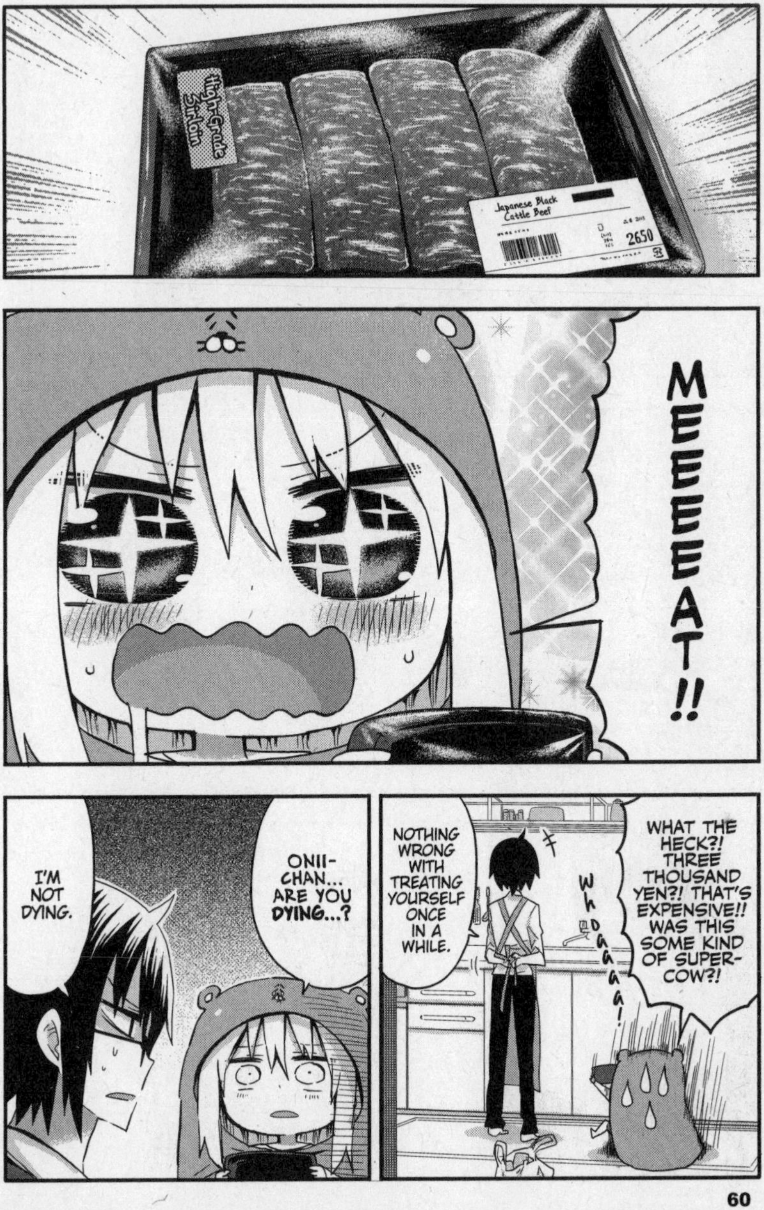
High-Grade Sirloin
Japanese Black Cattle Beef
2650
MEEEEEAT!!
WHAT THE HECK?! THREE THOUSAND YEN?! THAT'S EXPENSIVE!! WAS THIS SOME KIND OF SUPER-COW?!
Whaaaaaa!
NOTHING WRONG WITH TREATING YOURSELF ONCE IN A WHILE.
ONII-CHAN... ARE YOU **DYING...?**
I'M NOT DYING.

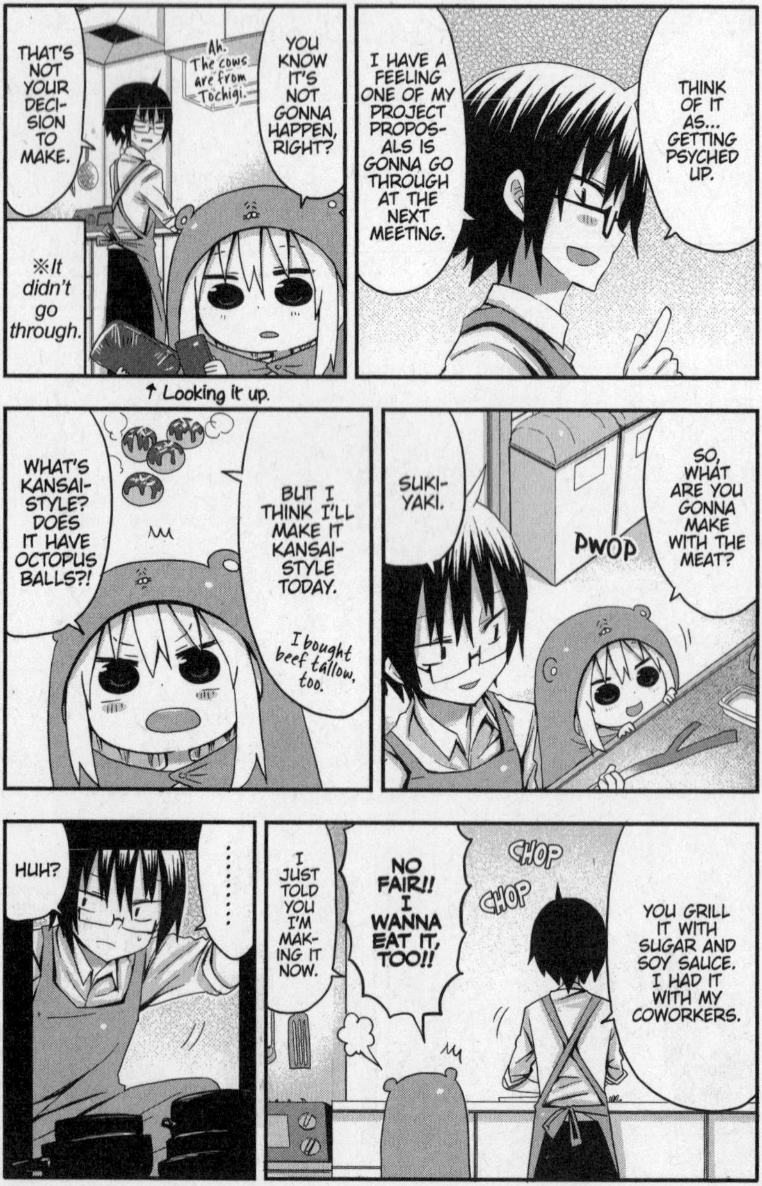
THINK OF IT AS... GETTING PSYCHED UP.
I HAVE A FEELING ONE OF MY PROJECT PROPOSALS IS GONNA GO THROUGH AT THE NEXT MEETING.
YOU KNOW IT'S NOT GONNA HAPPEN, RIGHT?
Ah. The cows are from Tochigi.
THAT'S NOT YOUR DECISION TO MAKE.
※It didn't go through.
↑ Looking it up.
SO, WHAT ARE YOU GONNA MAKE WITH THE MEAT?
PWOP
SUKI-YAKI.
BUT I THINK I'LL MAKE IT KANSAI-STYLE TODAY.
I bought beef tallow, too.
WHAT'S KANSAI-STYLE? DOES IT HAVE OCTOPUS BALLS?!
YOU GRILL IT WITH SUGAR AND SOY SAUCE. I HAD IT WITH MY COWORKERS.
CHOP
CHOP
NO FAIR!! I WANNA EAT IT, TOO!!
I JUST TOLD YOU I'M MAKING IT NOW.
....
HUH?

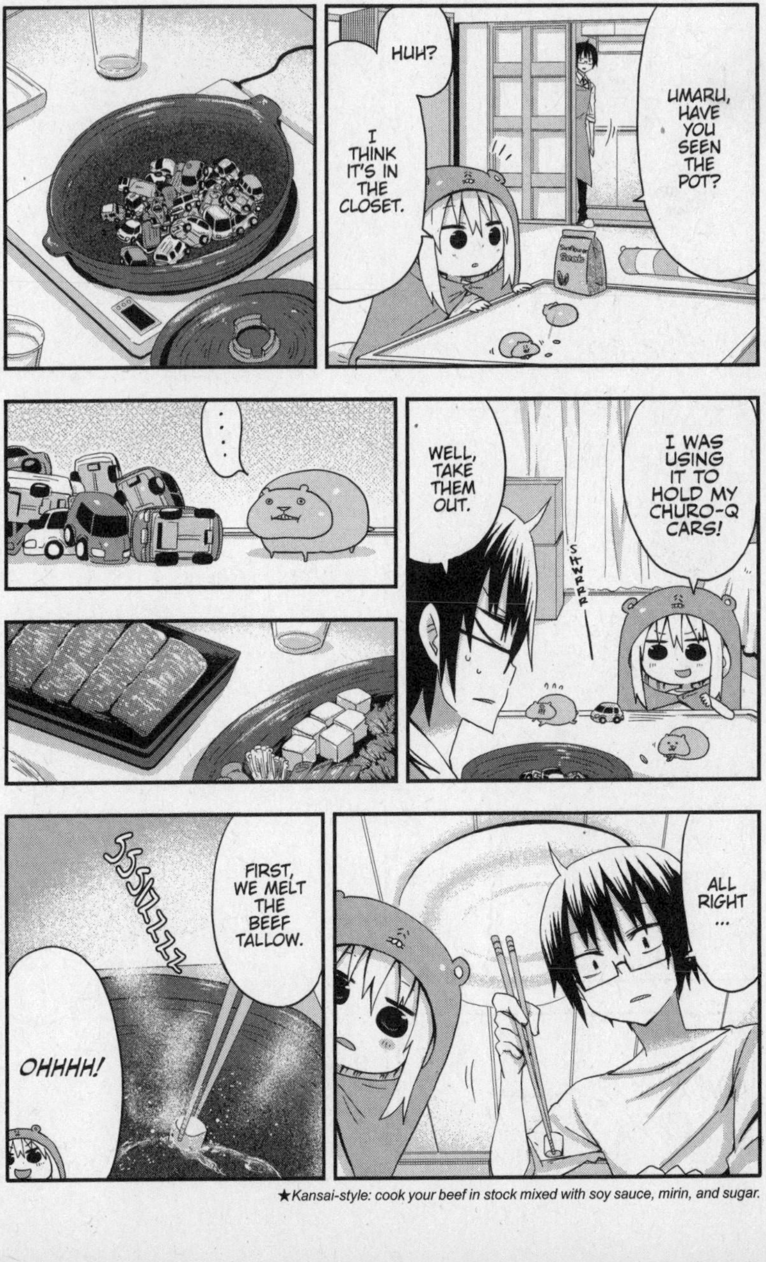
UMARU, HAVE YOU SEEN THE POT?
HUH?
I THINK IT'S IN THE CLOSET.
I WAS USING IT TO HOLD MY CHURO-Q CARS!
SHWRRR
WELL, TAKE THEM OUT.
...
ALL RIGHT ...
FIRST, WE MELT THE BEEF TALLOW.
OHHHH!

★*Kansai-style: cook your beef in stock mixed with soy sauce, mirin, and sugar.*

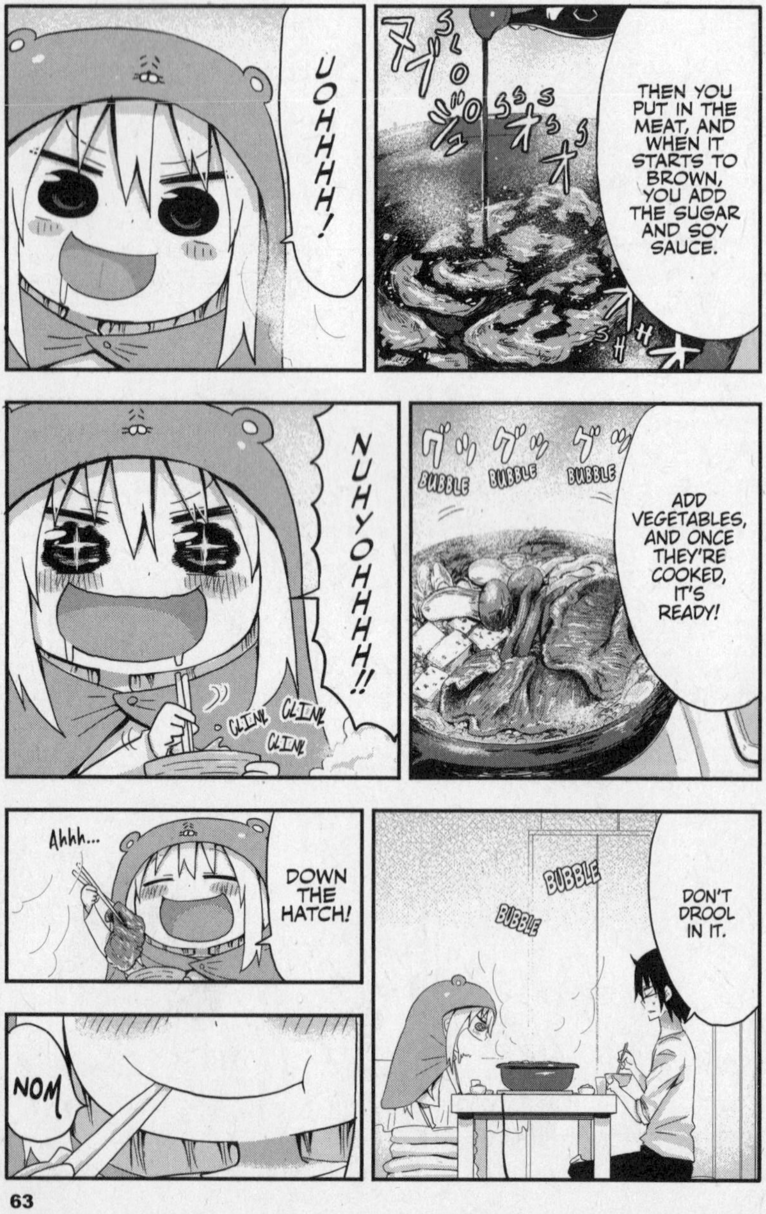
THEN YOU PUT IN THE MEAT, AND WHEN IT STARTS TO BROWN, YOU ADD THE SUGAR AND SOY SAUCE.
UOHHHHH!
ADD VEGETABLES, AND ONCE THEY'RE COOKED, IT'S READY!
BUBBLE BUBBLE BUBBLE
NUHYOHHHHH!!
CLINK CLINK CLINK
DON'T DROOL IN IT.
BUBBLE BUBBLE
Ahhh...
DOWN THE HATCH!
NOM

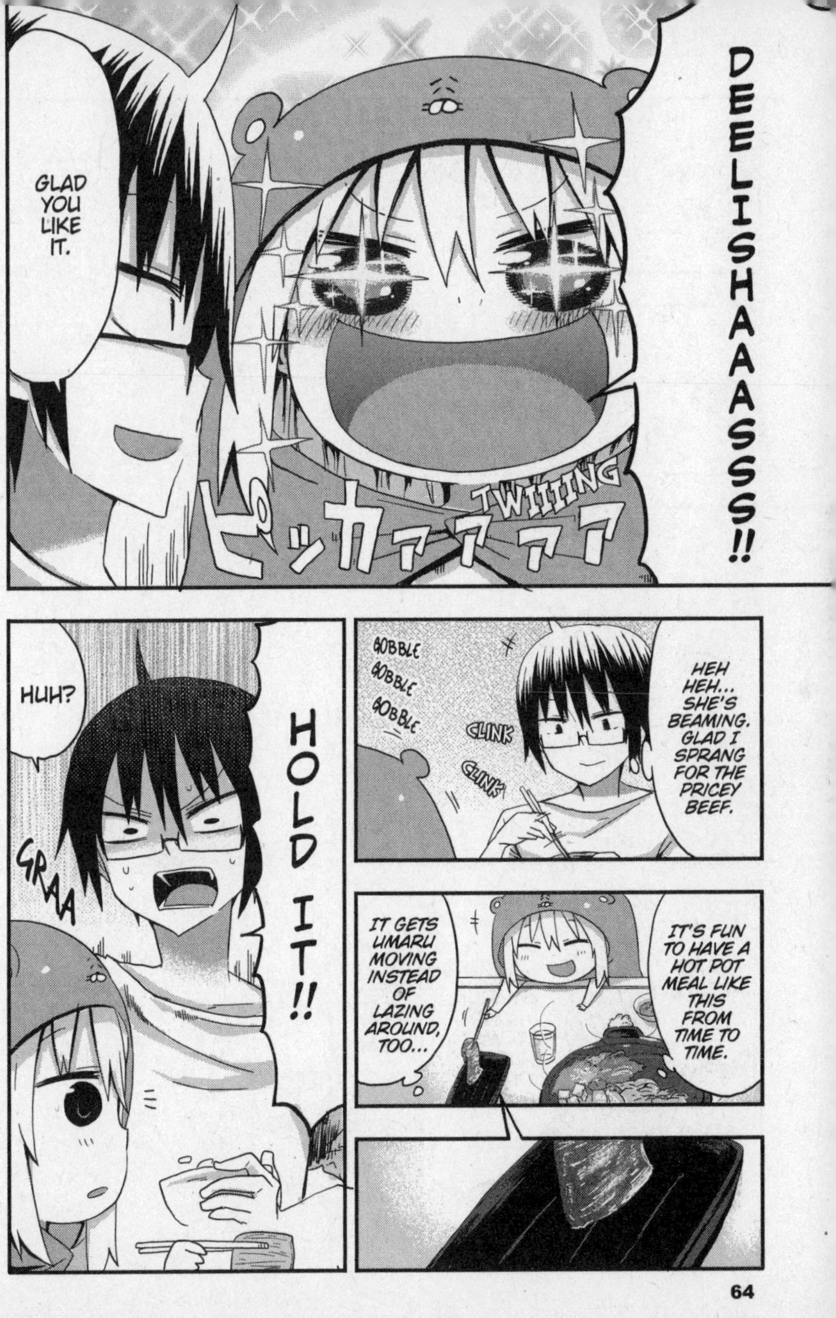
DEELISHAAAASSS!!
TWIIIING
ピッカァアアア
GLAD YOU LIKE IT.
HEH HEH... SHE'S BEAMING. GLAD I SPRANG FOR THE PRICEY BEEF.
GOBBLE GOBBLE GOBBLE
CLINK CLINK
IT'S FUN TO HAVE A HOT POT MEAL LIKE THIS FROM TIME TO TIME.
IT GETS UMARU MOVING INSTEAD OF LAZING AROUND, TOO...
HOLD IT!!
HUH?
GRAA

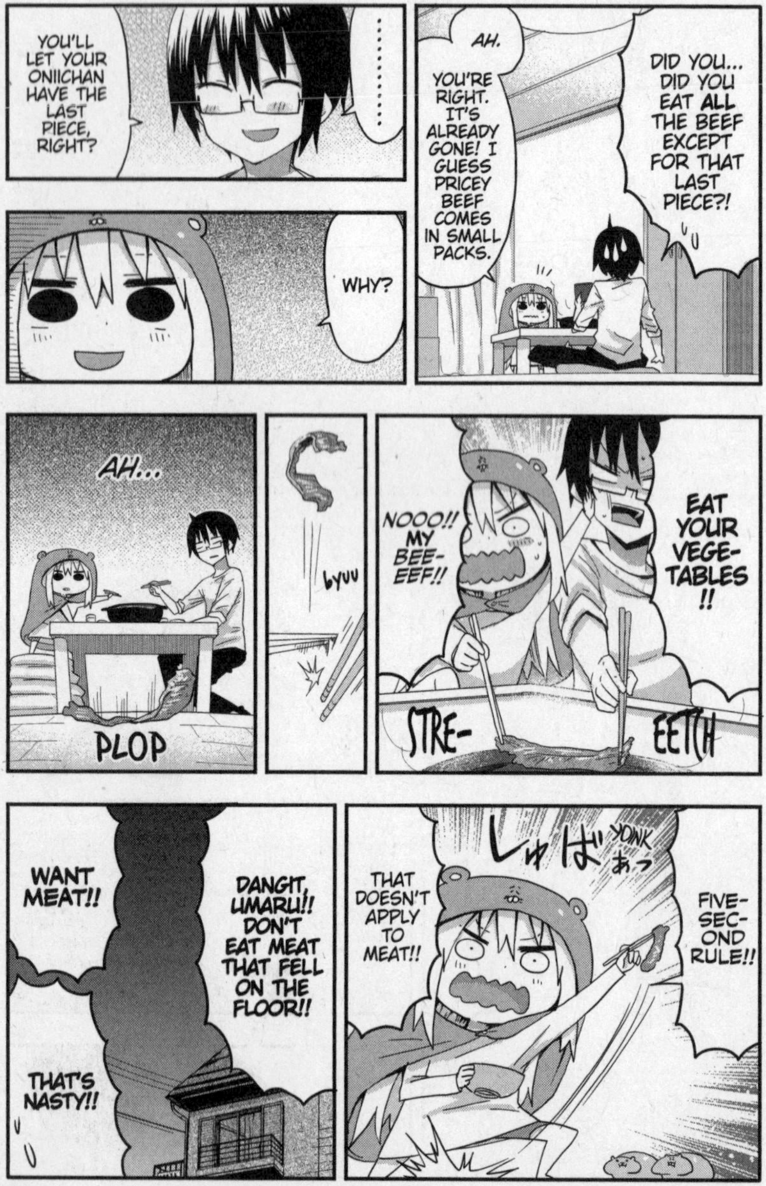
DID YOU... DID YOU EAT ALL THE BEEF EXCEPT FOR THAT LAST PIECE?!
AH.
YOU'RE RIGHT. IT'S ALREADY GONE! I GUESS PRICEY BEEF COMES IN SMALL PACKS.
......
YOU'LL LET YOUR ONIICHAN HAVE THE LAST PIECE, RIGHT?
WHY?
EAT YOUR VEGE-TABLES!!
NOOO!! MY BEE-EEF!!
STRE-
EETCH
byuu
AH...
PLOP
FIVE-SEC-OND RULE!!
しゅばあっ
YOINK
THAT DOESN'T APPLY TO MEAT!!
DANGIT, UMARU!! DON'T EAT MEAT THAT FELL ON THE FLOOR!!
WANT MEAT!!
THAT'S NASTY!!

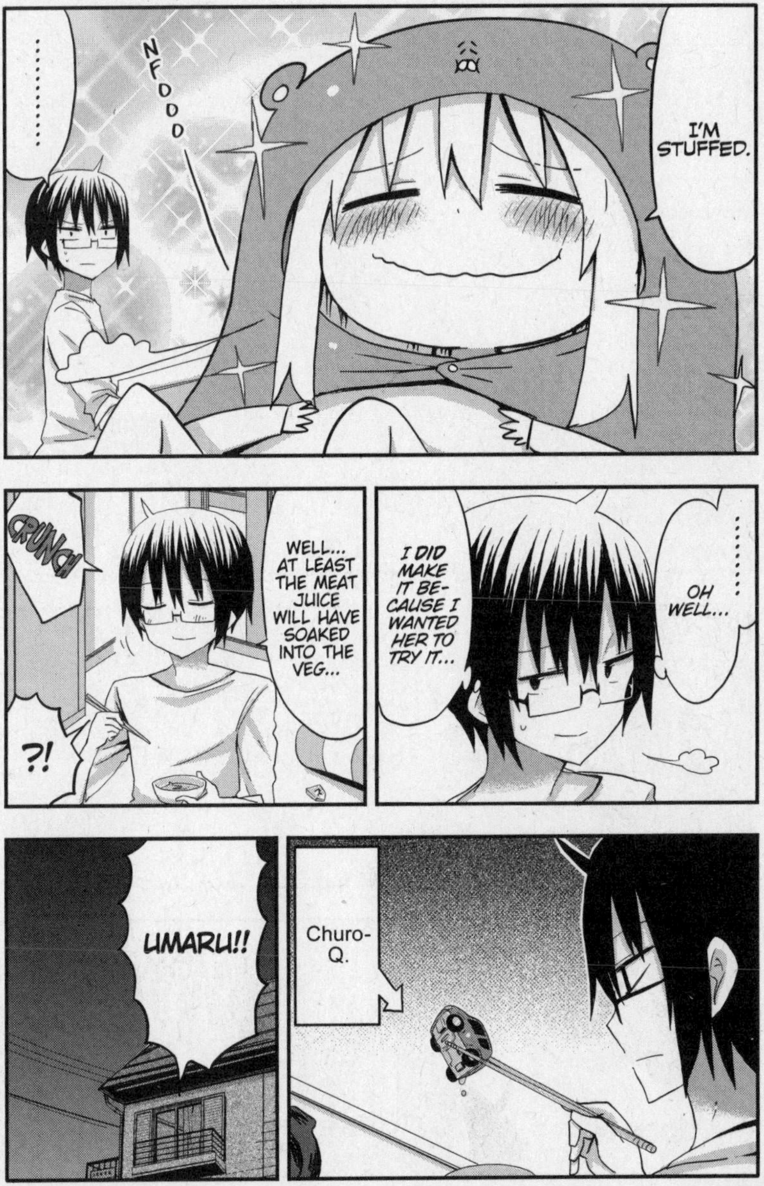
I'M STUFFED.
NFDDDD
......
......
OH WELL...
I DID MAKE IT BE-CAUSE I WANTED HER TO TRY IT...
WELL... AT LEAST THE MEAT JUICE WILL HAVE SOAKED INTO THE VEG...
CRUNCH
?!
Churo-Q.
UMARU!!

No. 8 Umaru & a Friend

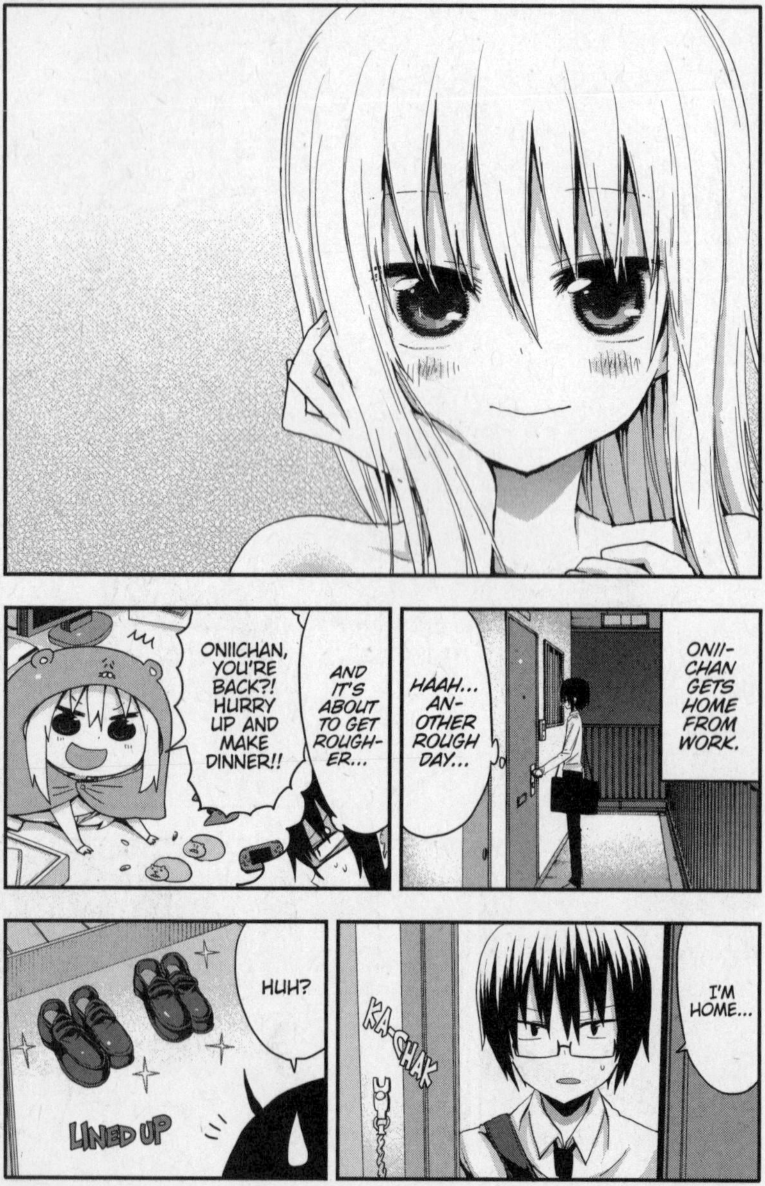
ONII-CHAN GETS HOME FROM WORK.
HAAH... AN-OTHER ROUGH DAY...
AND IT'S ABOUT TO GET ROUGH-ER...
ONIICHAN, YOU'RE BACK?! HURRY UP AND MAKE DINNER!!
I'M HOME...
KA-CHAK
HUH?
LINED UP

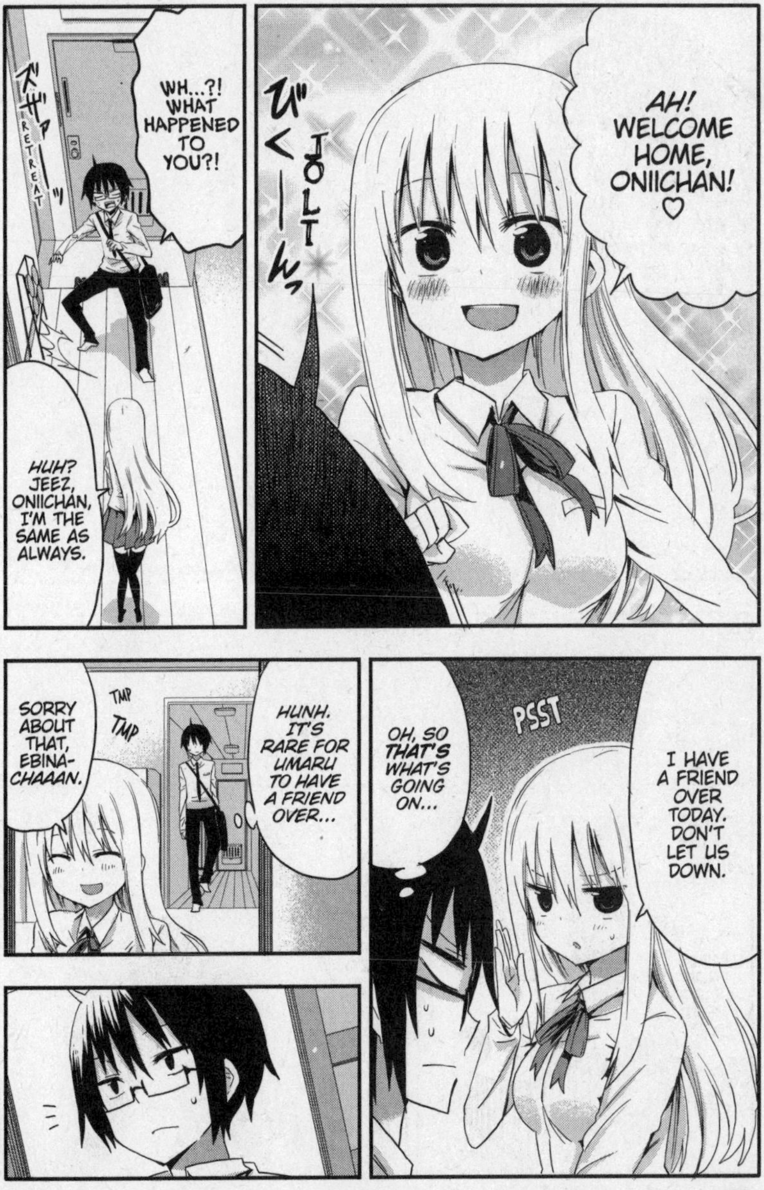
AH! WELCOME HOME, ONIICHAN! ♡
びくーんっ
JOLT
WH...?! WHAT HAPPENED TO YOU?!
ズザァーッ
RETREAT
HUH? JEEZ, ONIICHAN, I'M THE SAME AS ALWAYS.
I HAVE A FRIEND OVER TODAY. DON'T LET US DOWN.
PSST
OH, SO THAT'S WHAT'S GOING ON...
HUNH. IT'S RARE FOR UMARU TO HAVE A FRIEND OVER...
TMP
TMP
SORRY ABOUT THAT, EBINA-CHAAAN.
SORRY

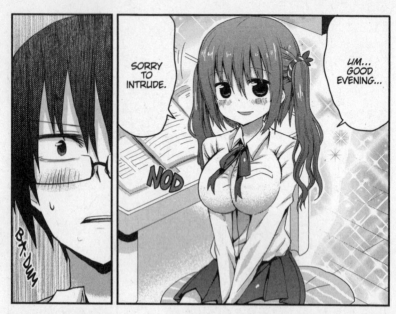

UM... GOOD EVENING...
SORRY TO INTRUDE.
NOD
BA-DUM
TWIIIIING
ピッカァァッ
WHAT'S GOING ON? THE APARTMENT'S SPARKLING CLEAN!!
EBINA-CHAN AND I ARE HAVING A STUDY PARTY.
HUH?
WAIT... EBINA-SAN? FROM OUR APARTMENT BUILDING?
I thought the name was familiar...
AH... YES...
I'M EBINA FROM APARTMENT 301...
Yoshida Apartments
Now Leasing!

Umaru-chan & Oniichan live in 201.

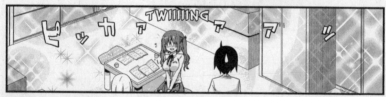

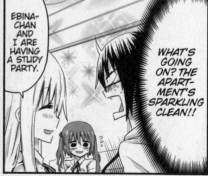

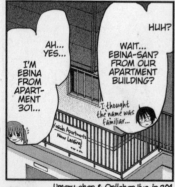

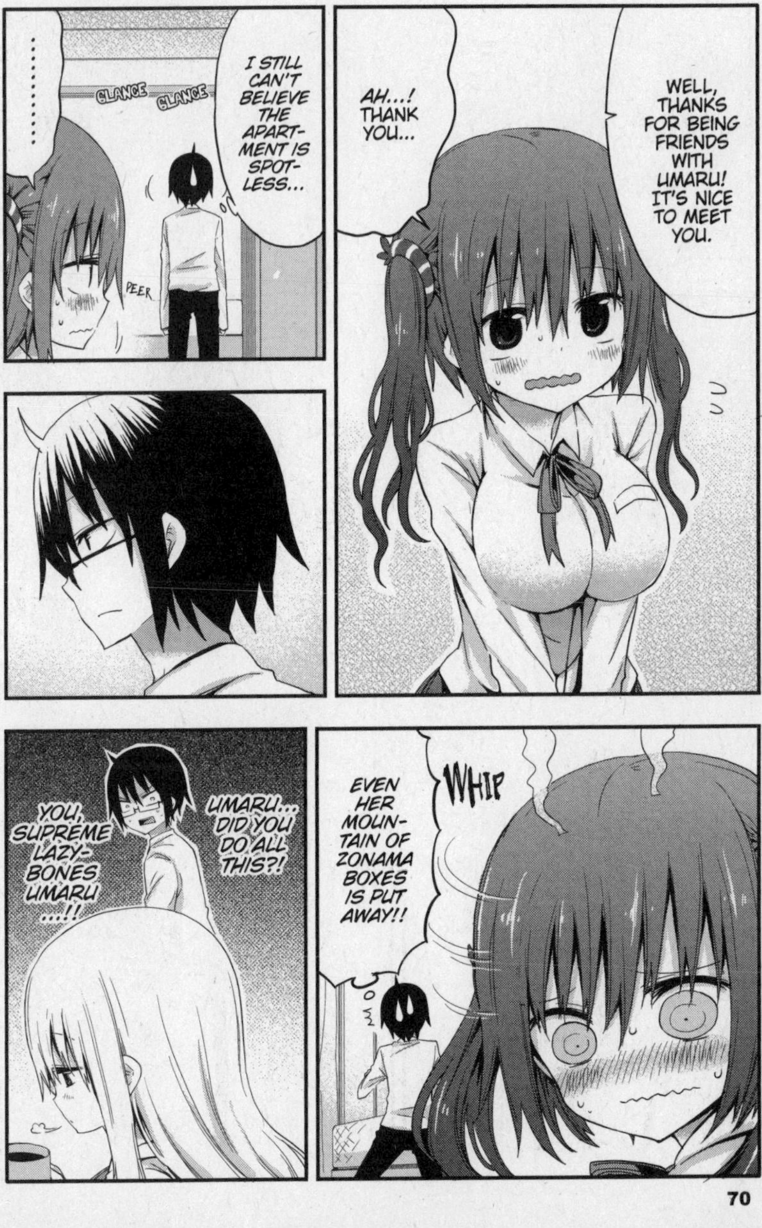

WELL, THANKS FOR BEING FRIENDS WITH UMARU! IT'S NICE TO MEET YOU.
AH...! THANK YOU...
I STILL CAN'T BELIEVE THE APARTMENT IS SPOTLESS...
GLANCE
GLANCE
PEER
......
EVEN HER MOUNTAIN OF ZONAMA BOXES IS PUT AWAY!!
WHIP
UMARU... DID YOU DO ALL THIS?!
YOU, SUPREME LAZYBONES UMARU ...!!

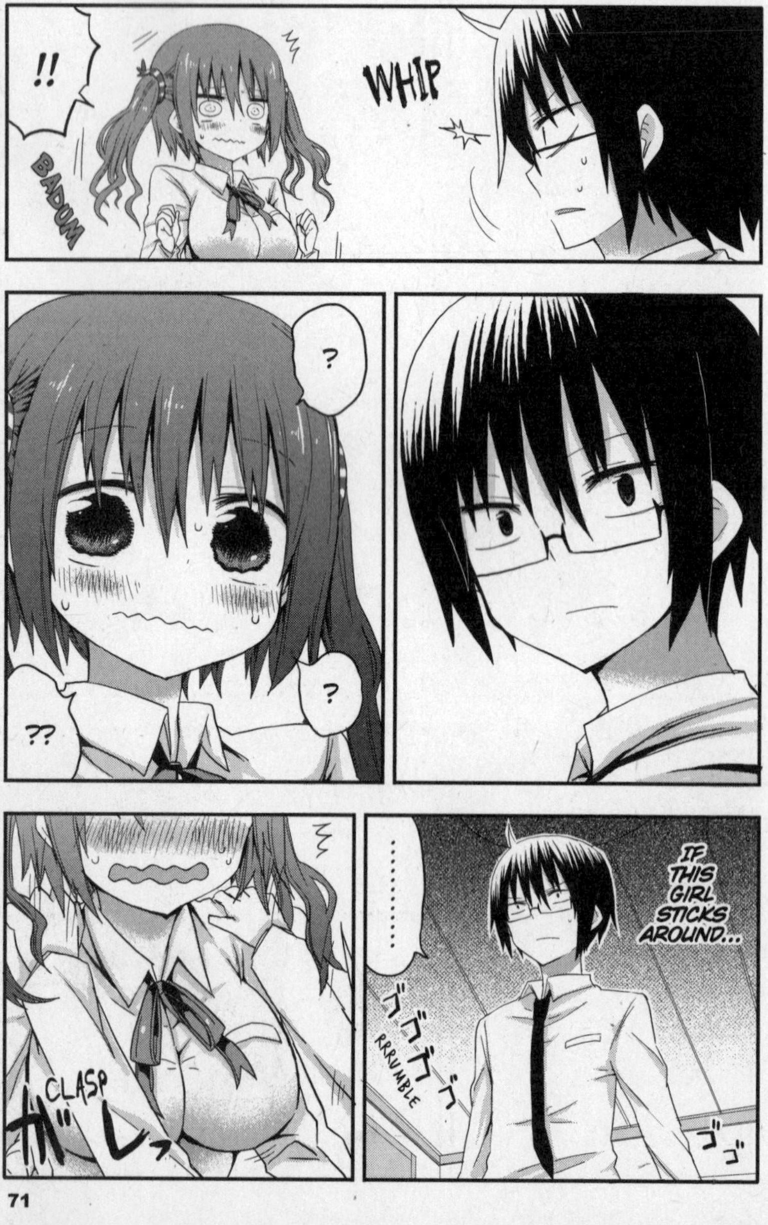
WHIP
!!
BADUM
?
?
??
......
IF THIS GIRL STICKS AROUND...
ゴゴゴゴ
RRRUMBLE
ゴゴ
CLASP
ガシッ

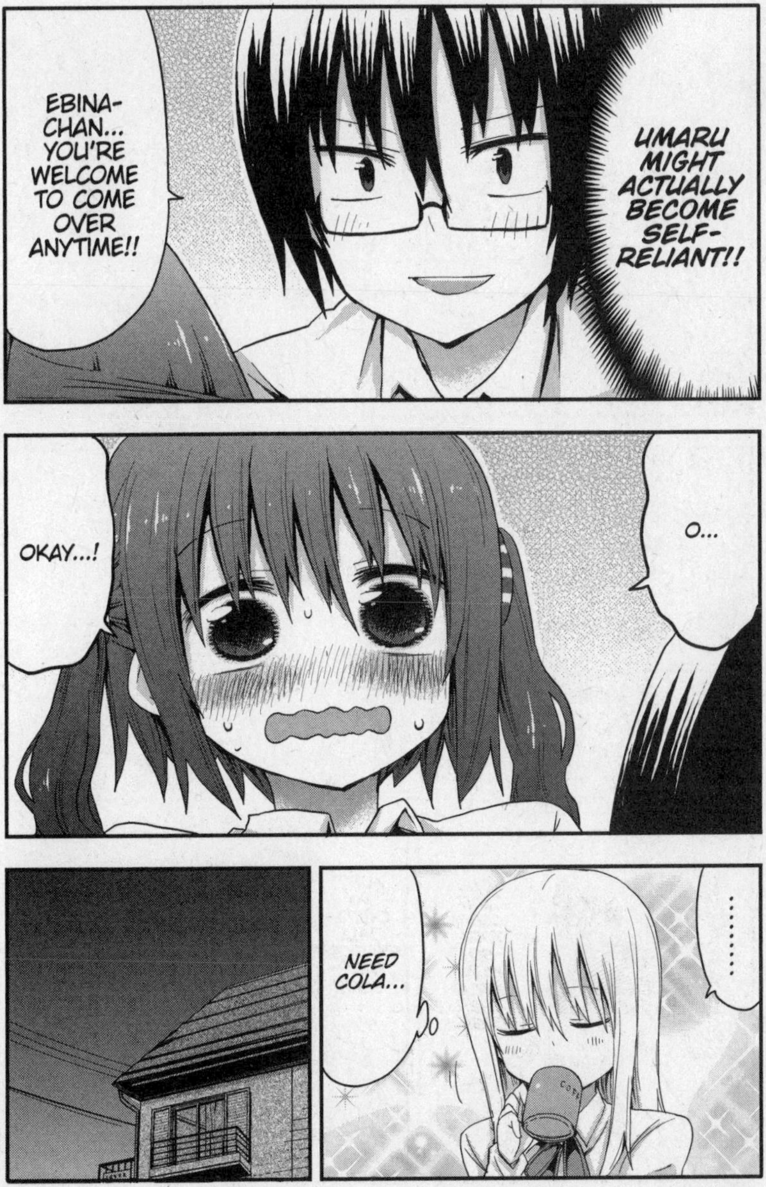
UMARU MIGHT ACTUALLY BECOME SELF-RELIANT!!
EBINA-CHAN... YOU'RE WELCOME TO COME OVER ANYTIME!!
O...
OKAY...!
......
NEED COLA...

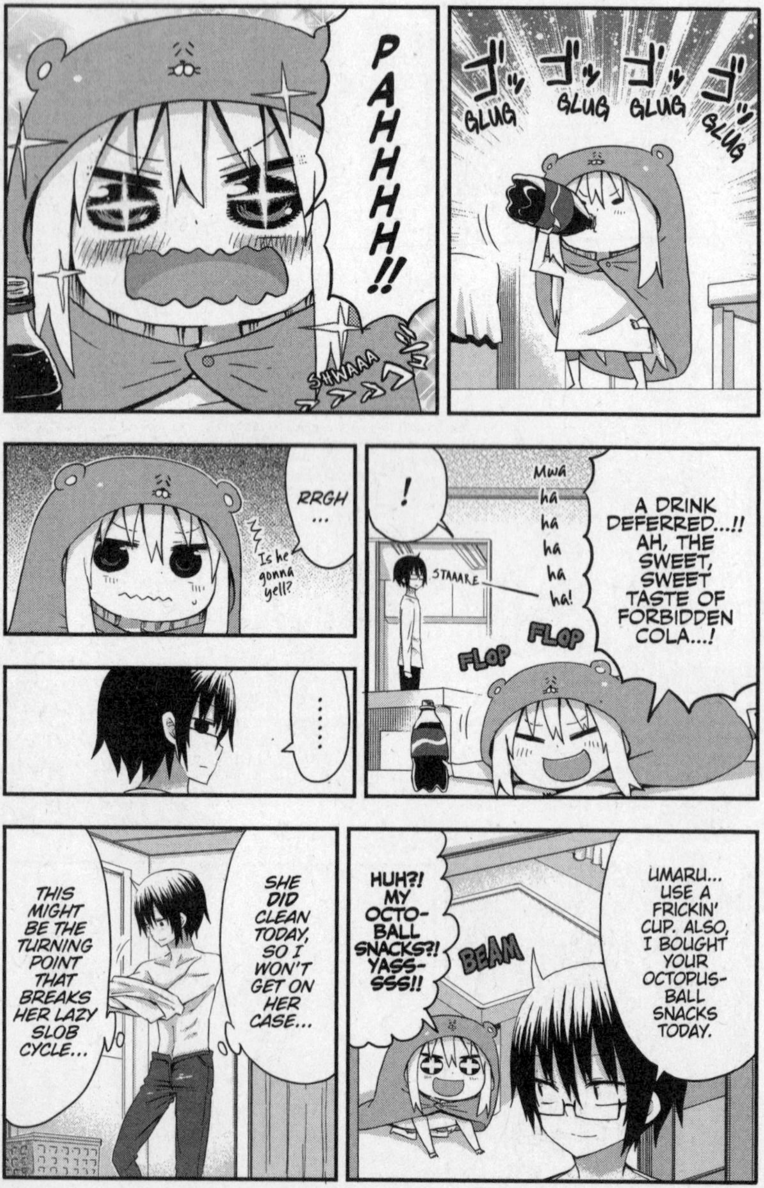
ゴッ ゴッ ゴッ ゴッ
GLUG GLUG GLUG GLUG
PAHHHHH!!
SHWAAA
A DRINK DEFERRED...!! AH, THE SWEET, SWEET TASTE OF FORBIDDEN COLA...!
Mwa ha ha ha ha ha!
!
STAAARE
FLOP FLOP
RRGH ...
Is he gonna yell?
......
UMARU... USE A FRICKIN' CUP. ALSO, I BOUGHT YOUR OCTOPUS-BALL SNACKS TODAY.
HUH?! MY OCTO-BALL SNACKS?! YASS-SSS!!
BEAM
SHE DID CLEAN TODAY, SO I WON'T GET ON HER CASE...
THIS MIGHT BE THE TURNING POINT THAT BREAKS HER LAZY SLOB CYCLE...

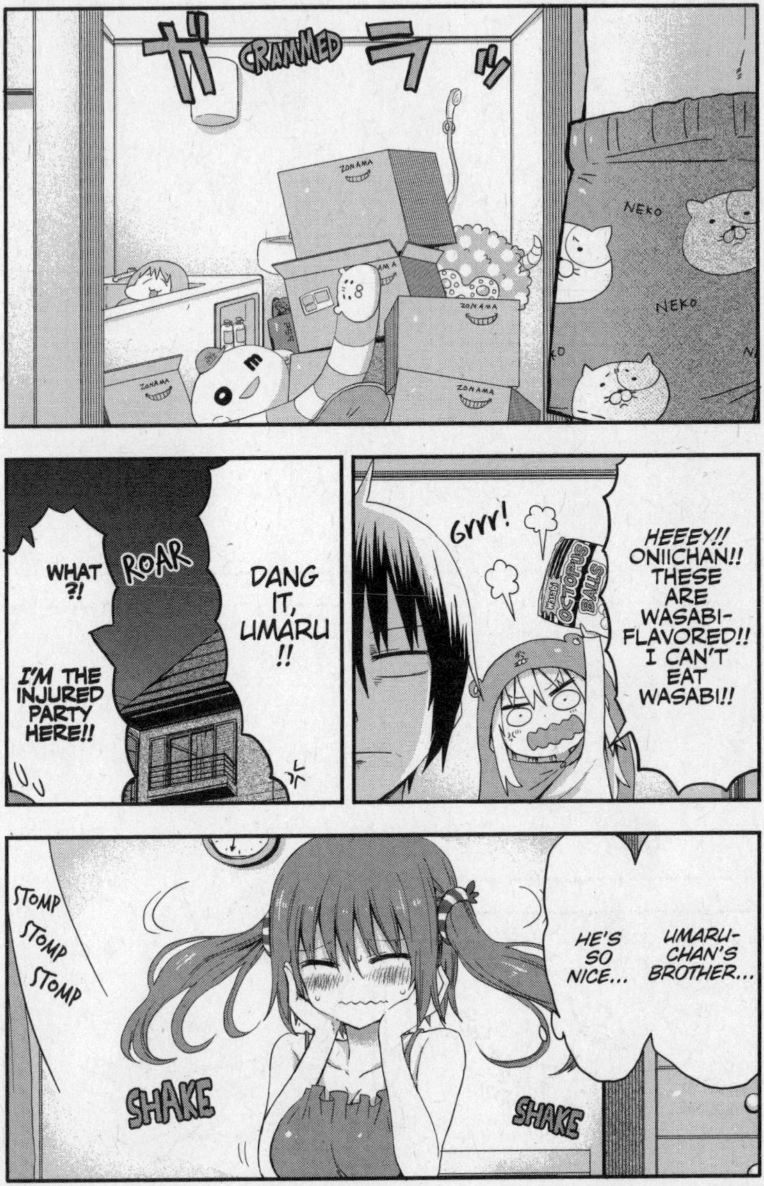
ガ
CRAMMED
ラ
ッ
ZONAMA
NEKO
NEKO
Oniichan's butt
HEEEY!! ONIICHAN!! THESE ARE WASABI-FLAVORED!! I CAN'T EAT WASABI!!
WASABI OCTOPUS BALLS
Grrr!
DANG IT, UMARU!!
ROAR
WHAT?!
I'M THE INJURED PARTY HERE!!
UMARU-CHAN'S BROTHER...
HE'S SO NICE...
STOMP
STOMP
STOMP
SHAKE
SHAKE

No. 9 Umaru & the Rock-Paper-Scissors Contest

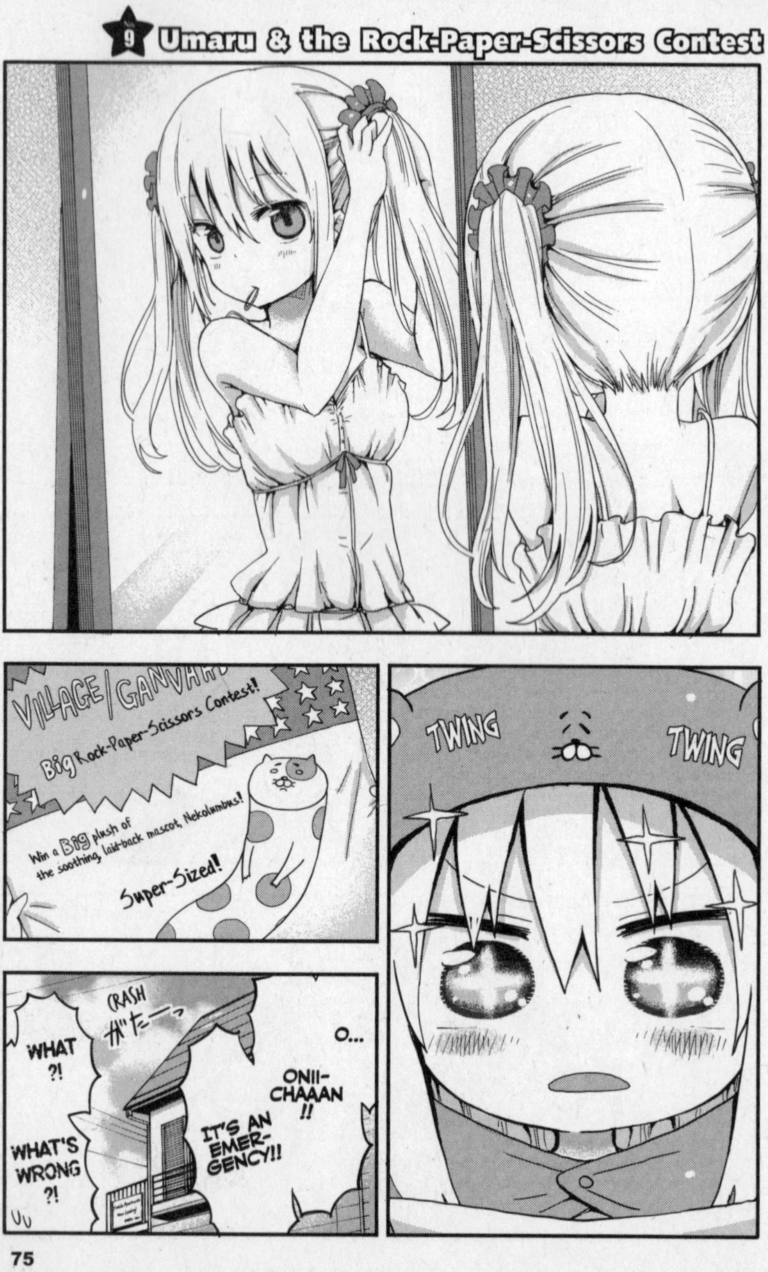
TWING
TWING
VILLAGE/GANVAN
Big Rock-Paper-Scissors Contest!
Win a Big plush of the soothing, laid-back mascot, Nekolumbus!
Super-Sized!
O...
ONII-CHAAAN!!
IT'S AN EMERGENCY!!
CRASH
WHAT?!
WHAT'S WRONG?!

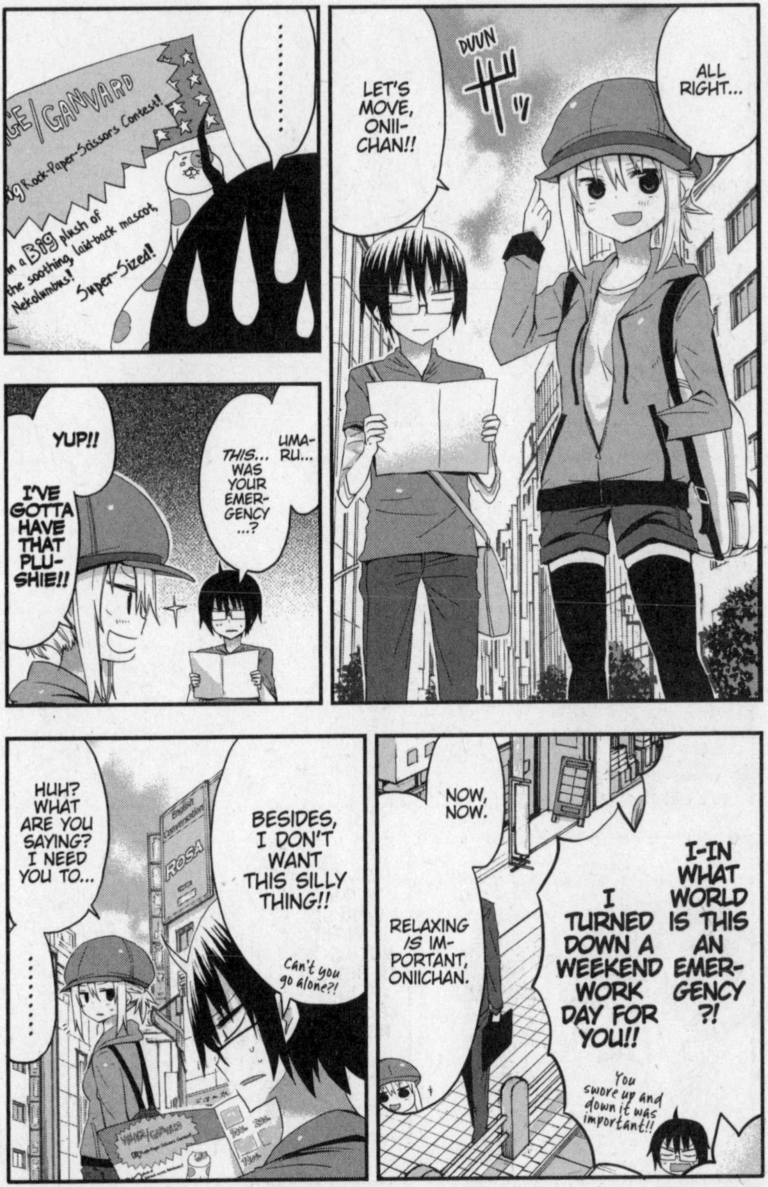
ALL RIGHT...
DUUN
LET'S MOVE, ONII-CHAN!!
GE/GANVARD
Big Rock-Paper-Scissors Contest!
in a Big plush of the soothing, laid-back mascot, Nekolumbus!
Super-Sized!
......
UMARU...
THIS... WAS YOUR EMERGENCY ...?
YUP!!
I'VE GOTTA HAVE THAT PLUSHIE!!
I-IN WHAT WORLD IS THIS AN EMERGENCY?!
I TURNED DOWN A WEEKEND WORK DAY FOR YOU!!
You swore up and down it was important!!
NOW, NOW.
RELAXING *IS* IMPORTANT, ONIICHAN.
BESIDES, I DON'T WANT THIS SILLY THING!!
Can't you go alone?!
HUH? WHAT ARE YOU SAYING? I NEED YOU TO...
......

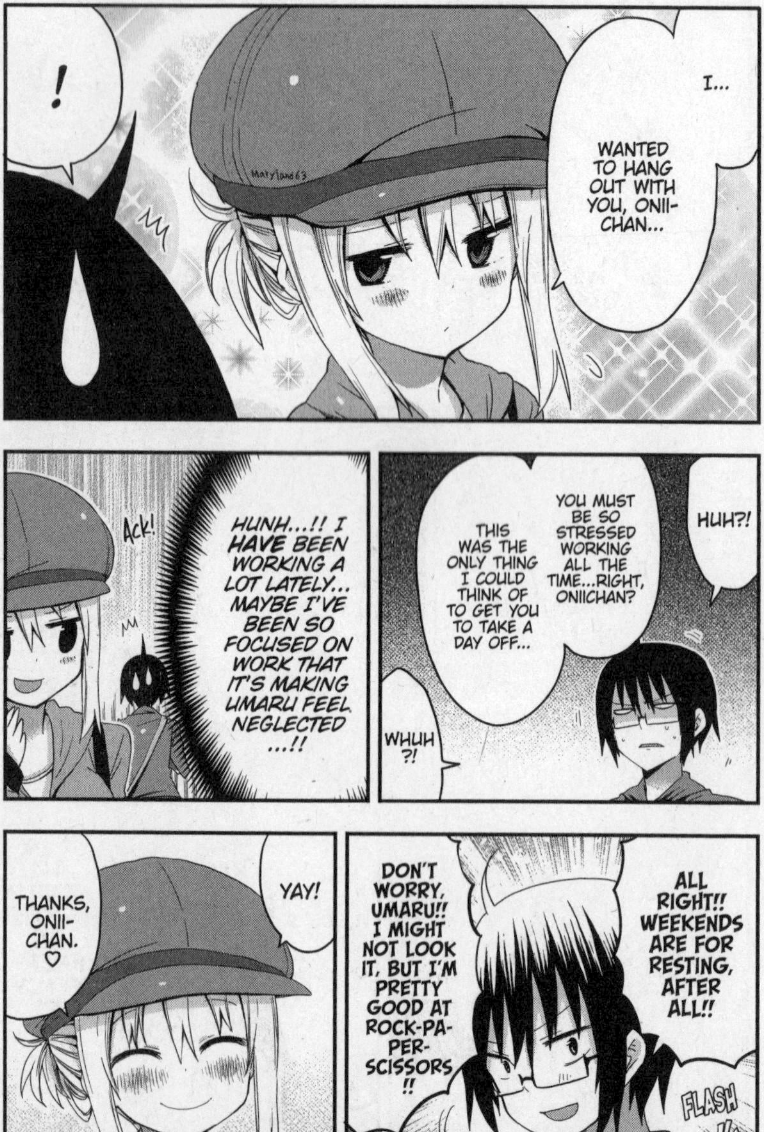
I...
WANTED TO HANG OUT WITH YOU, ONII-CHAN...
!
HUH?!
YOU MUST BE SO STRESSED WORKING ALL THE TIME...RIGHT, ONIICHAN?
THIS WAS THE ONLY THING I COULD THINK OF TO GET YOU TO TAKE A DAY OFF...
WHUH ?!
HUNH...!! I **HAVE** BEEN WORKING A LOT LATELY... MAYBE I'VE BEEN SO FOCUSED ON WORK THAT IT'S MAKING UMARU FEEL NEGLECTED ...!!
ACK!
ALL RIGHT!! WEEKENDS ARE FOR RESTING, AFTER ALL!!
DON'T WORRY, UMARU!! I MIGHT NOT LOOK IT, BUT I'M PRETTY GOOD AT ROCK-PA-PER-SCISSORS !!
FLASH
YAY!
THANKS, ONII-CHAN. ♡

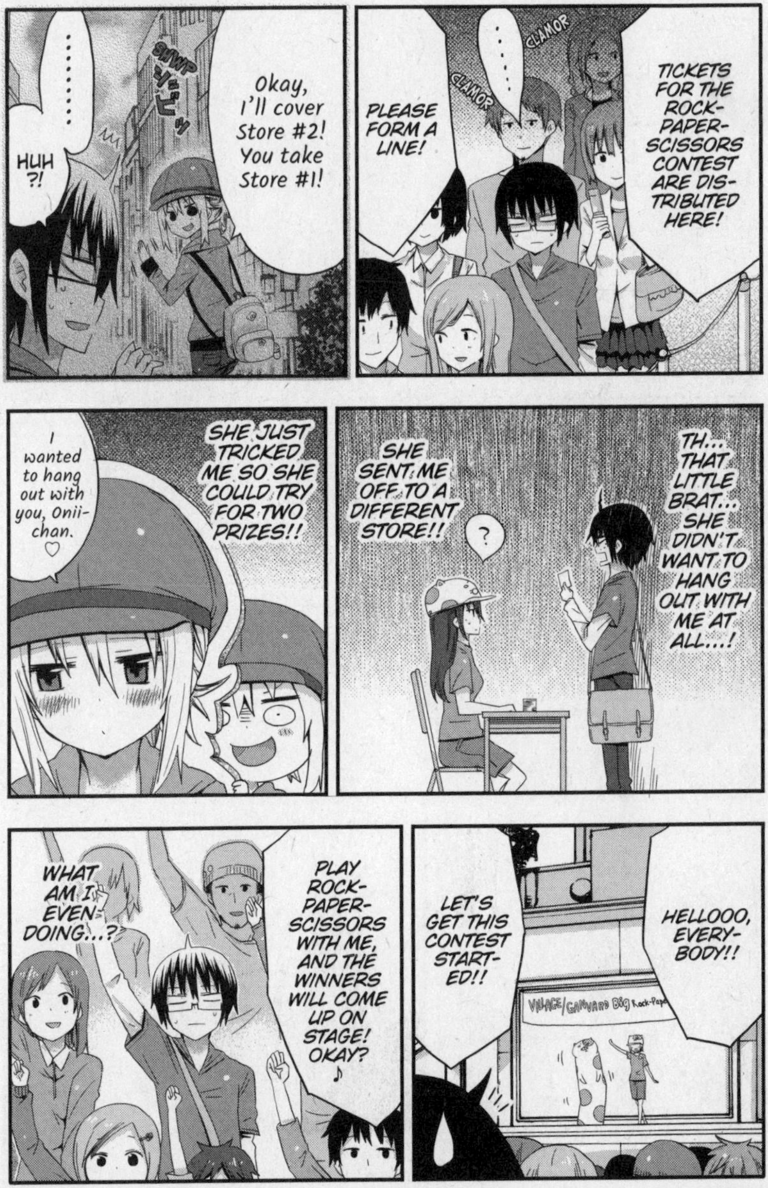
TICKETS FOR THE ROCK-PAPER-SCISSORS CONTEST ARE DISTRIBUTED HERE!
CLAMOR
......
CLAMOR
PLEASE FORM A LINE!
Okay, I'll cover Store #2! You take Store #1!
SHWP
......
HUH?!
TH... THAT LITTLE BRAT... SHE DIDN'T WANT TO HANG OUT WITH ME AT ALL...!
SHE SENT ME OFF TO A DIFFERENT STORE!!
?
SHE JUST TRICKED ME SO SHE COULD TRY FOR TWO PRIZES!!
I wanted to hang out with you, Onii-chan. ♡
HELLOOO, EVERYBODY!!
LET'S GET THIS CONTEST STARTED!!
VILLAGE/GANVARD Big
PLAY ROCK-PAPER-SCISSORS WITH ME, AND THE WINNERS WILL COME UP ON STAGE! OKAY? ♪
WHAT AM I EVEN DOING...?

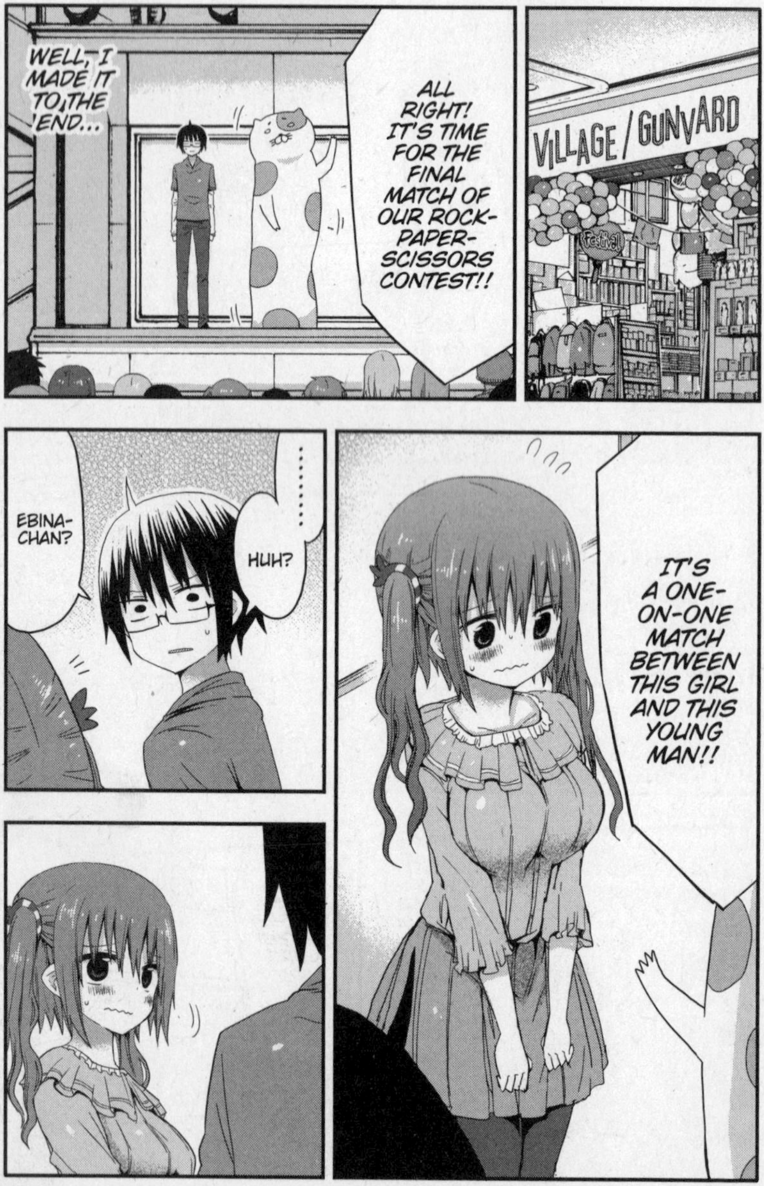
VILLAGE / GUNVARD
Festival
ALL RIGHT! IT'S TIME FOR THE FINAL MATCH OF OUR ROCK-PAPER-SCISSORS CONTEST!!
WELL, I MADE IT TO THE END...
IT'S A ONE-ON-ONE MATCH BETWEEN THIS GIRL AND THIS YOUNG MAN!!
......
HUH?
EBINA-CHAN?

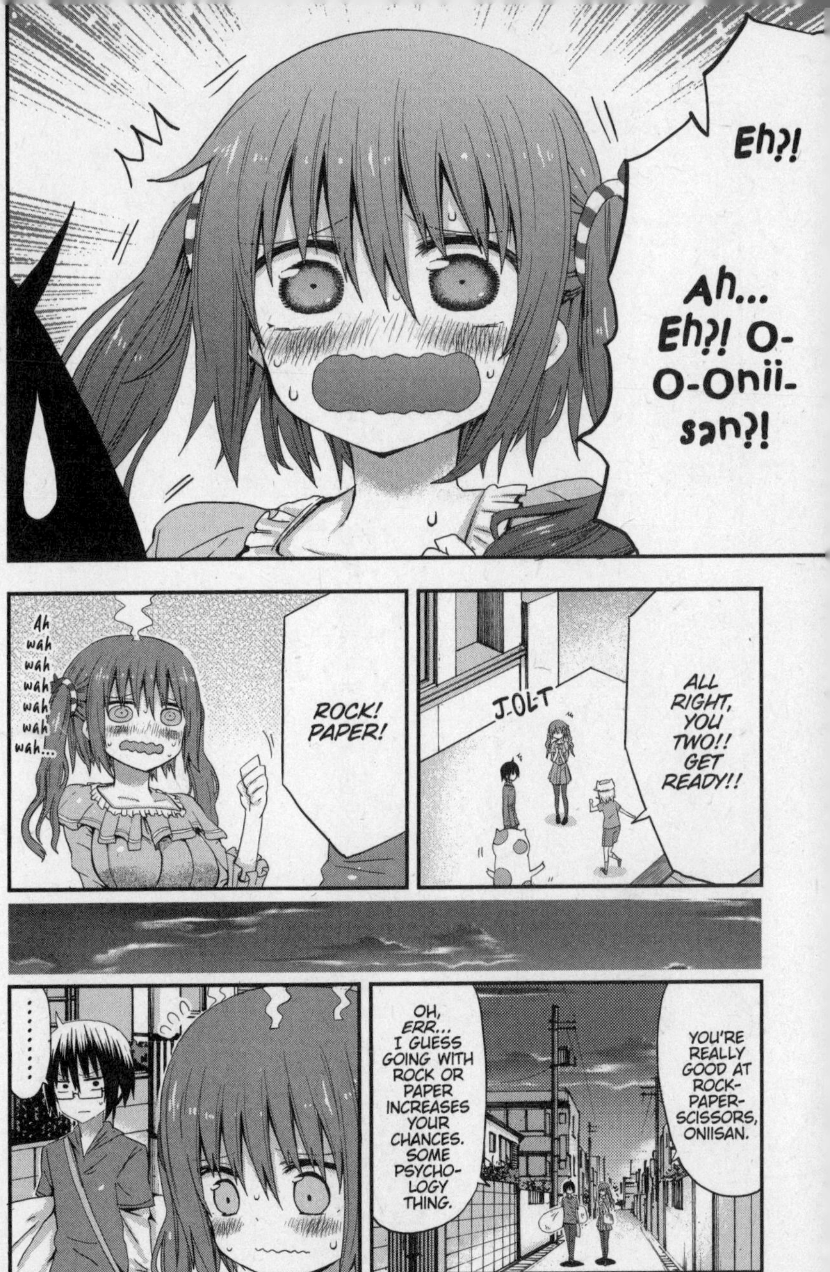
Eh?!
Ah... Eh?! O-O-Onii-san?!
ALL RIGHT, YOU TWO!! GET READY!!
J-OLT
ROCK! PAPER!
Ah wah wah wah wah wah wah...
YOU'RE REALLY GOOD AT ROCK-PAPER-SCISSORS, ONIISAN.
OH, ERR... I GUESS GOING WITH ROCK OR PAPER INCREASES YOUR CHANCES. SOME PSYCHOLOGY THING.
....

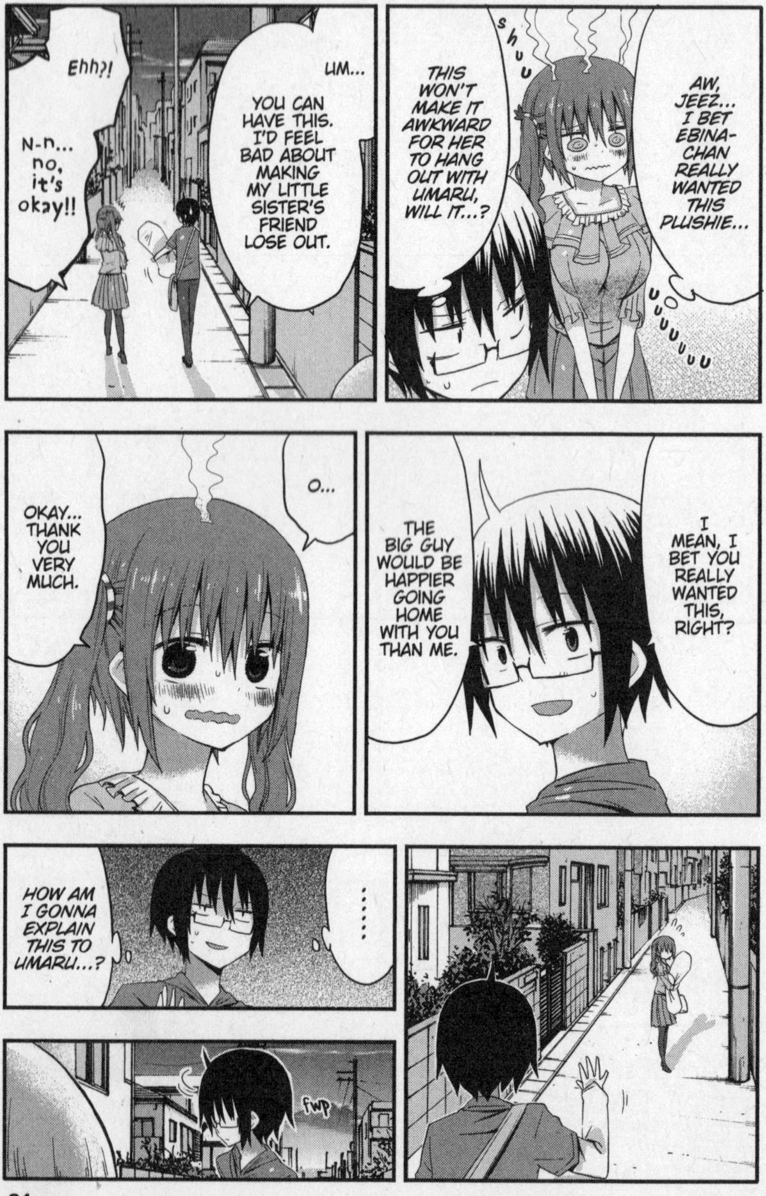
AW, JEEZ... I BET EBINA-CHAN REALLY WANTED THIS PLUSHIE...
shuu
THIS WON'T MAKE IT AWKWARD FOR HER TO HANG OUT WITH UMARU, WILL IT...?
uuuuuuuuu
UM...
YOU CAN HAVE THIS. I'D FEEL BAD ABOUT MAKING MY LITTLE SISTER'S FRIEND LOSE OUT.
Ehh?!
N-n... no, it's okay!!
I MEAN, I BET YOU REALLY WANTED THIS, RIGHT?
THE BIG GUY WOULD BE HAPPIER GOING HOME WITH YOU THAN ME.
O...
OKAY... THANK YOU VERY MUCH.
......
HOW AM I GONNA EXPLAIN THIS TO UMARU...?
fwp

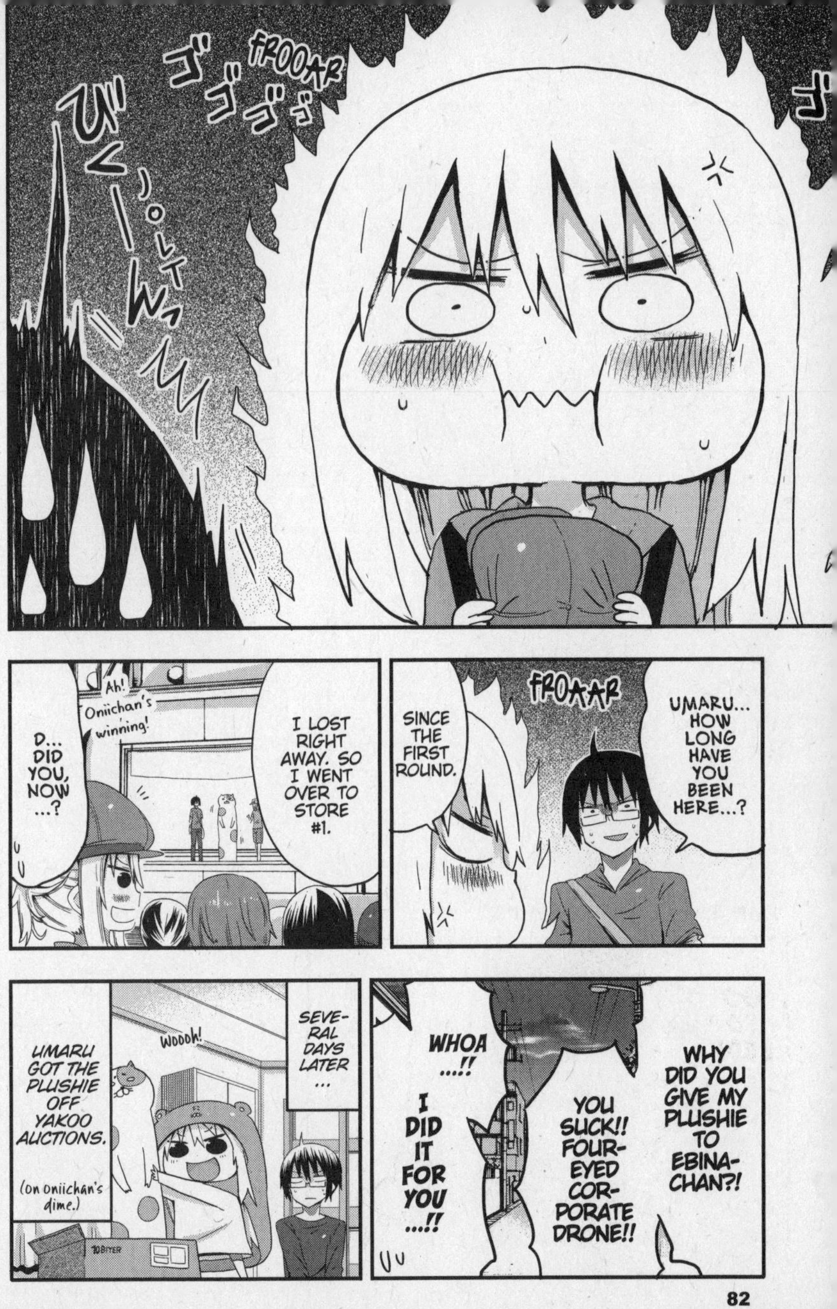
FROOAR
FROAAR
UMARU... HOW LONG HAVE YOU BEEN HERE...?
SINCE THE FIRST ROUND.
I LOST RIGHT AWAY. SO I WENT OVER TO STORE #1.
Ah! Oniichan's winning!
D... DID YOU, NOW ...?
WHY DID YOU GIVE MY PLUSHIE TO EBINA-CHAN?!
YOU SUCK!! FOUR-EYED CORPORATE DRONE!!
WHOA ....!!
I DID IT FOR YOU ....!!
SEVE-RAL DAYS LATER ...
UMARU GOT THE PLUSHIE OFF YAKOO AUCTIONS.
Woooh!
(on Oniichan's dime.)

But She's Awake at Night

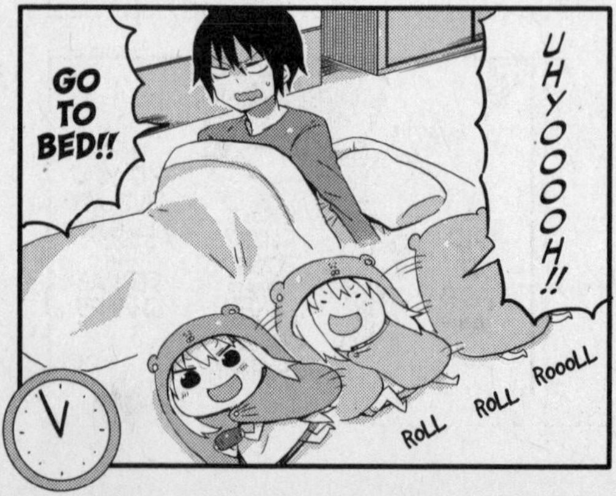
UHYOOOOOH!!
GO TO BED!!
ROOOLL
ROLL
ROLL

HIMOUTO! UMARU-CHAN

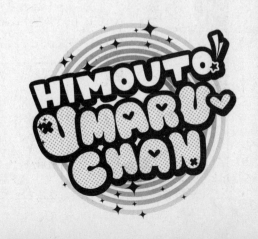

No. 10 Umaru & Golden Week

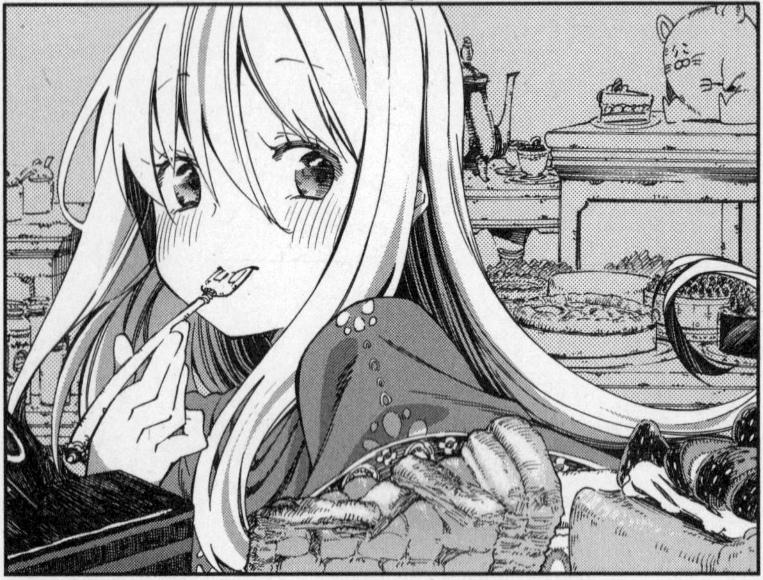

Guest Illustrator: Abara Heiki

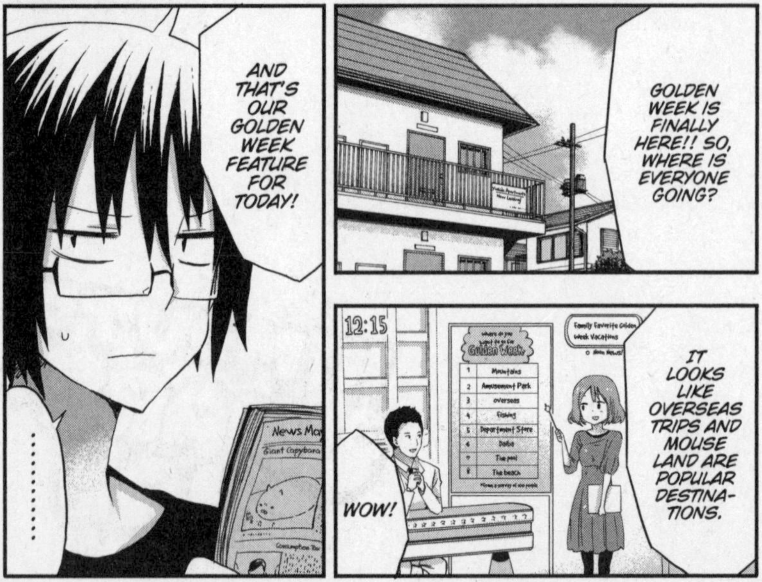
GOLDEN WEEK IS FINALLY HERE!! SO, WHERE IS EVERYONE GOING?
12:15
Family Favorite Golden Week Vacations
Golden Week
1 Mountains
2 Amusement Park
3 overseas
4 Fishing
5 Department Store
7 The pool
8 The beach
IT LOOKS LIKE OVERSEAS TRIPS AND MOUSE LAND ARE POPULAR DESTINATIONS.
WOW!
AND THAT'S OUR GOLDEN WEEK FEATURE FOR TODAY!
News
Giant Capybara
......

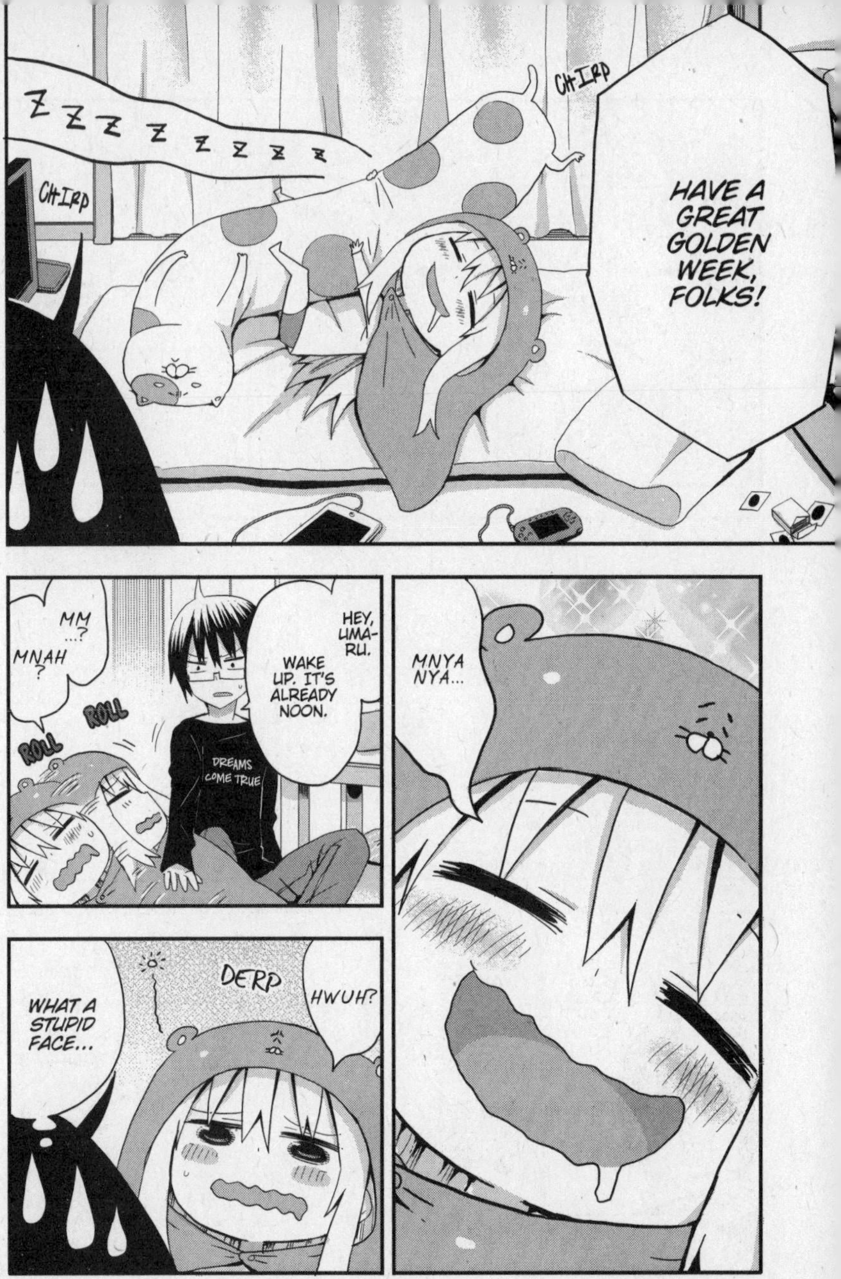
HAVE A GREAT GOLDEN WEEK, FOLKS!
CHIRP
ZZZZZZZZ
CHIRP
MNYA NYA...
HEY, UMARU.
WAKE UP. IT'S ALREADY NOON.
MM ...?
MNAH ?
ROLL
ROLL
DREAMS COME TRUE
HWUH?
DERP
WHAT A STUPID FACE...

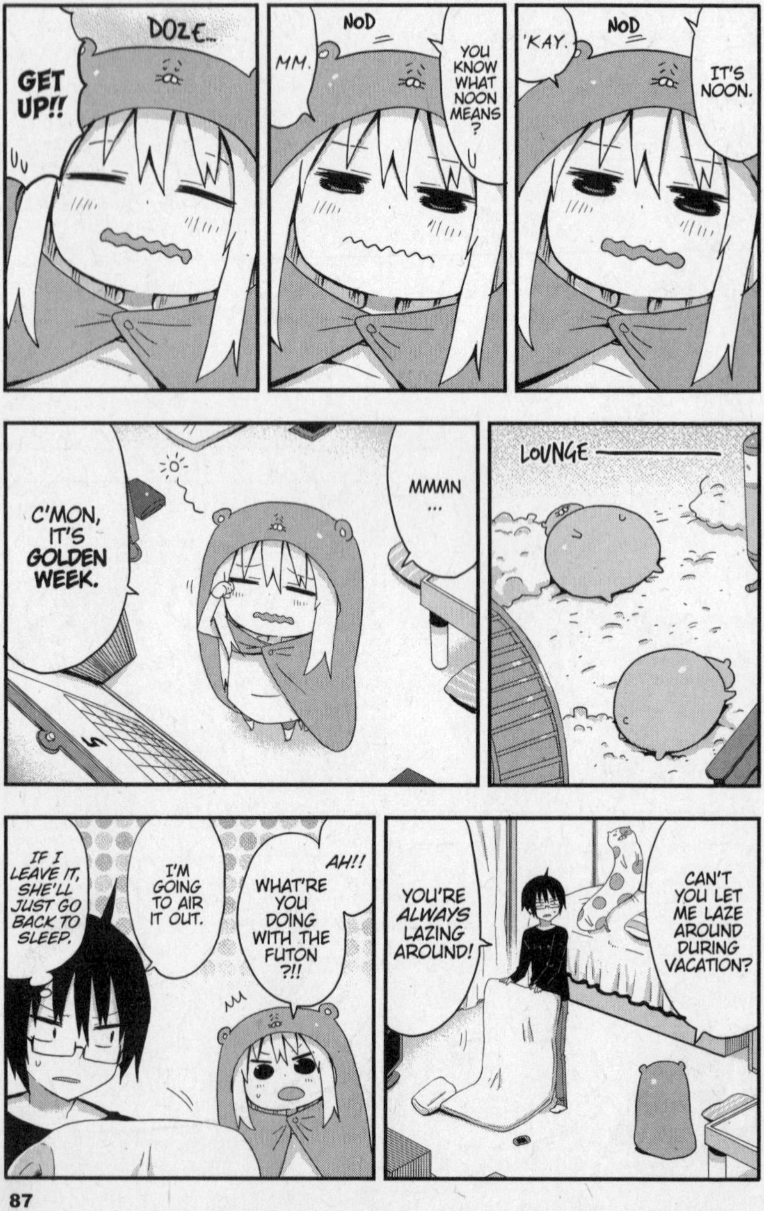
IT'S NOON.
'KAY.
NOD
YOU KNOW WHAT NOON MEANS?
MM.
NOD
GET UP!!
DOZE...
LOUNGE
MMMN...
C'MON, IT'S GOLDEN WEEK.
CAN'T YOU LET ME LAZE AROUND DURING VACATION?
YOU'RE ALWAYS LAZING AROUND!
AH!!
WHAT'RE YOU DOING WITH THE FUTON?!!
I'M GOING TO AIR IT OUT.
IF I LEAVE IT, SHE'LL JUST GO BACK TO SLEEP.

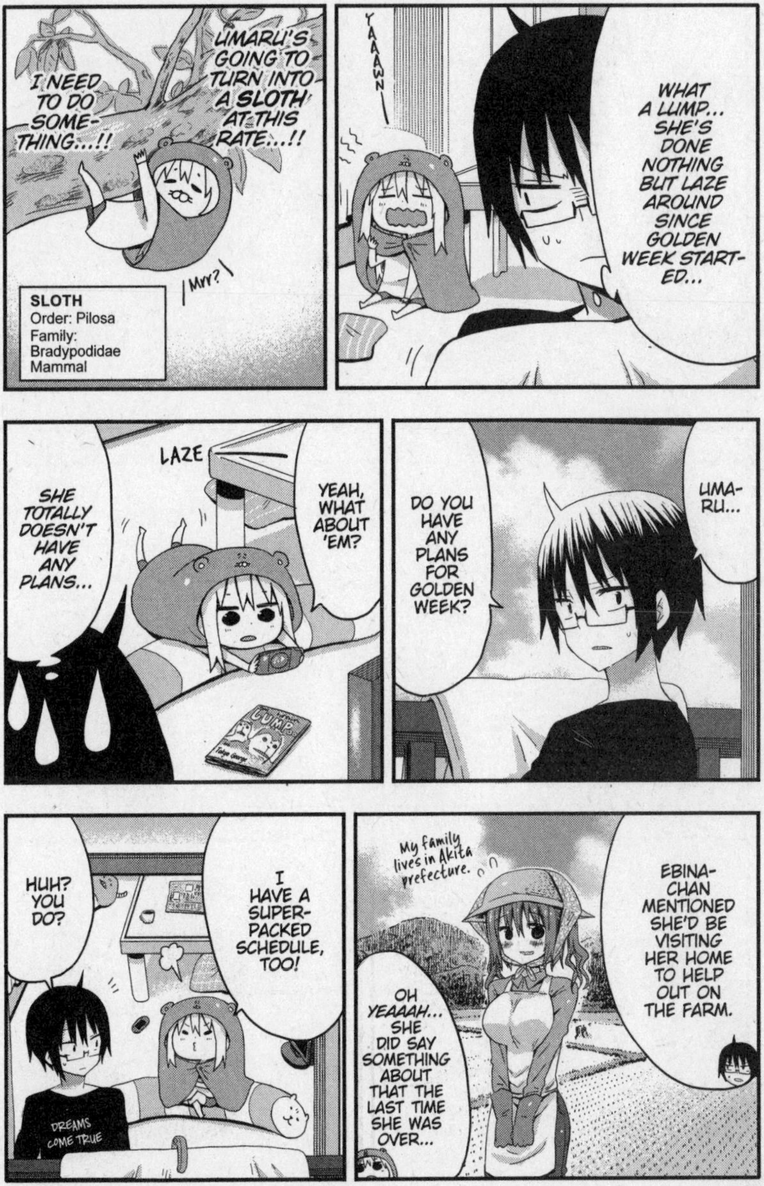
YAAAAWN
WHAT A LUMP... SHE'S DONE NOTHING BUT LAZE AROUND SINCE GOLDEN WEEK STARTED...
UMARU'S GOING TO TURN INTO A SLOTH AT THIS RATE...!!
I NEED TO DO SOMETHING...!!
Mrr?
SLOTH
Order: Pilosa
Family: Bradypodidae
Mammal
UMARU...
DO YOU HAVE ANY PLANS FOR GOLDEN WEEK?
LAZE
YEAH, WHAT ABOUT 'EM?
SHE TOTALLY DOESN'T HAVE ANY PLANS...
EBINA-CHAN MENTIONED SHE'D BE VISITING HER HOME TO HELP OUT ON THE FARM.
My family lives in Akita prefecture.
OH YEAAAH... SHE DID SAY SOMETHING ABOUT THAT THE LAST TIME SHE WAS OVER...
I HAVE A SUPER-PACKED SCHEDULE, TOO!
HUH? YOU DO?
DREAMS COME TRUE

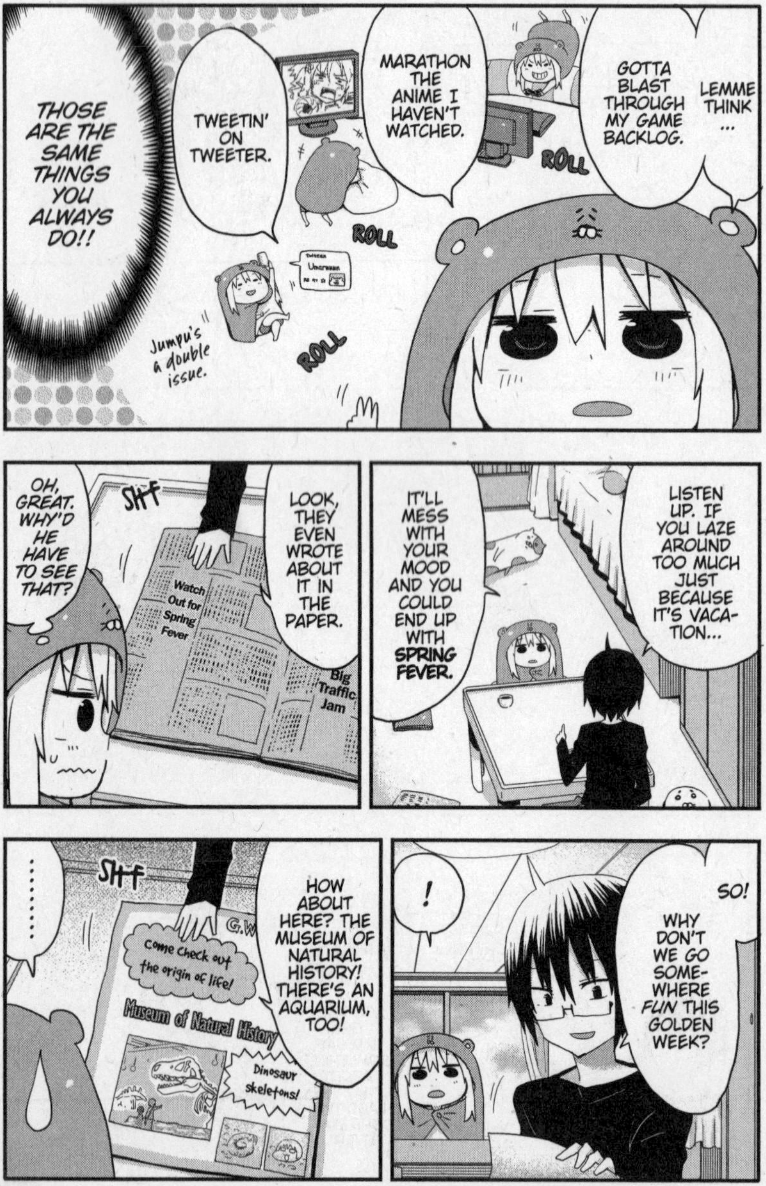
LEMME THINK ...
GOTTA BLAST THROUGH MY GAME BACKLOG.
MARATHON THE ANIME I HAVEN'T WATCHED.
ROLL
TWEETIN' ON TWEETER.
ROLL
ROLL
Jumpu's a double issue.
THOSE ARE THE SAME THINGS YOU ALWAYS DO!!
LISTEN UP. IF YOU LAZE AROUND TOO MUCH JUST BECAUSE IT'S VACATION...
IT'LL MESS WITH YOUR MOOD AND YOU COULD END UP WITH **SPRING FEVER.**
LOOK, THEY EVEN WROTE ABOUT IT IN THE PAPER.
SHF
Watch Out for Spring Fever
Big Traffic Jam
OH, GREAT. WHY'D HE HAVE TO SEE THAT?
SO!
WHY DON'T WE GO SOMEWHERE *FUN* THIS GOLDEN WEEK?
!
HOW ABOUT HERE? THE MUSEUM OF NATURAL HISTORY! THERE'S AN AQUARIUM, TOO!
SHF
Come check out the origin of life!
Museum of Natural History
Dinosaur skeletons!
....

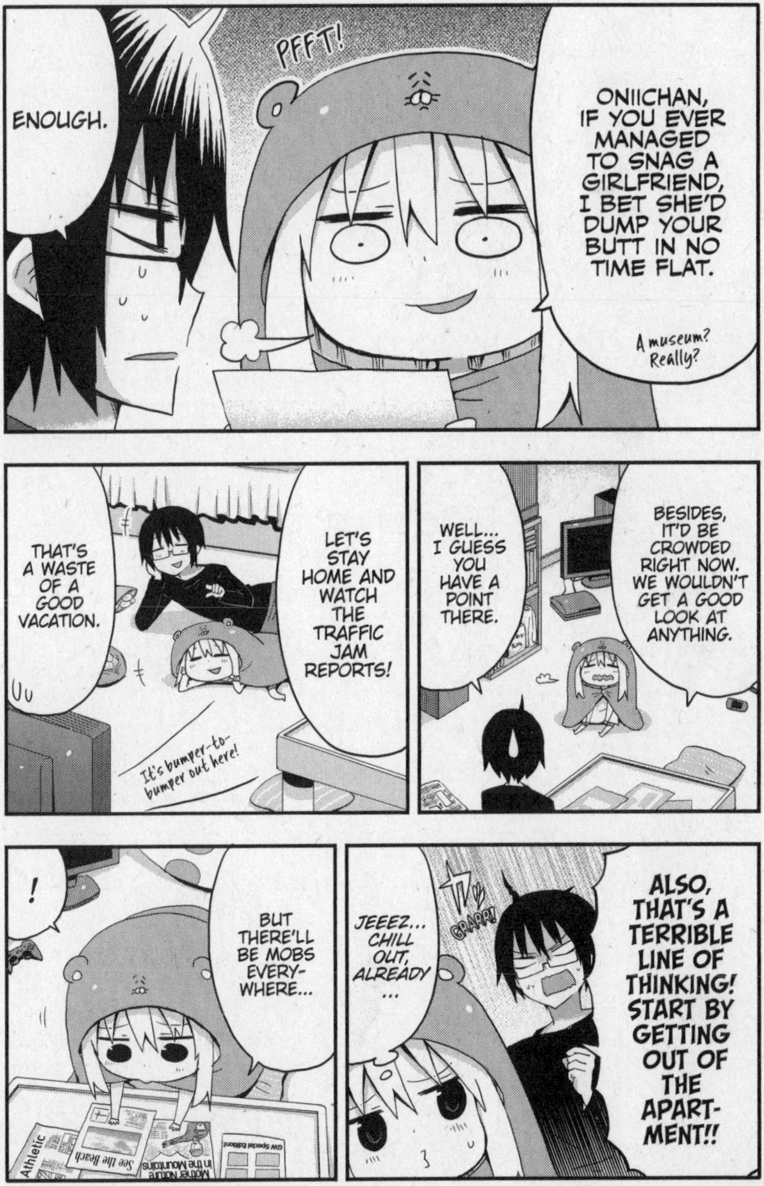
ONIICHAN, IF YOU EVER MANAGED TO SNAG A GIRLFRIEND, I BET SHE'D DUMP YOUR BUTT IN NO TIME FLAT.
PFFT!
A museum? Really?
ENOUGH.
BESIDES, IT'D BE CROWDED RIGHT NOW. WE WOULDN'T GET A GOOD LOOK AT ANYTHING.
WELL... I GUESS YOU HAVE A POINT THERE.
LET'S STAY HOME AND WATCH THE TRAFFIC JAM REPORTS!
THAT'S A WASTE OF A GOOD VACATION.
It's bumper-to-bumper out here!
ALSO, THAT'S A TERRIBLE LINE OF THINKING! START BY GETTING OUT OF THE APARTMENT!!
GRARR!
JEEEZ... CHILL OUT, ALREADY...
BUT THERE'LL BE MOBS EVERYWHERE...
!
GW Special Edition
Mother Nature in the Mountains
See the Beach
Athletic

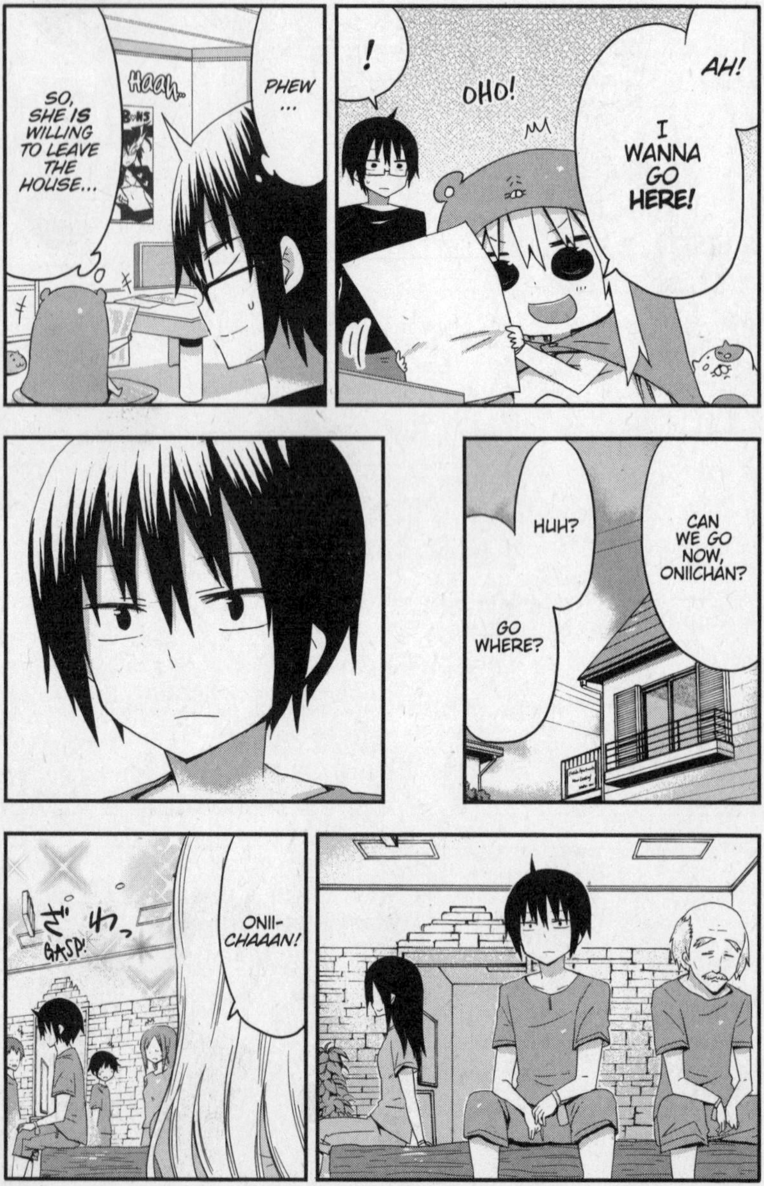
AH!
I WANNA GO HERE!
OHO!
!
PHEW ...
Haah..
SO, SHE IS WILLING TO LEAVE THE HOUSE...
CAN WE GO NOW, ONIICHAN?
HUH?
GO WHERE?
ONII-CHAAAN!
ざわっ
GASP!

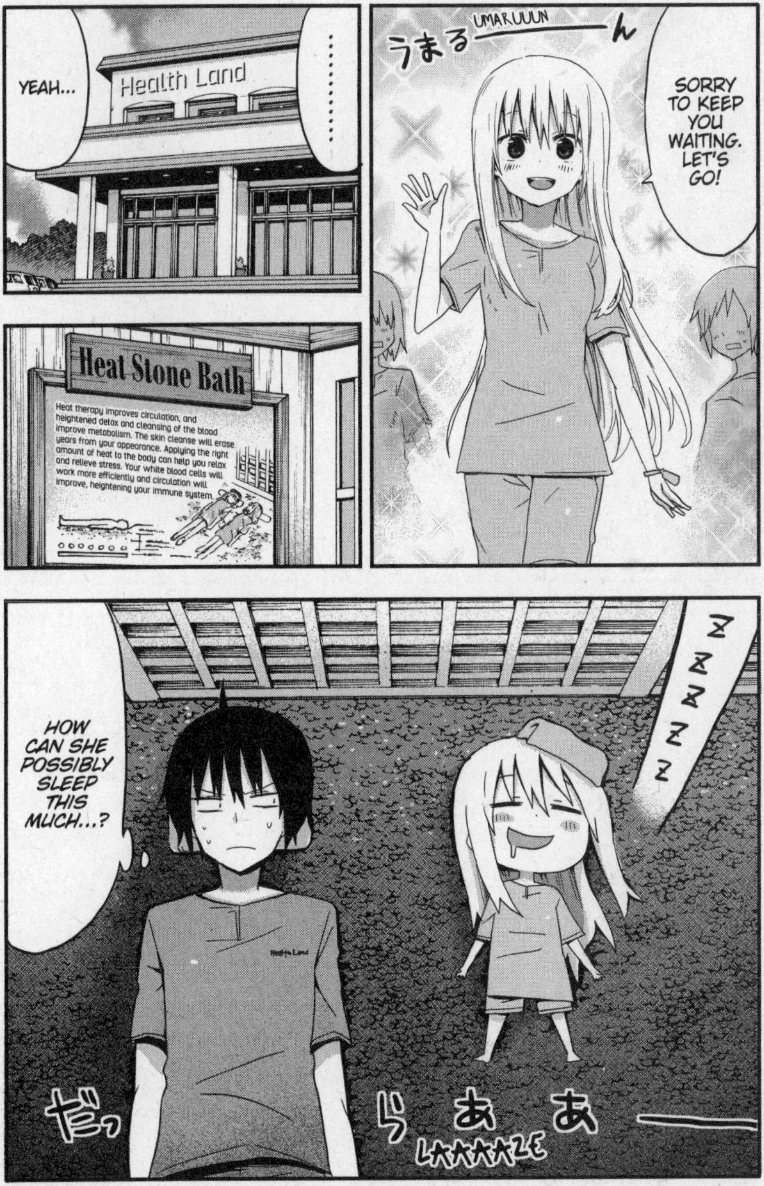
うまる――ん
UMARUUUN
SORRY TO KEEP YOU WAITING. LET'S GO!
......
YEAH...
Health Land
Heat Stone Bath
Heat therapy improves circulation, and heightened detox and cleansing of the blood improve metabolism. The skin cleanse will erase years from your appearance. Applying the right amount of heat to the body can help you relax and relieve stress. Your white blood cells will work more efficiently and circulation will improve, heightening your immune system.
ZZZZZ
HOW CAN SHE POSSIBLY SLEEP THIS MUCH...?
Health Land
だっらあああ―
LAAAAZE

No. 11 Umaru & the Fight

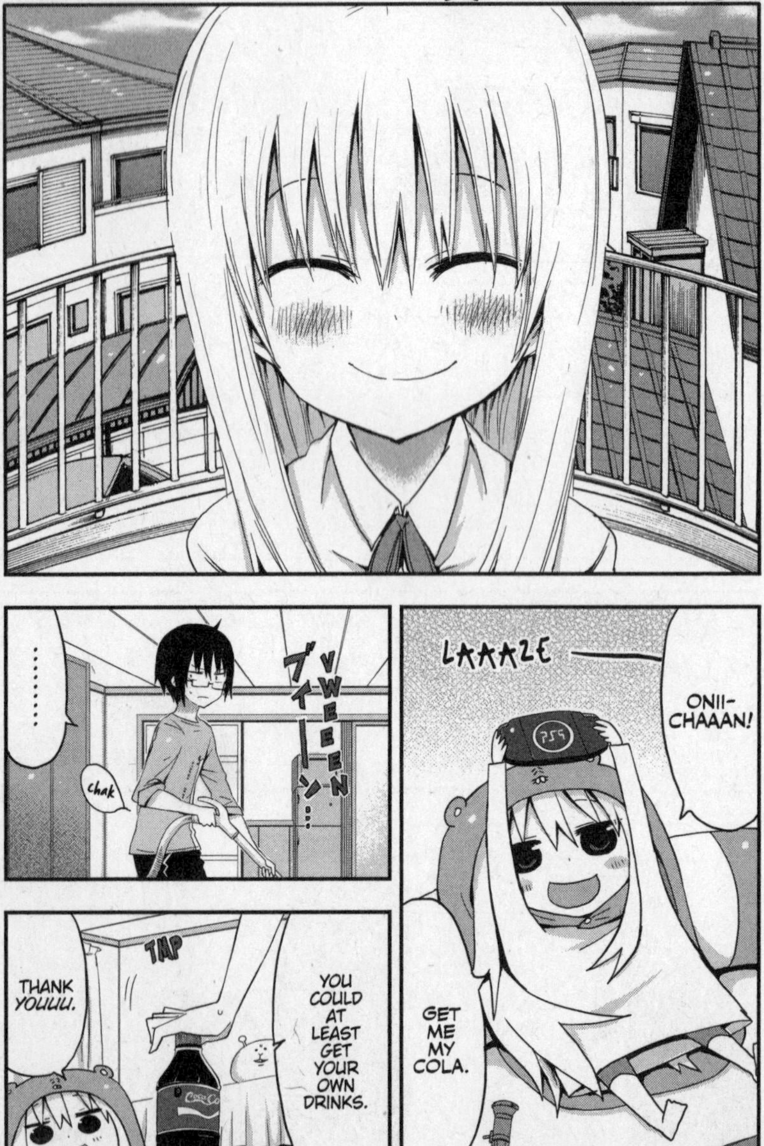
LAAAZE —
ONII-CHAAAN!
GET ME MY COLA.
......
VWEEN
ブイーン…
chak
TMP
YOU COULD AT LEAST GET YOUR OWN DRINKS.
THANK YOUUU.

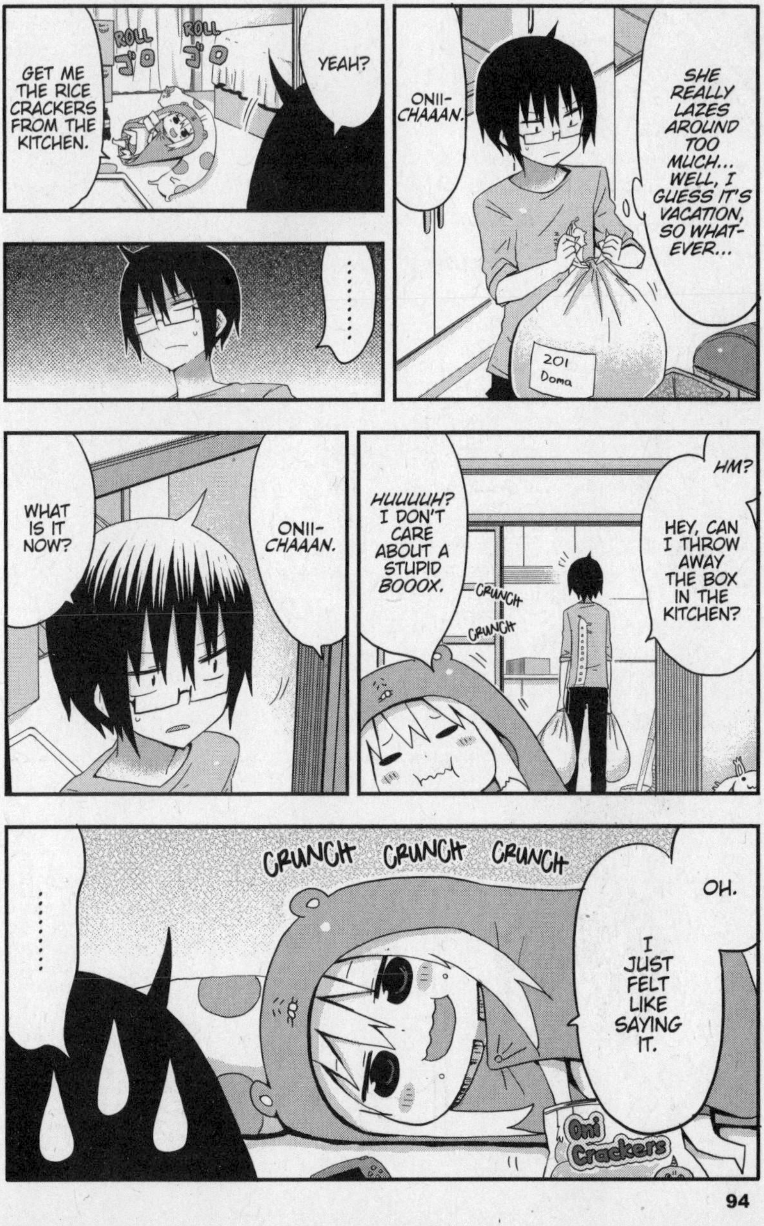
SHE REALLY LAZES AROUND TOO MUCH... WELL, I GUESS IT'S VACATION, SO WHATEVER...
ONII-CHAAAN.
201 Doma
YEAH?
ROLL ゴロ
ROLL ゴロ
GET ME THE RICE CRACKERS FROM THE KITCHEN.
......
HM?
HEY, CAN I THROW AWAY THE BOX IN THE KITCHEN?
HUUUUH? I DON'T CARE ABOUT A STUPID BOOOX.
CRUNCH
CRUNCH
ONII-CHAAAN.
WHAT IS IT NOW?
OH.
I JUST FELT LIKE SAYING IT.
CRUNCH CRUNCH CRUNCH
Oni Crackers
......

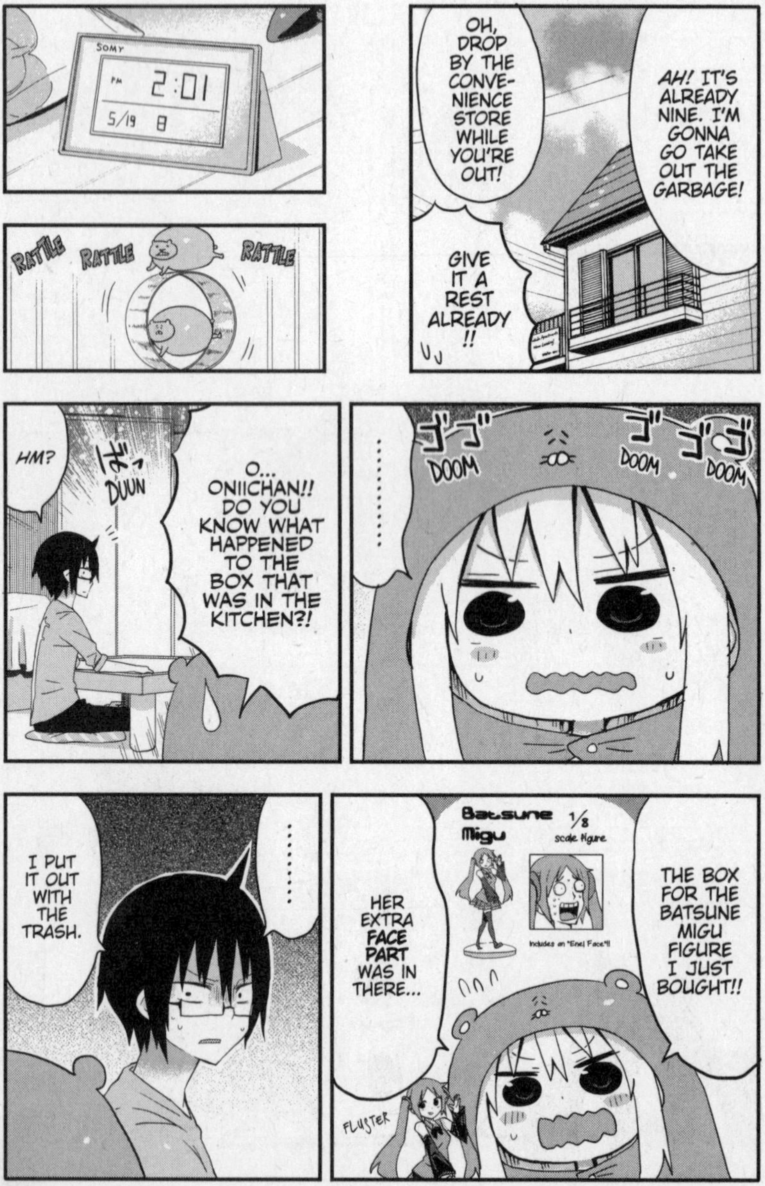
AH! IT'S ALREADY NINE. I'M GONNA GO TAKE OUT THE GARBAGE!
OH, DROP BY THE CONVENIENCE STORE WHILE YOU'RE OUT!
GIVE IT A REST ALREADY !!
SOMY
PM 2:01
5/19
RATTLE
RATTLE
RATTLE
ゴゴ DOOM
ゴゴゴ DOOM DOOM
......
O... ONIICHAN!! DO YOU KNOW WHAT HAPPENED TO THE BOX THAT WAS IN THE KITCHEN?!
ばっ DUUN
HM?
THE BOX FOR THE BATSUNE MIGU FIGURE I JUST BOUGHT!!
Batsune Migu 1/8 scale figure
Includes an "Enel Face"!!
HER EXTRA FACE PART WAS IN THERE...
FLUSTER
......
I PUT IT OUT WITH THE TRASH.

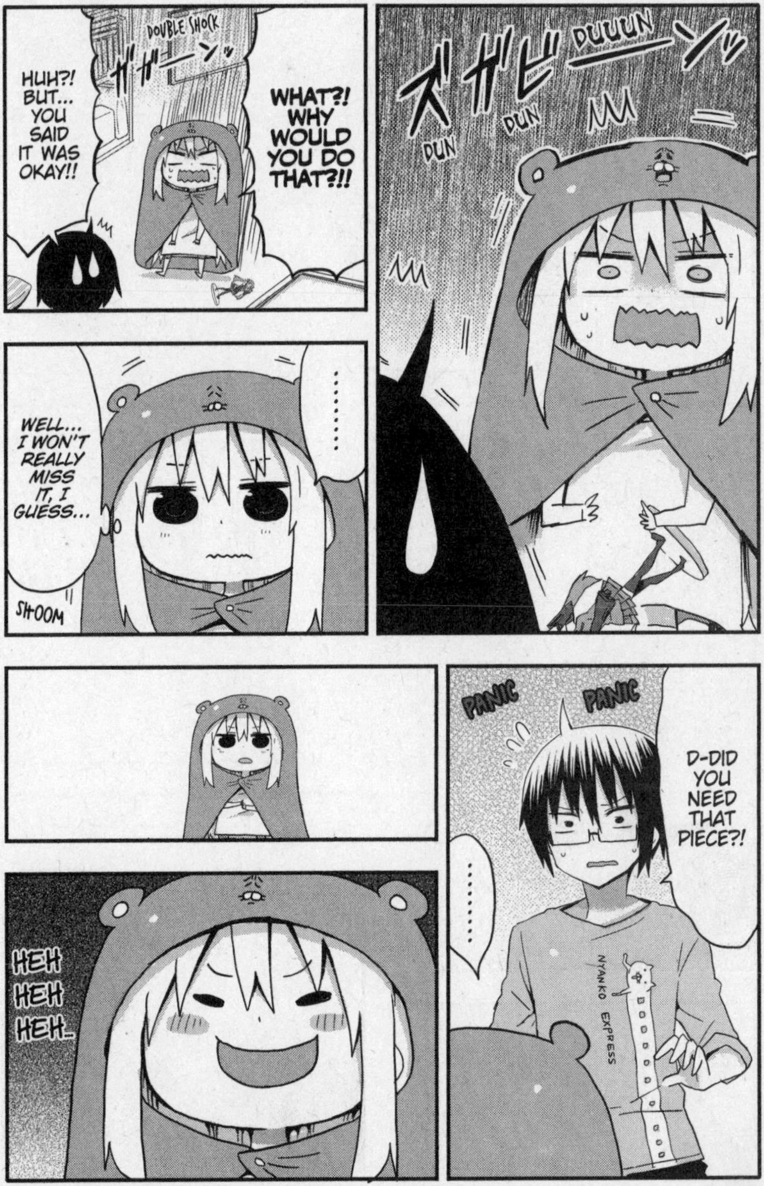

DUUUN
ズガビーーンッ
DUN
DUN
DOUBLE SHOCK
ガガーンッ
WHAT?! WHY WOULD YOU DO THAT?!!
HUH?! BUT... YOU SAID IT WAS OKAY!!
....
WELL... I WON'T REALLY MISS IT, I GUESS...
SHOOM
PANIC
PANIC
D-DID YOU NEED THAT PIECE?!
....
NYANKO EXPRESS
HEH HEH HEH..

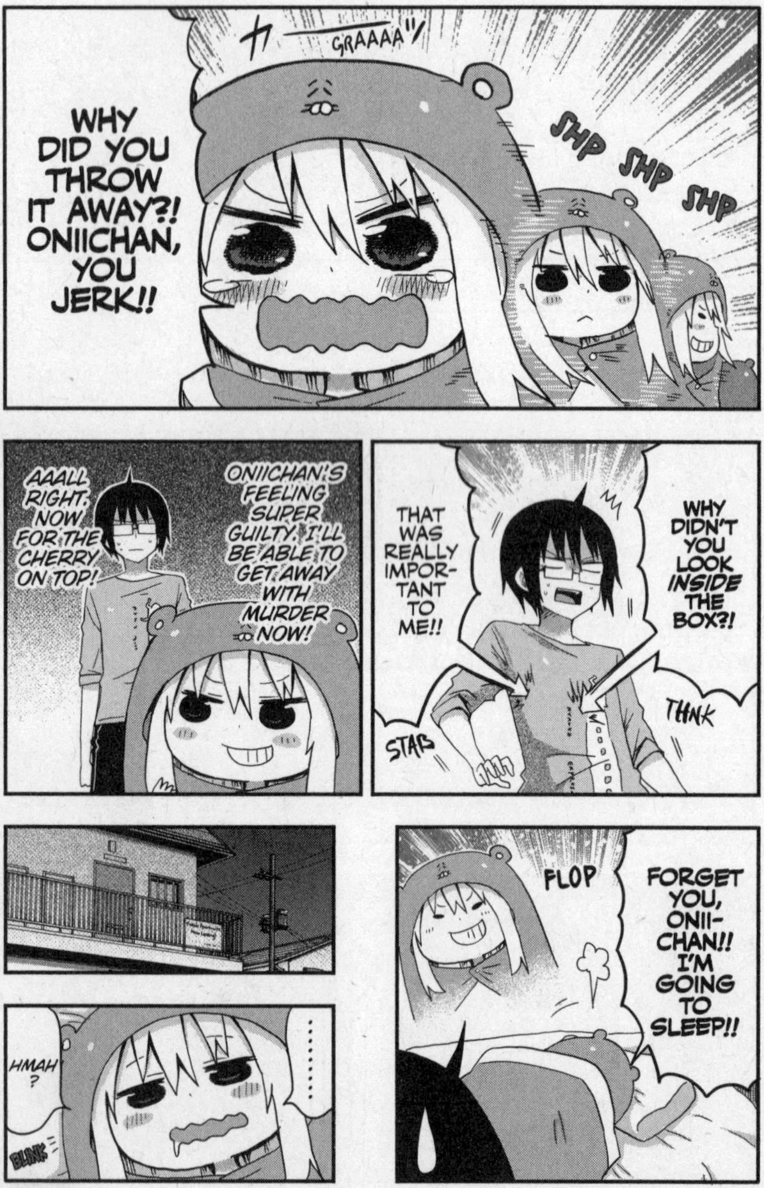

GRAAAA
SHP SHP SHP
WHY DID YOU THROW IT AWAY?! ONIICHAN, YOU JERK!!
WHY DIDN'T YOU LOOK INSIDE THE BOX?!
THAT WAS REALLY IMPORTANT TO ME!!
THNK
STAB
ONIICHAN'S FEELING SUPER GUILTY. I'LL BE ABLE TO GET AWAY WITH MURDER NOW!
AAALL RIGHT. NOW FOR THE CHERRY ON TOP!
FORGET YOU, ONII-CHAN!! I'M GOING TO SLEEP!!
FLOP
......
HMAH?
BLINK

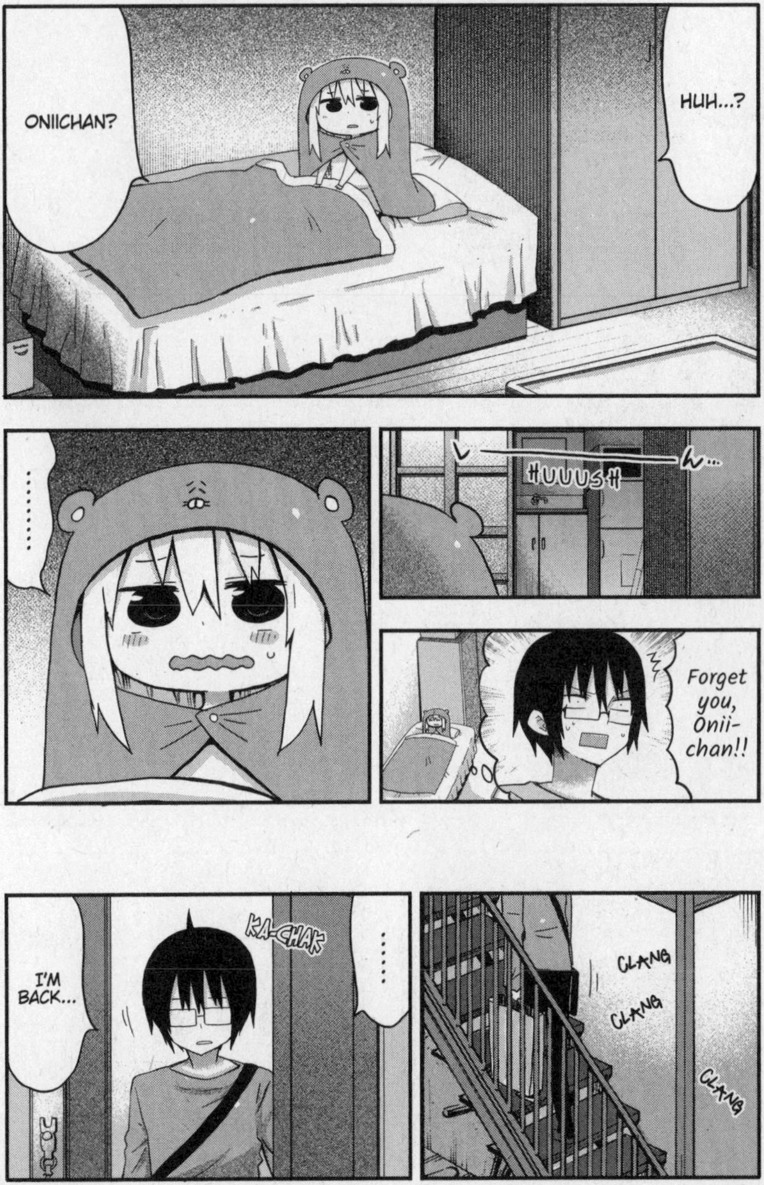

HUH...?
ONIICHAN?
L————W...
HUUUSH
Forget you, Onii-chan!!
......
CLANG
CLANG
CLANG
......
KA-CHAK
I'M BACK...

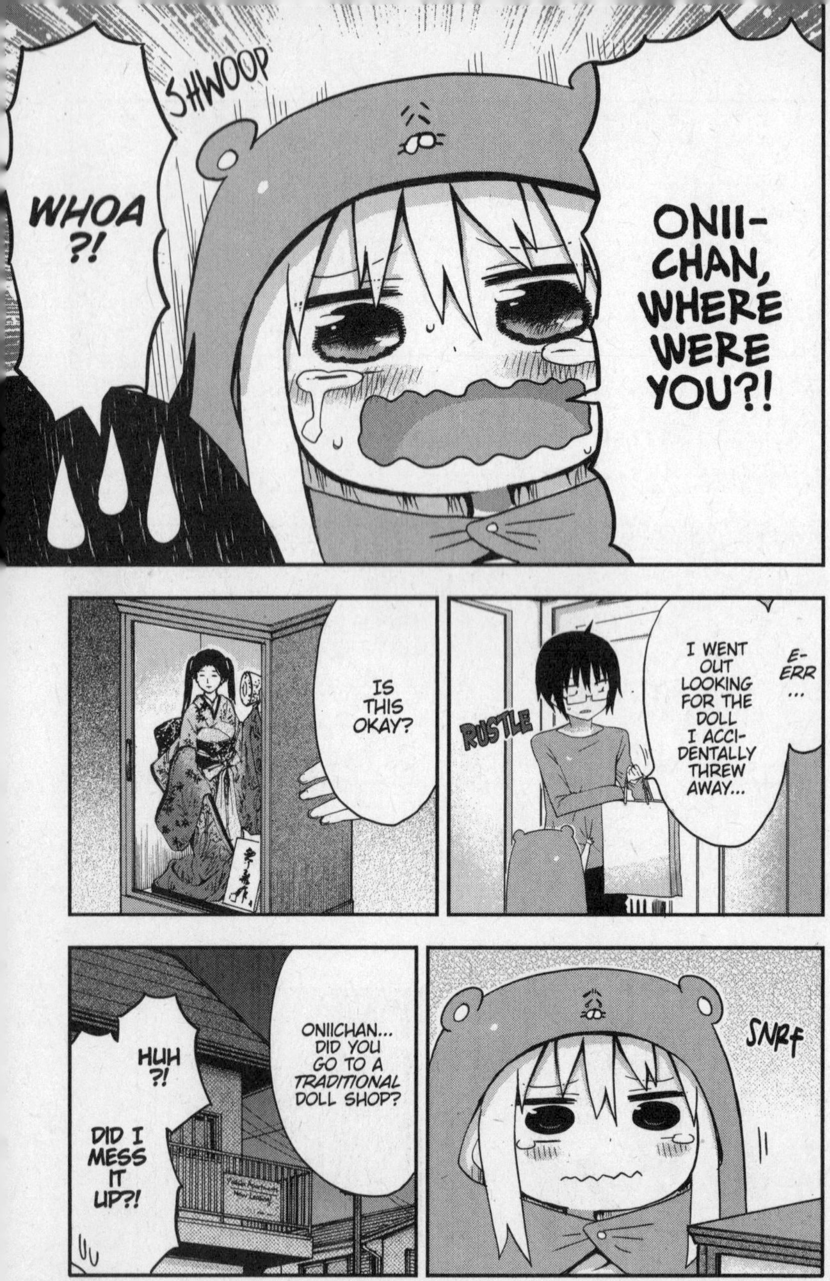
ONII-CHAN, WHERE WERE YOU?!
SHWOOP
WHOA ?!
E-ERR ...
I WENT OUT LOOKING FOR THE DOLL I ACCIDENTALLY THREW AWAY...
RUSTLE
IS THIS OKAY?
SNRF
ONIICHAN... DID YOU GO TO A *TRADITIONAL* DOLL SHOP?
HUH ?!
DID I MESS IT UP?!

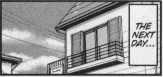

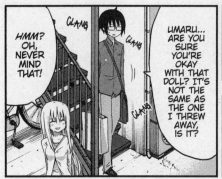

THE NEXT DAY...
COME ON, ONIICHAN! YOU'LL BE LATE FOR WORK!
R-RIGHT...
UMARU... ARE YOU SURE YOU'RE OKAY WITH THAT DOLL? IT'S NOT THE SAME AS THE ONE I THREW AWAY, IS IT?
CLANG
CLANG
CLANG
HMM? OH, NEVER MIND THAT!
BESIDES, I DIDN'T REALLY CARE THAT YOU THREW IT AWAY.
?!
WHAT?! THEN WHY WERE YOU CRYING?!
ONII-CHAN...
HMM? WHAT'S UP?
HEH HEH HEH. JUST WANTED TO SAY IT!

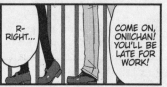

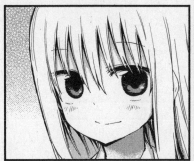

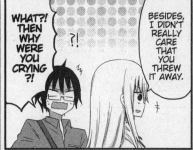

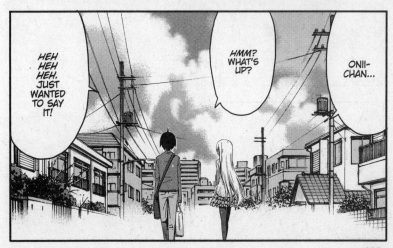

No. 12 Umaru & the Arcade

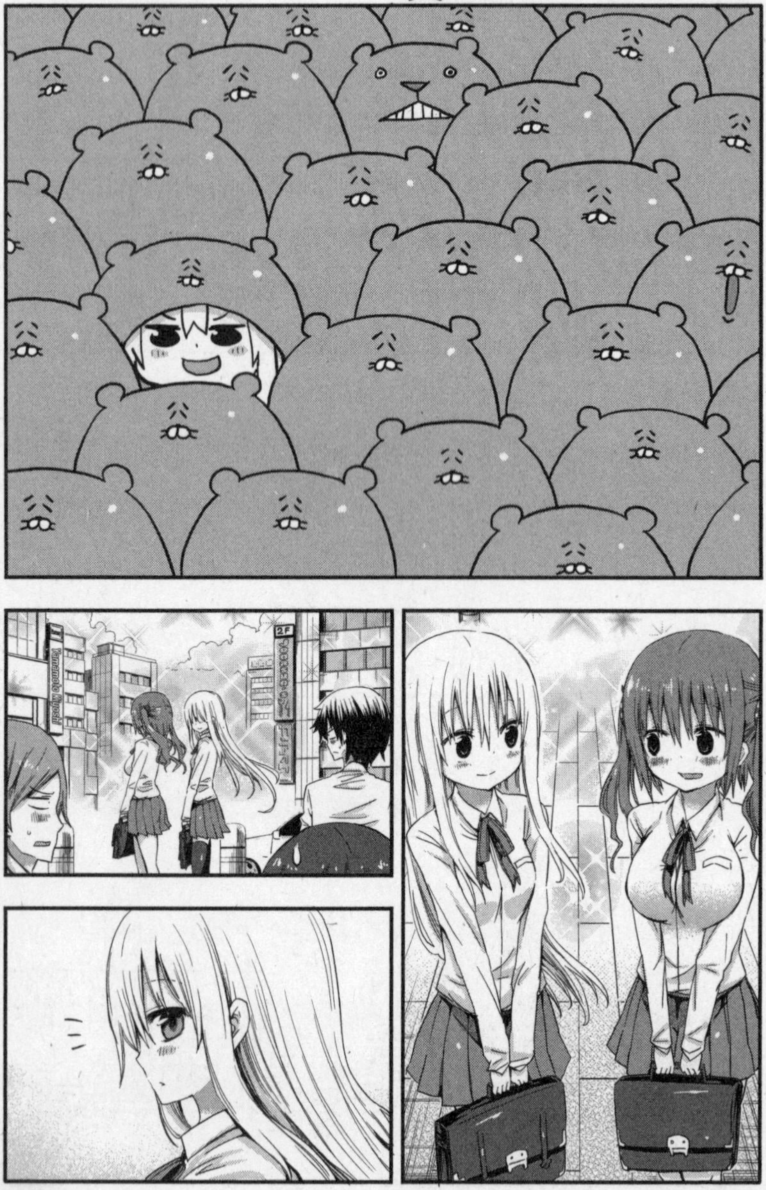
Yamamoto Kiyoshi
2F

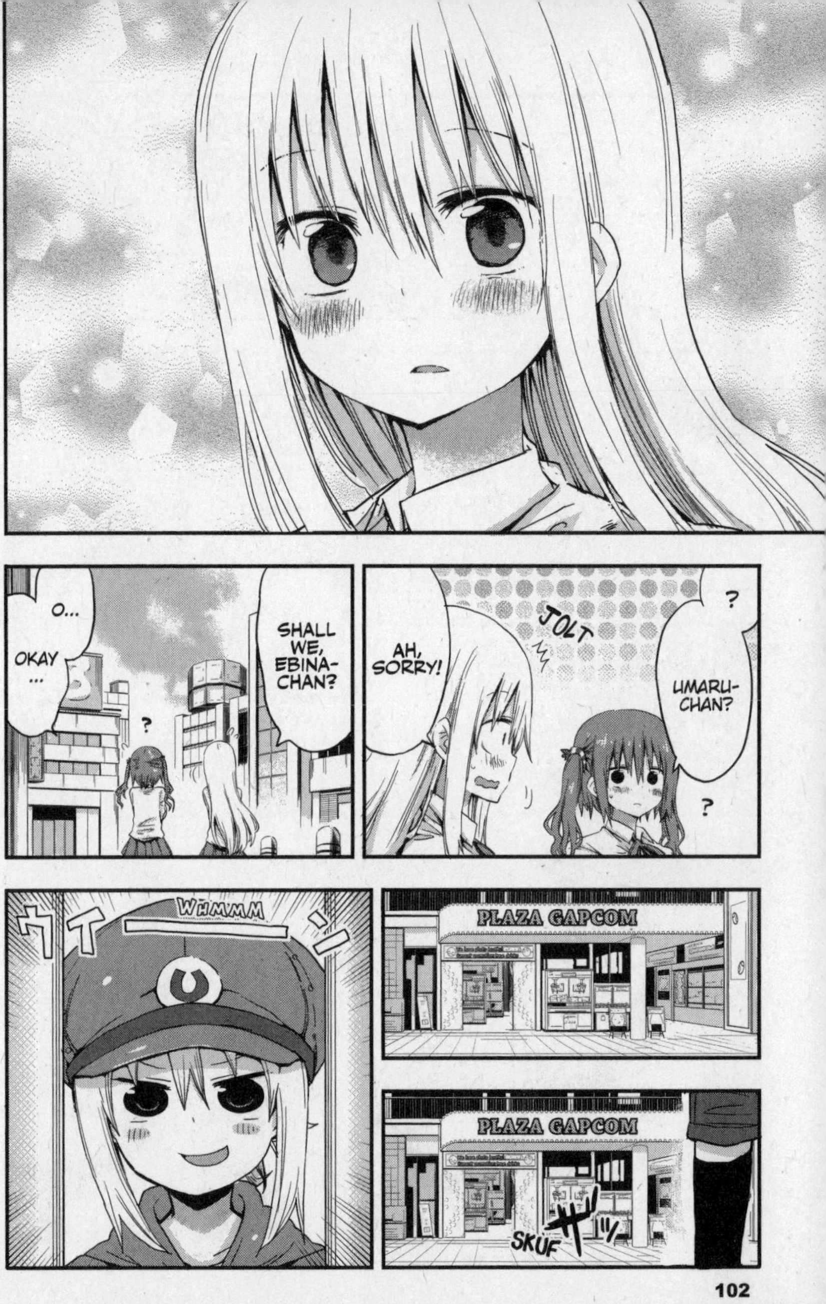
?
UMARU-CHAN?
JOLT
AH, SORRY!
?
SHALL WE, EBINA-CHAN?
O... OKAY ...
?
PLAZA GAPCOM
PLAZA GAPCOM
SKÜF
WHMMM

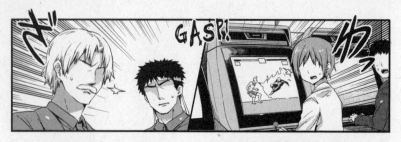

GASP!

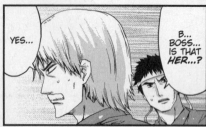

YES...

B... BOSS... IS THAT HER...?

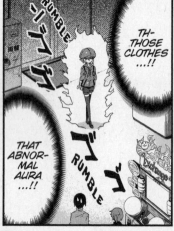

TH-THOSE CLOTHES ...!!

THAT ABNORMAL AURA ...!!

RUMBLE

RUMBLE

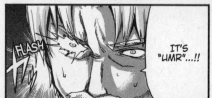

FLASH

IT'S "UMR"...!!

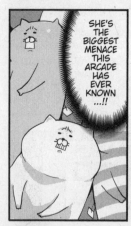

SHE'S THE BIGGEST MENACE THIS ARCADE HAS EVER KNOWN ...!!

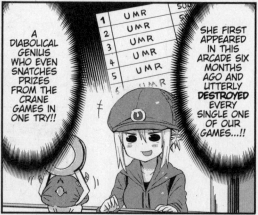

A DIABOLICAL GENIUS WHO EVEN SNATCHES PRIZES FROM THE CRANE GAMES IN ONE TRY!!

1	UMR	500
2	UMR	5
3	UMR	
4	UMR	
5	UMR	
6	UMR	

SHE FIRST APPEARED IN THIS ARCADE SIX MONTHS AGO AND UTTERLY **DESTROYED** EVERY SINGLE ONE OF OUR GAMES...!!

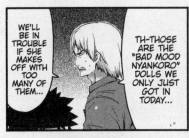

キラ
TWING
キラ
TWING
TH-THOSE ARE THE "BAD MOOD NYANKORO" DOLLS WE ONLY JUST GOT IN TODAY...
WE'LL BE IN TROUBLE IF SHE MAKES OFF WITH TOO MANY OF THEM...
NOT TO WORRY, BOSS ...!
I'VE SET UP THAT MACHINE TO BE EXTRA CHAL-LENGING!
TEN TEN TEN TILLO ♪
SHE GOT THREE OF THEM.
GRAAA
MY GOD... SHE USED "TAG HOOK"...!! IT'S A HIGH-LEVEL TECHNIQUE WHERE YOU LIFT THE PLUSHIES BY HOOKING THE TAG ...!!
Hella Mad Huffin' Puffin' Migu
Hella Mad Huffin' Puffin' Migu
Collect All 6

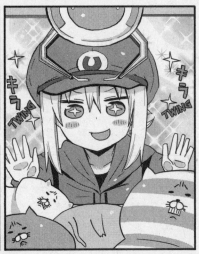

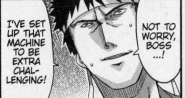

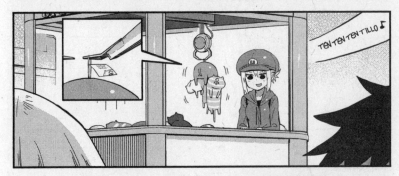

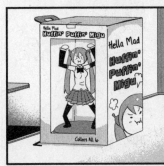

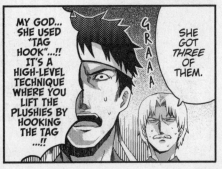

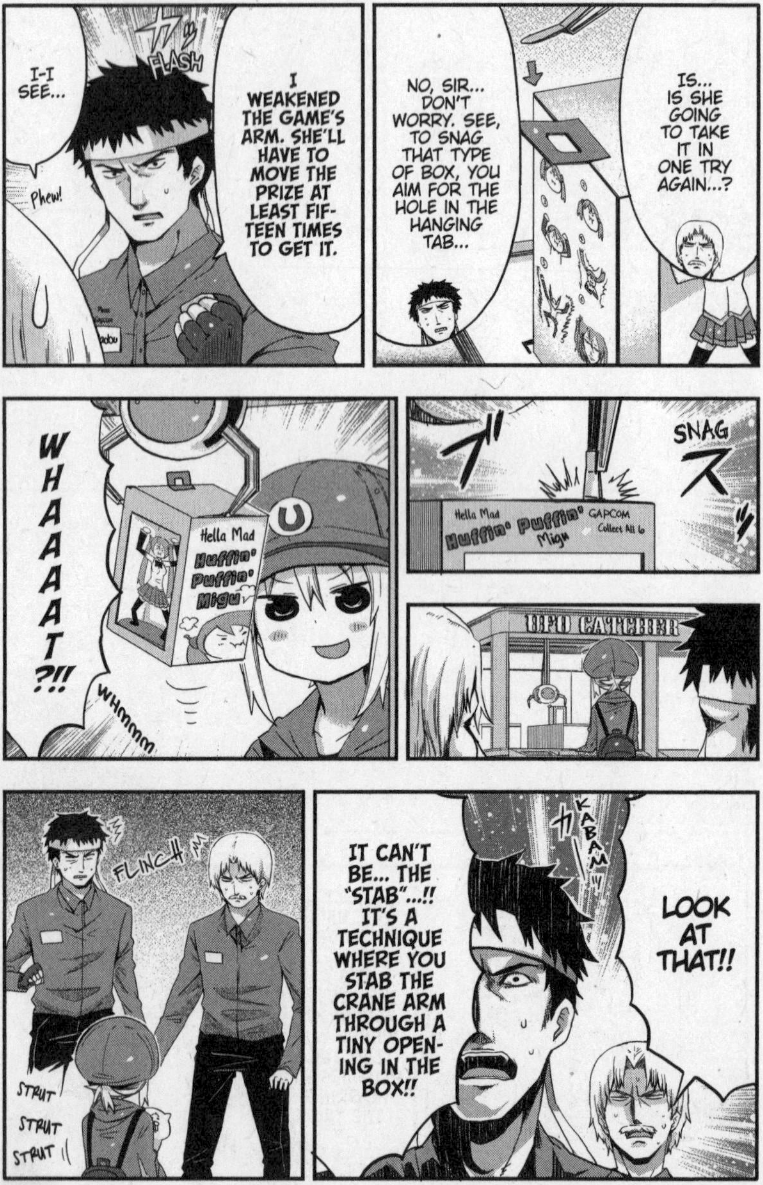
IS... IS SHE GOING TO TAKE IT IN ONE TRY AGAIN...?
NO, SIR... DON'T WORRY. SEE, TO SNAG THAT TYPE OF BOX, YOU AIM FOR THE HOLE IN THE HANGING TAB...
FLASH
I WEAKENED THE GAME'S ARM. SHE'LL HAVE TO MOVE THE PRIZE AT LEAST FIF-TEEN TIMES TO GET IT.
I-I SEE...
Phew!
SNAG
Hella Mad
Huffin' Puffin' Migu
GAPCOM
Collect All 6
UFO CATCHER
WHAAAAAT?!!
Hella Mad
Huffin' Puffin' Migu
WHmmmm
LOOK AT THAT!!
KABAM
IT CAN'T BE... THE "STAB"...!! IT'S A TECHNIQUE WHERE YOU STAB THE CRANE ARM THROUGH A TINY OPEN-ING IN THE BOX!!
FLINCH
STRUT
STRUT
STRUT

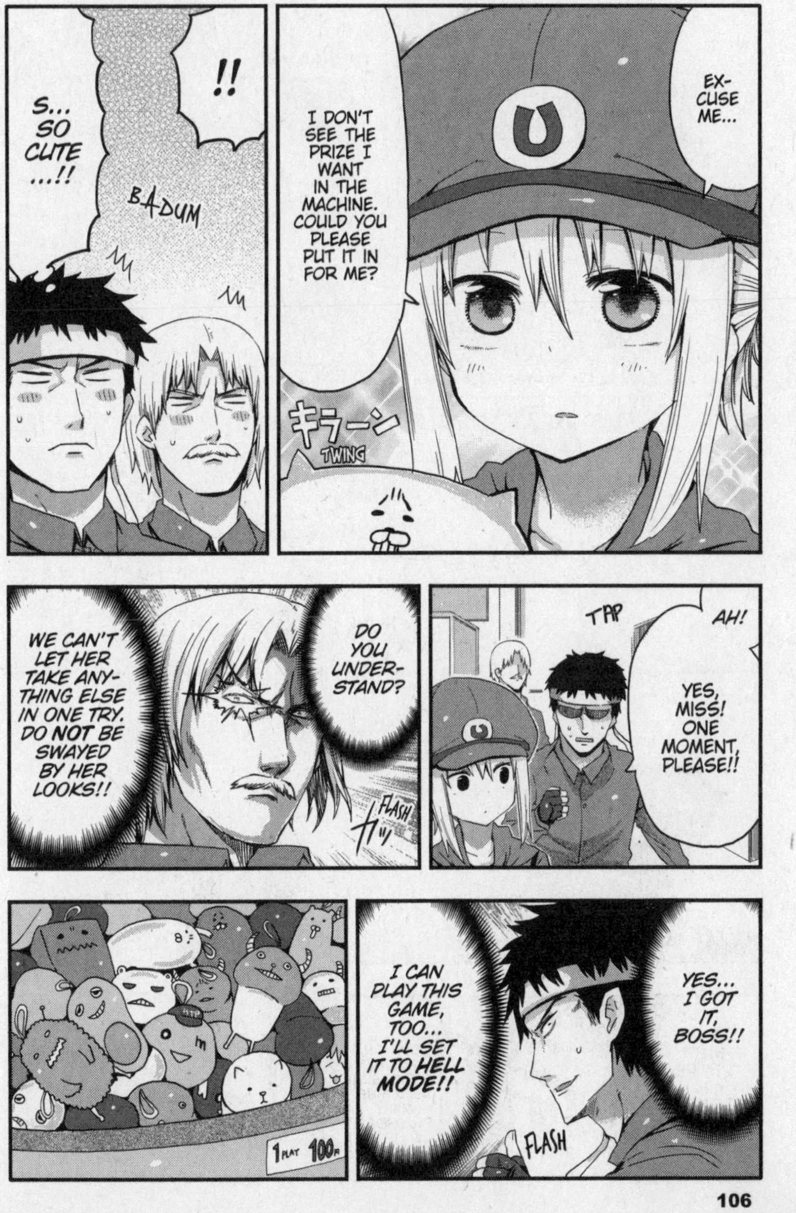

EX-
CUSE
ME...
I DON'T SEE THE PRIZE I WANT IN THE MACHINE. COULD YOU PLEASE PUT IT IN FOR ME?
キラーン
TWING
!!
S... SO CUTE ...!!
BADUM
AH!
TAP
YES, MISS! ONE MOMENT, PLEASE!!
DO YOU UNDER-STAND?
WE CAN'T LET HER TAKE ANY-THING ELSE IN ONE TRY. DO **NOT** BE SWAYED BY HER LOOKS!!
FLASH
ガッ
YES... I GOT IT, BOSS!!
I CAN PLAY THIS GAME, TOO... I'LL SET IT TO **HELL MODE!!**
FLASH
1 PLAY 100円

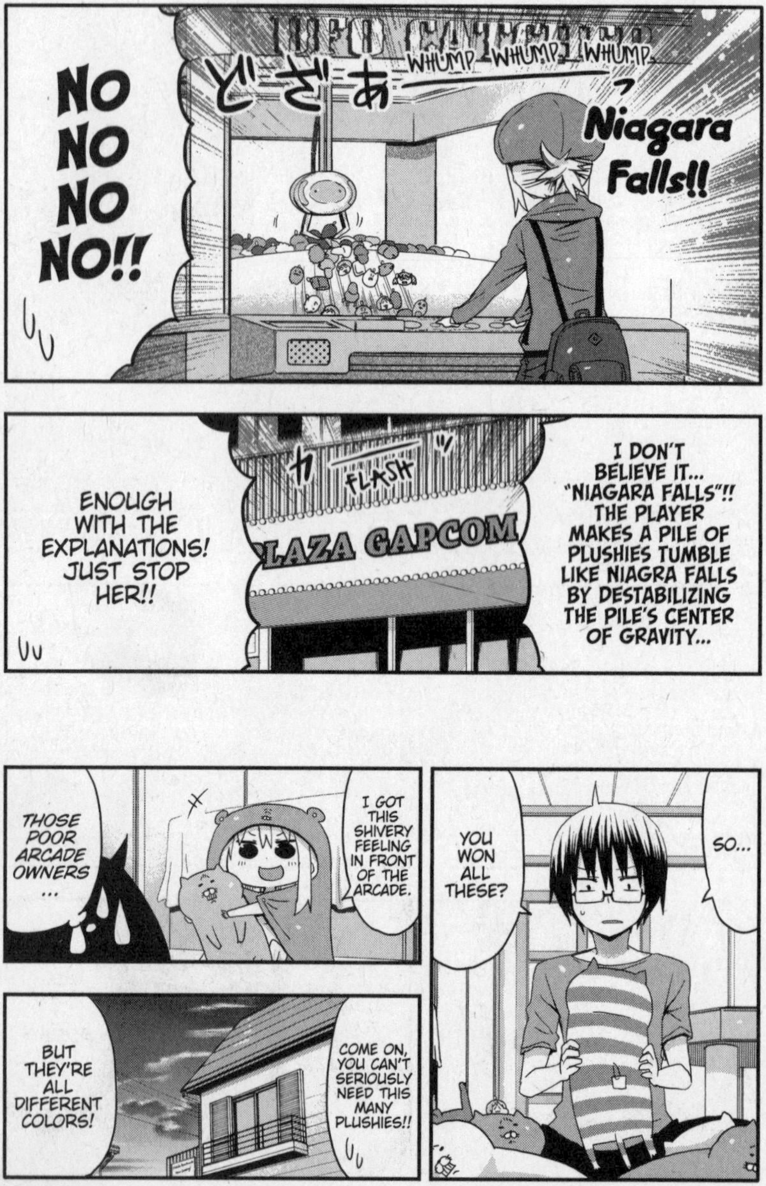
Niagara Falls!!
どざあ WHUMP WHUMP WHUMP
NO NO NO NO!!
I DON'T BELIEVE IT... "NIAGARA FALLS"!! THE PLAYER MAKES A PILE OF PLUSHIES TUMBLE LIKE NIAGRA FALLS BY DESTABILIZING THE PILE'S CENTER OF GRAVITY...
カッ FLASH
PLAZA GAPCOM
ENOUGH WITH THE EXPLANATIONS! JUST STOP HER!!
SO...
YOU WON ALL THESE?
I GOT THIS SHIVERY FEELING IN FRONT OF THE ARCADE.
THOSE POOR ARCADE OWNERS...
COME ON, YOU CAN'T SERIOUSLY NEED THIS MANY PLUSHIES!!
BUT THEY'RE ALL DIFFERENT COLORS!

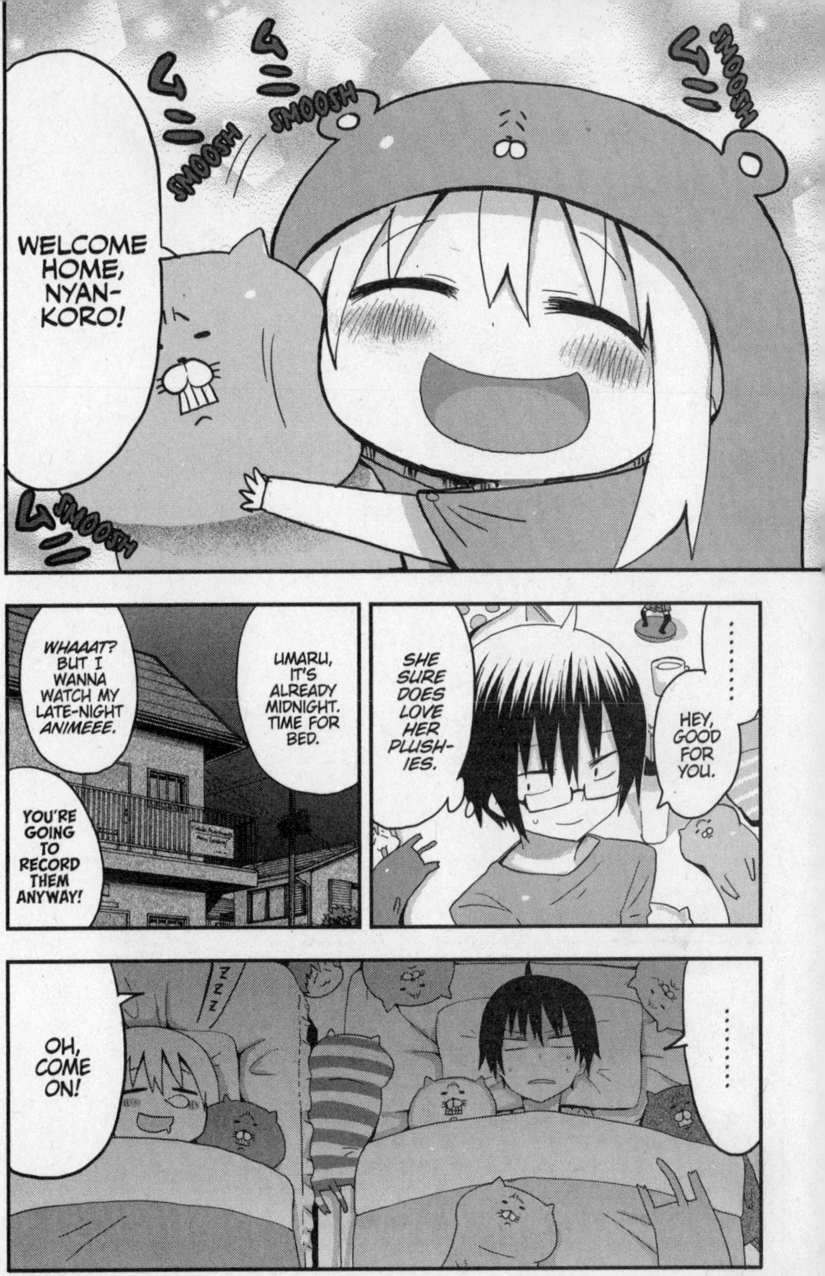
SMOOSH
SMOOSH
SMOOSH
WELCOME HOME, NYAN-KORO!
SMOOSH
....
HEY, GOOD FOR YOU.
SHE SURE DOES LOVE HER PLUSHIES.
UMARU, IT'S ALREADY MIDNIGHT. TIME FOR BED.
WHAAAT? BUT I WANNA WATCH MY LATE-NIGHT ANIMEEE.
YOU'RE GOING TO RECORD THEM ANYWAY!
....
Z Z Z
OH, COME ON!

Collect All 6!

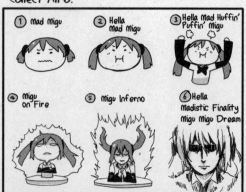

1. Mad Migu
2. Hella Mad Migu
3. Hella Mad Huffin' Puffin' Migu
4. Migu on Fire
5. Migu Inferno
6. Hella Madistic Finality Migu Migu Dream

HIMOUTO! UMARU-CHAN

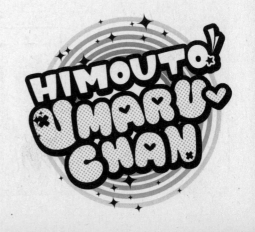

No. 13 Umaru & Dining Out

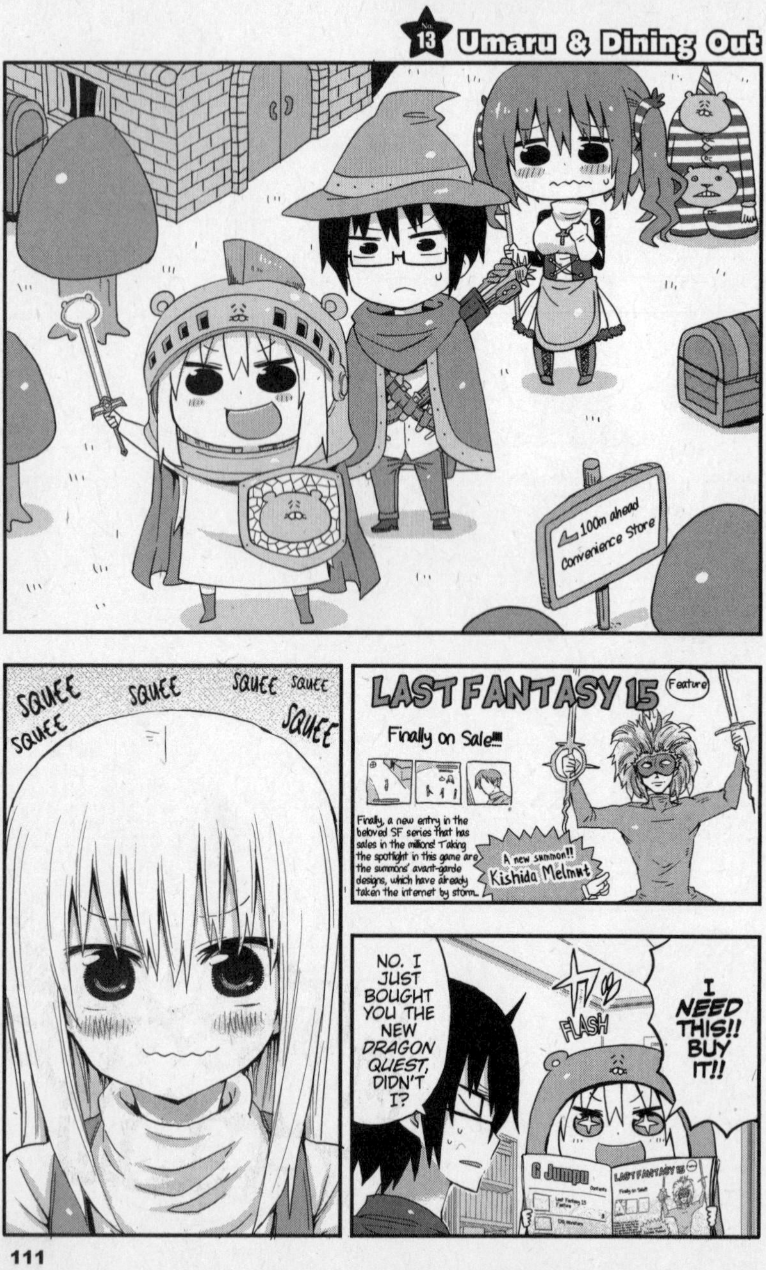

100m ahead
Convenience Store
LAST FANTASY 15
Feature
Finally on Sale!!!!
Finally, a new entry in the beloved SF series that has sales in the millions! Taking the spotlight in this game are the summons' avant-garde designs, which have already taken the internet by storm.
A new summon!! Kishida Melmut
I NEED THIS!! BUY IT!!
FLASH
NO. I JUST BOUGHT YOU THE NEW DRAGON QUEST, DIDN'T I?
G Jumpu
LAST FANTASY 15
SQUEE
SQUEE
SQUEE
SQUEE
SQUEE
SQUEE

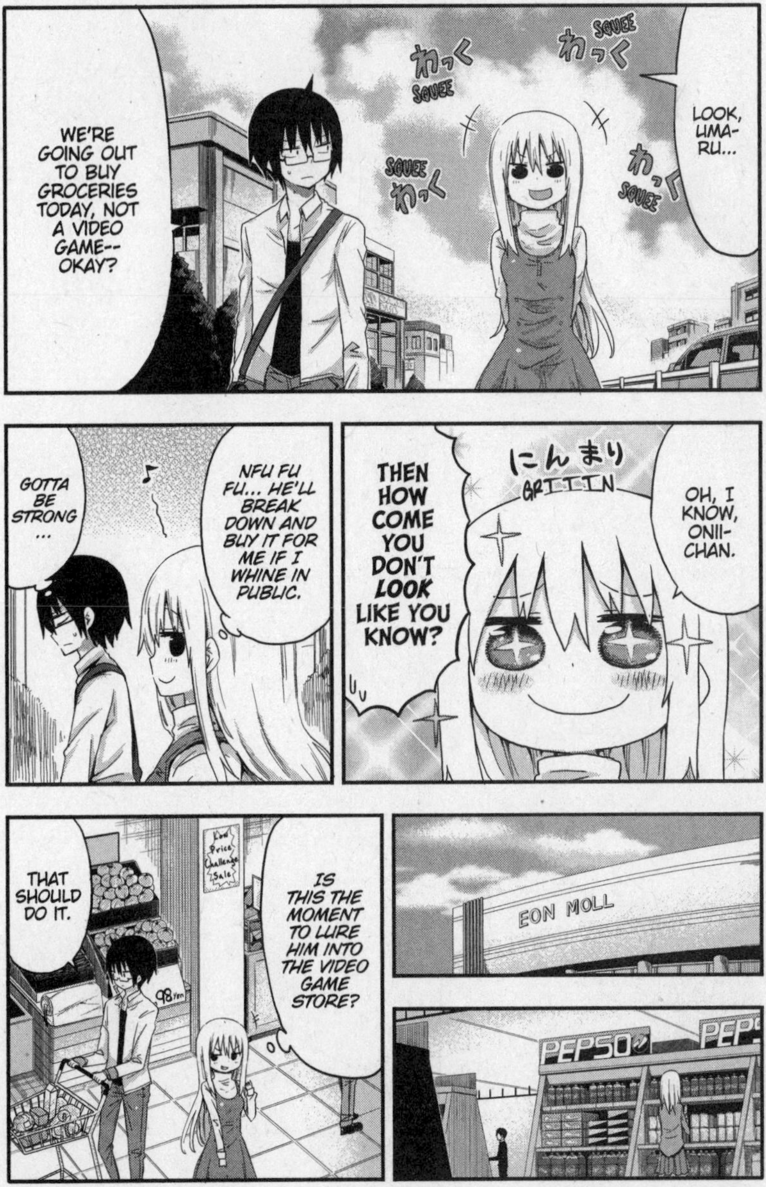
LOOK, UMA-RU...
わっく SQUEE
わっく SQUEE
わっく SQUEE
わっく SQUEE
WE'RE GOING OUT TO BUY GROCERIES TODAY, NOT A VIDEO GAME-- OKAY?
OH, I KNOW, ONII-CHAN.
にんまり GRIIIN
THEN HOW COME YOU DON'T LOOK LIKE YOU KNOW?
NFU FU FU... HE'LL BREAK DOWN AND BUY IT FOR ME IF I WHINE IN PUBLIC.
GOTTA BE STRONG...
EON MOLL
PEPSO
PEPS
IS THIS THE MOMENT TO LURE HIM INTO THE VIDEO GAME STORE?
Low Price Challenge Sale
THAT SHOULD DO IT.
98 Yen

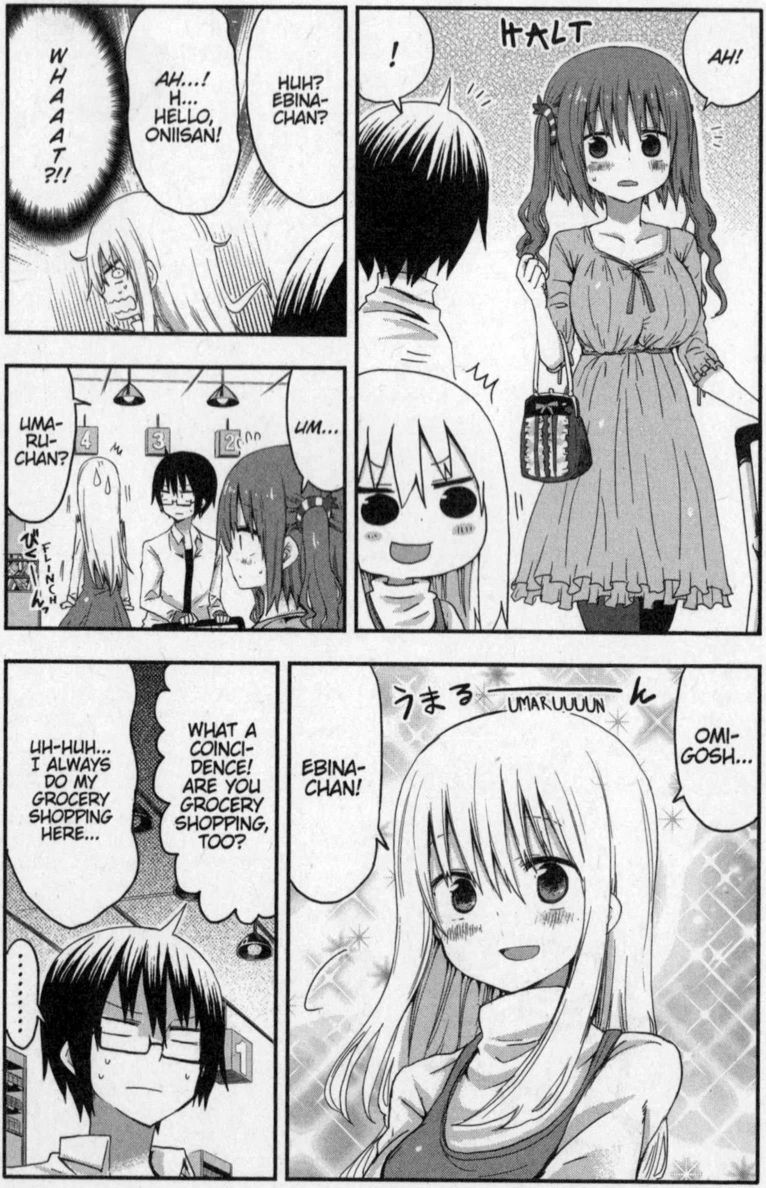
AH!
HALT
!
HUH? EBINA-CHAN?
AH...! H... HELLO, ONIISAN!
WHAAAAT?!!
UM...
UMARU-CHAN?
びくーん
FLINCH
OMI-GOSH...
うまる―ん
UMARUUUUN
EBINA-CHAN!
WHAT A COINCIDENCE! ARE YOU GROCERY SHOPPING, TOO?
UH-HUH... I ALWAYS DO MY GROCERY SHOPPING HERE...
......

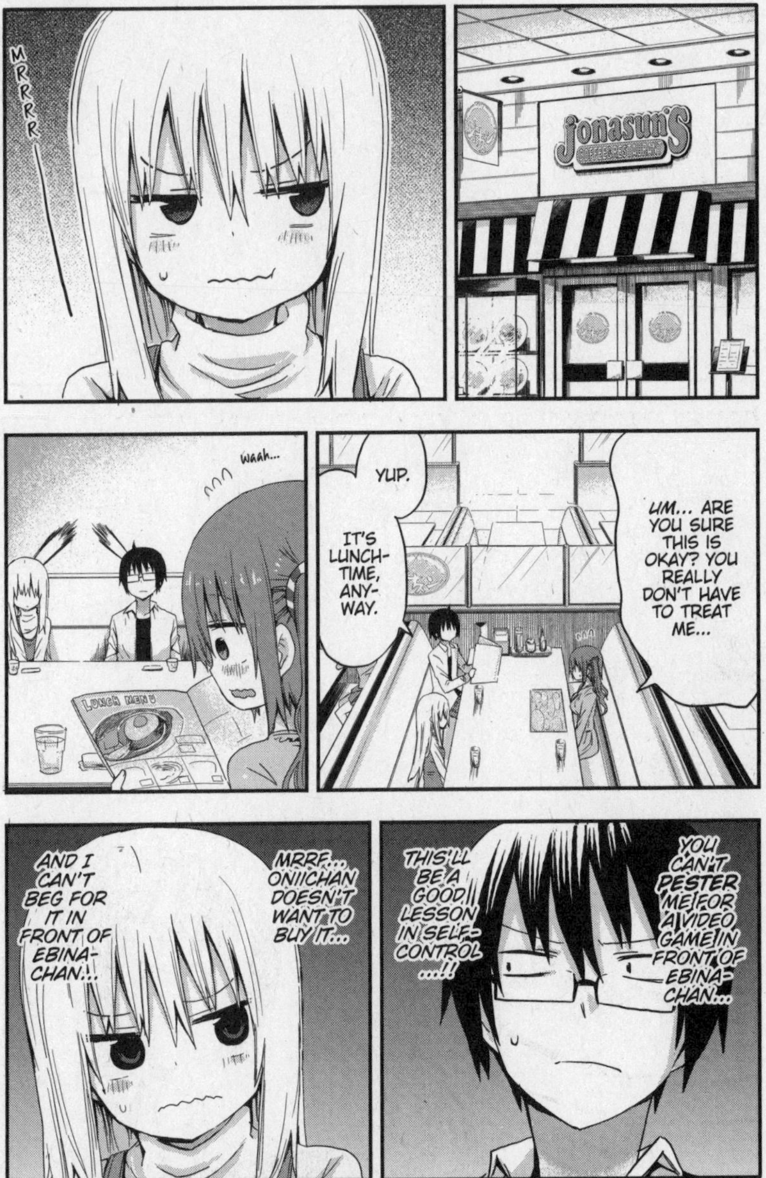
jonasun's
MRRRR
UM... ARE YOU SURE THIS IS OKAY? YOU REALLY DON'T HAVE TO TREAT ME...
YUP.
IT'S LUNCH-TIME, ANYWAY.
waah...
LUNCH MENU
YOU CAN'T PESTER ME FOR A VIDEO GAME IN FRONT OF EBINA-CHAN...
THIS'LL BE A GOOD LESSON IN SELF-CONTROL...!!
MRRF... ONIICHAN DOESN'T WANT TO BUY IT...
AND I CAN'T BEG FOR IT IN FRONT OF EBINA-CHAN...!

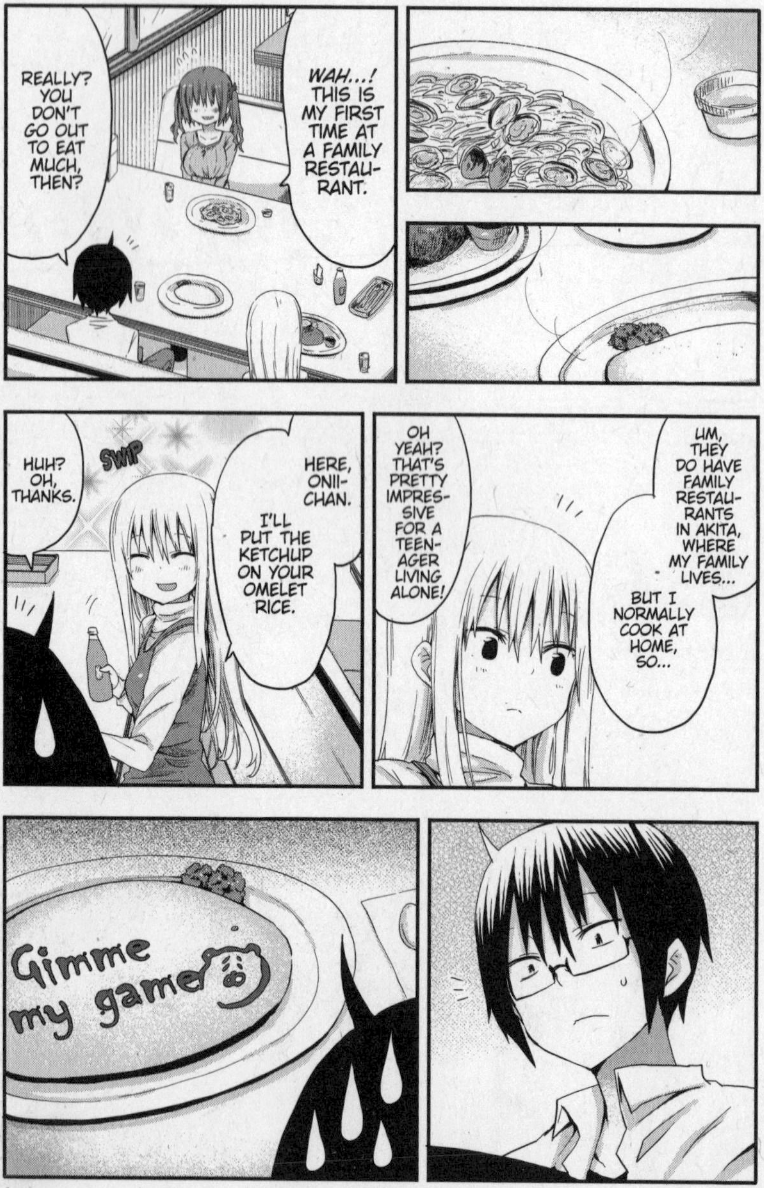
WAH...! THIS IS MY FIRST TIME AT A FAMILY RESTAURANT.
REALLY? YOU DON'T GO OUT TO EAT MUCH, THEN?
UM, THEY DO HAVE FAMILY RESTAURANTS IN AKITA, WHERE MY FAMILY LIVES...
BUT I NORMALLY COOK AT HOME, SO...
OH YEAH? THAT'S PRETTY IMPRESSIVE FOR A TEENAGER LIVING ALONE!
HERE, ONII-CHAN.
I'LL PUT THE KETCHUP ON YOUR OMELET RICE.
SWIP
HUH? OH, THANKS.
Gimme my game

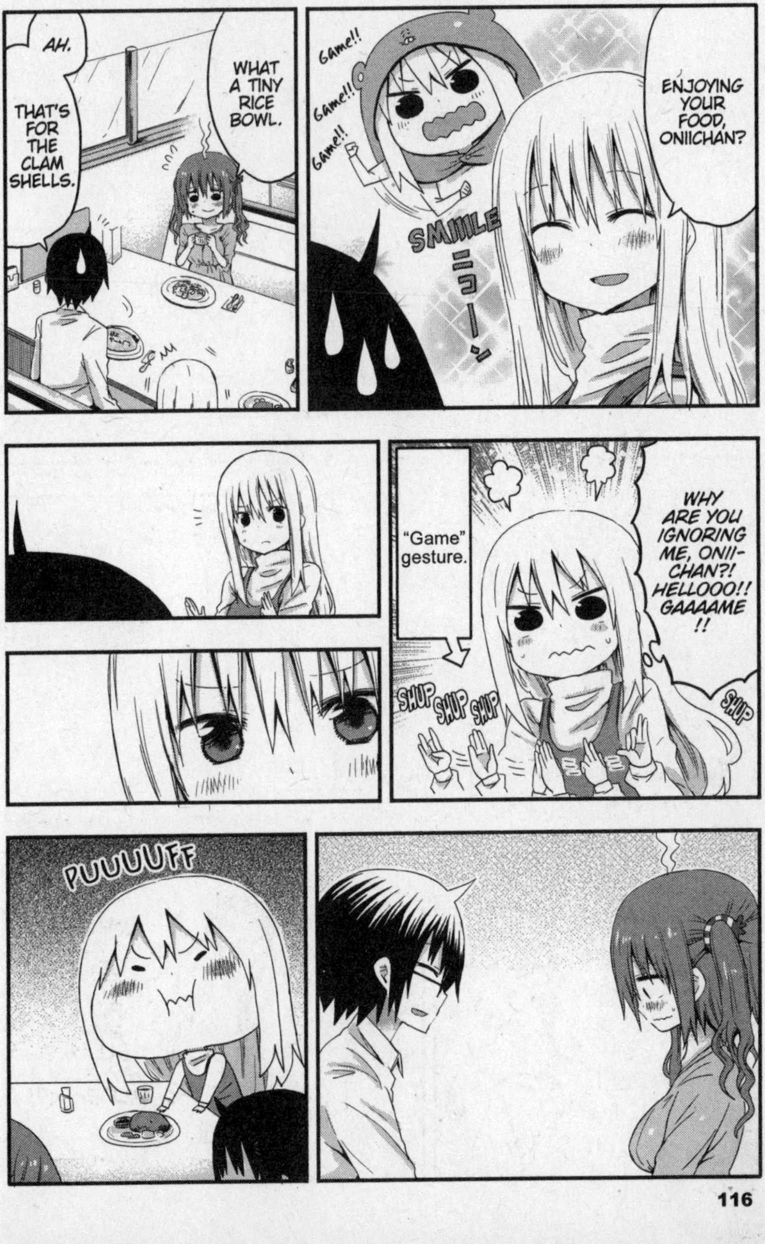
ENJOYING YOUR FOOD, ONIICHAN?
Game!!
Game!!
Game!!
SMIIILE
ニコーッ
WHAT A TINY RICE BOWL.
AH.
THAT'S FOR THE CLAM SHELLS.
WHY ARE YOU IGNORING ME, ONII-CHAN?! HELLOOO!! GAAAAME!!
"Game" gesture.
SHUP
SHUP SHUP SHUP
PUUUUFF

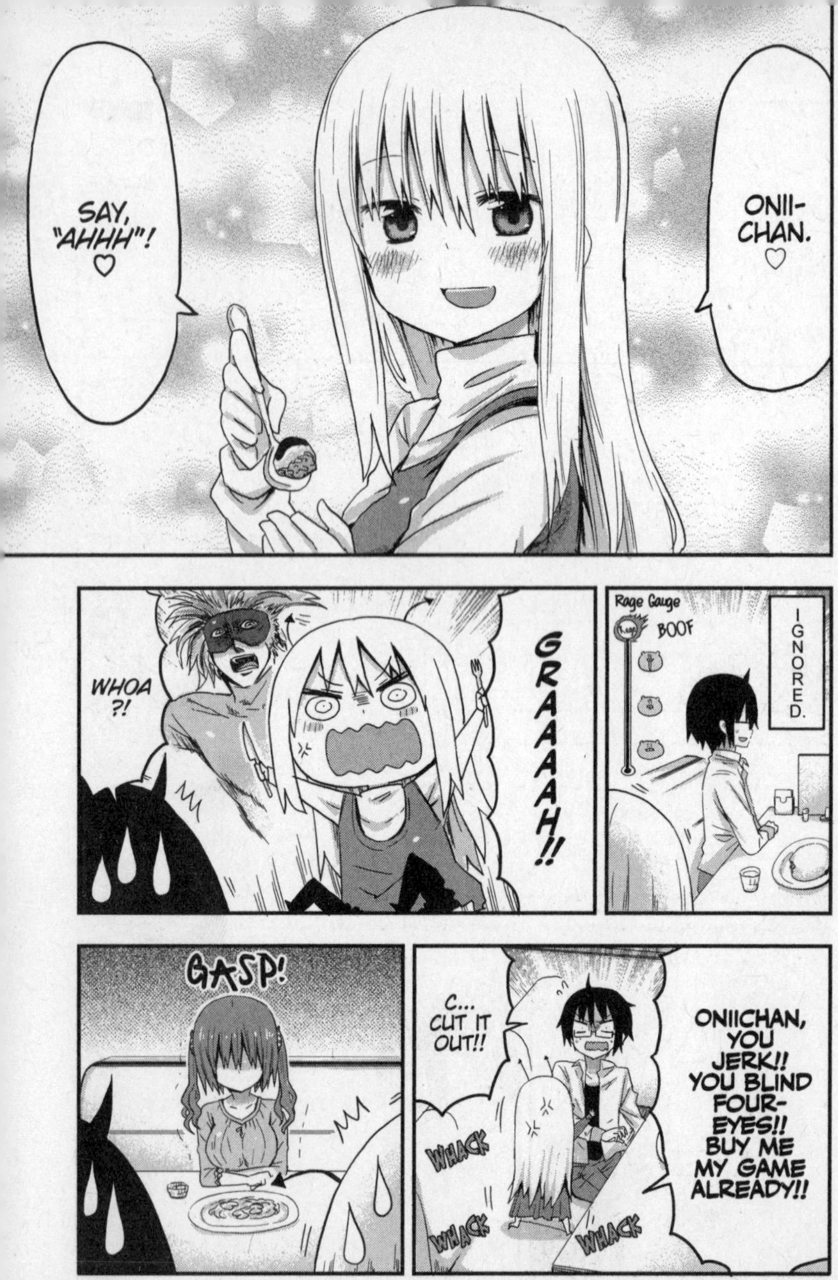
ONII-CHAN. ♡
SAY, "AHHH"! ♡
Rage Gauge
BOOF
IGNORED.
GRAAAAAH!!
WHOA ?!
ONIICHAN, YOU JERK!! YOU BLIND FOUR-EYES!! BUY ME MY GAME ALREADY!!
C... CUT IT OUT!!
WHACK
WHACK
WHACK
GASP!

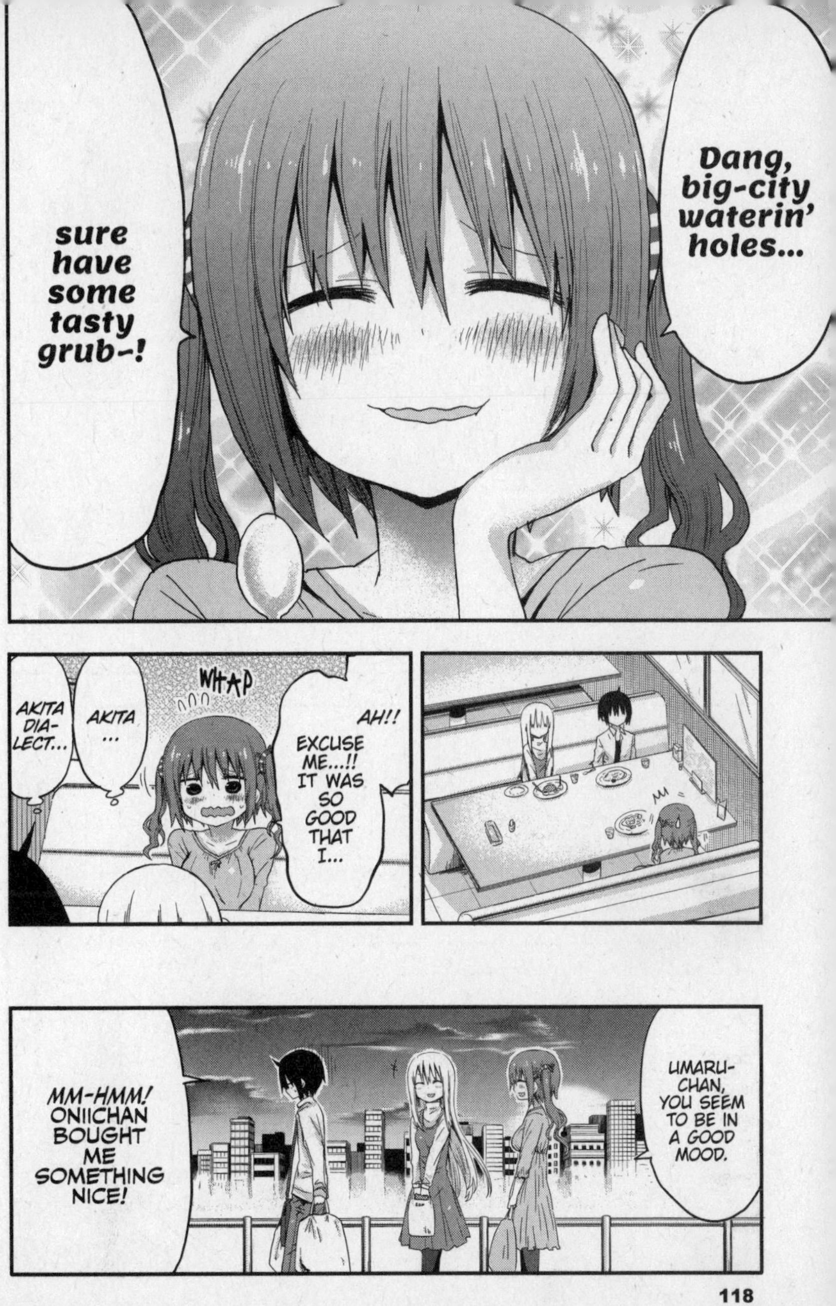
Dang, big-city waterin' holes...
sure have some tasty grub-!
AH!! EXCUSE ME...!! IT WAS SO GOOD THAT I...
WHAP
AKITA ...
AKITA DIALECT...
UMARU-CHAN, YOU SEEM TO BE IN A GOOD MOOD.
MM-HMM! ONIICHAN BOUGHT ME SOMETHING NICE!

14 A Day in the Life of Oniichan

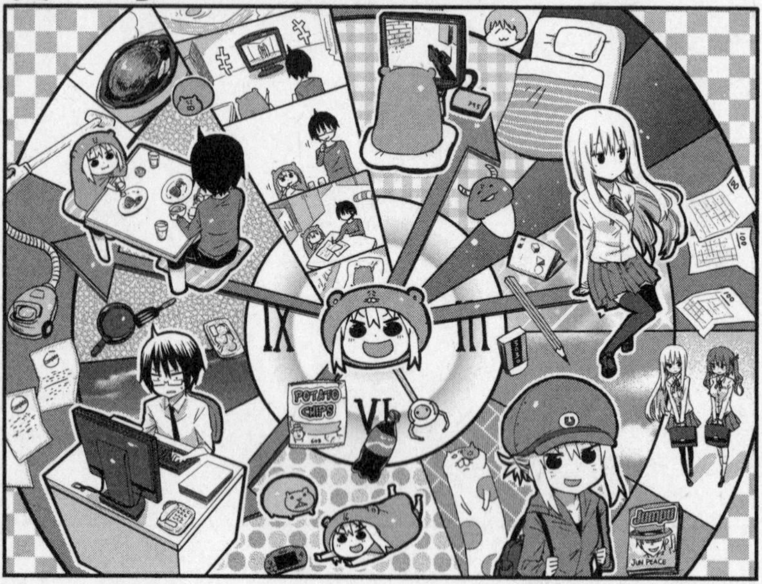
IX
III
VI
POTATO CHIPS
JUN PEACE

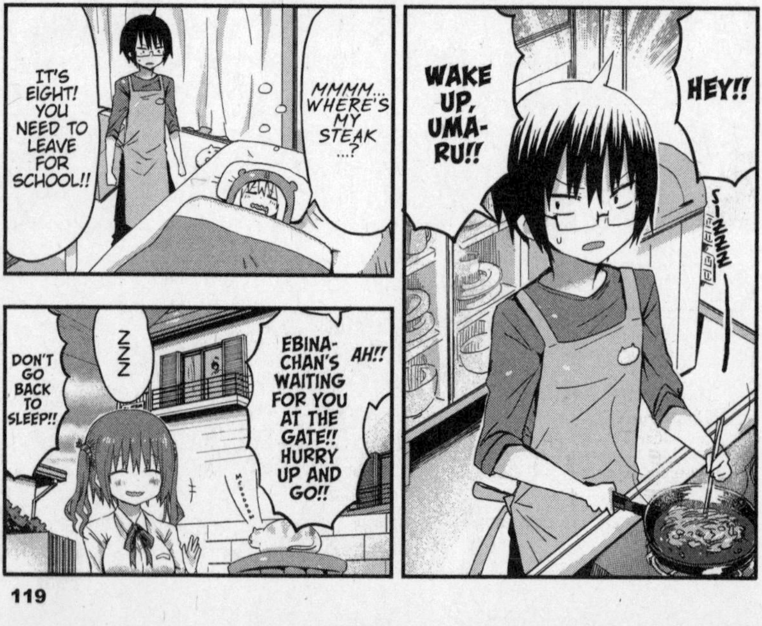
HEY!!
WAKE UP, UMA-RU!!
S-NNNN
MMMM... WHERE'S MY STEAK ...?
IT'S EIGHT! YOU NEED TO LEAVE FOR SCHOOL!!
AH!!
EBINA-CHAN'S WAITING FOR YOU AT THE GATE!! HURRY UP AND GO!!
ZZZ
DON'T GO BACK TO SLEEP!!

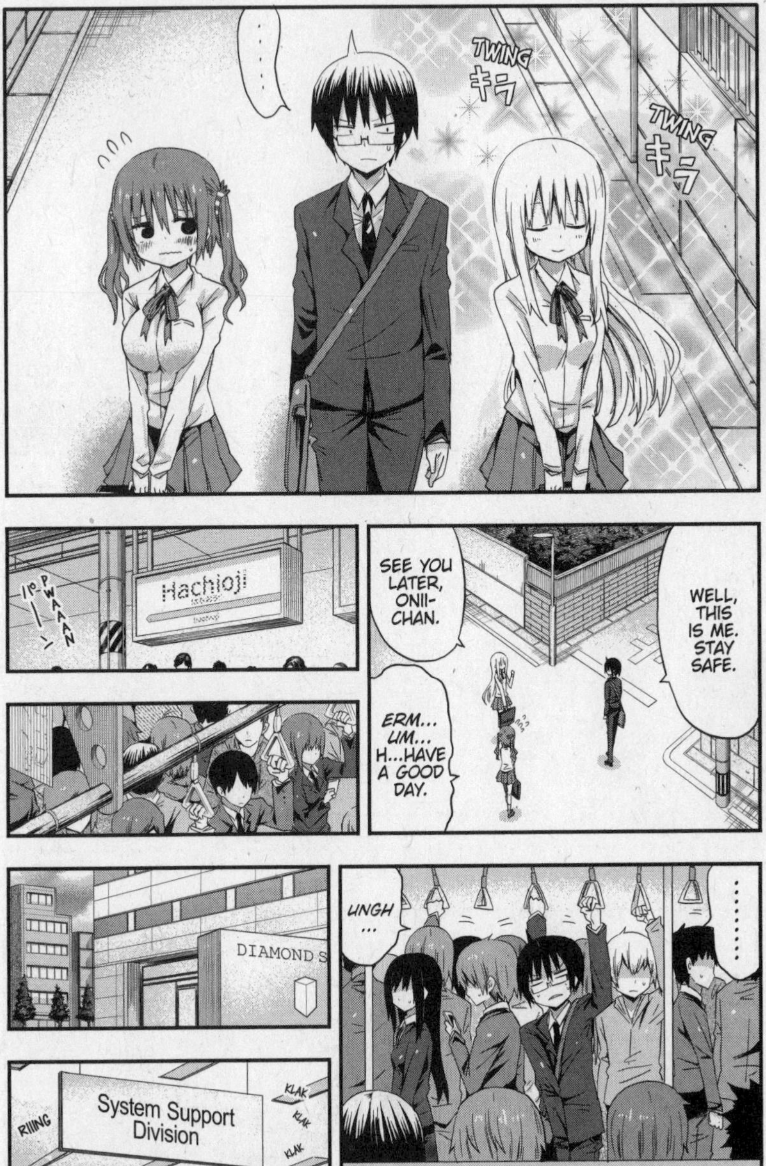
. . . . .
TWING
キラ
TWING
キラ
WELL, THIS IS ME. STAY SAFE.
SEE YOU LATER, ONII-CHAN.
ERM... UM... H...HAVE A GOOD DAY.
Hachioji
パー
PWAAAN
....
UNGH ...
DIAMOND S
System Support Division
RIIING
KLAK
KLAK
KLAK

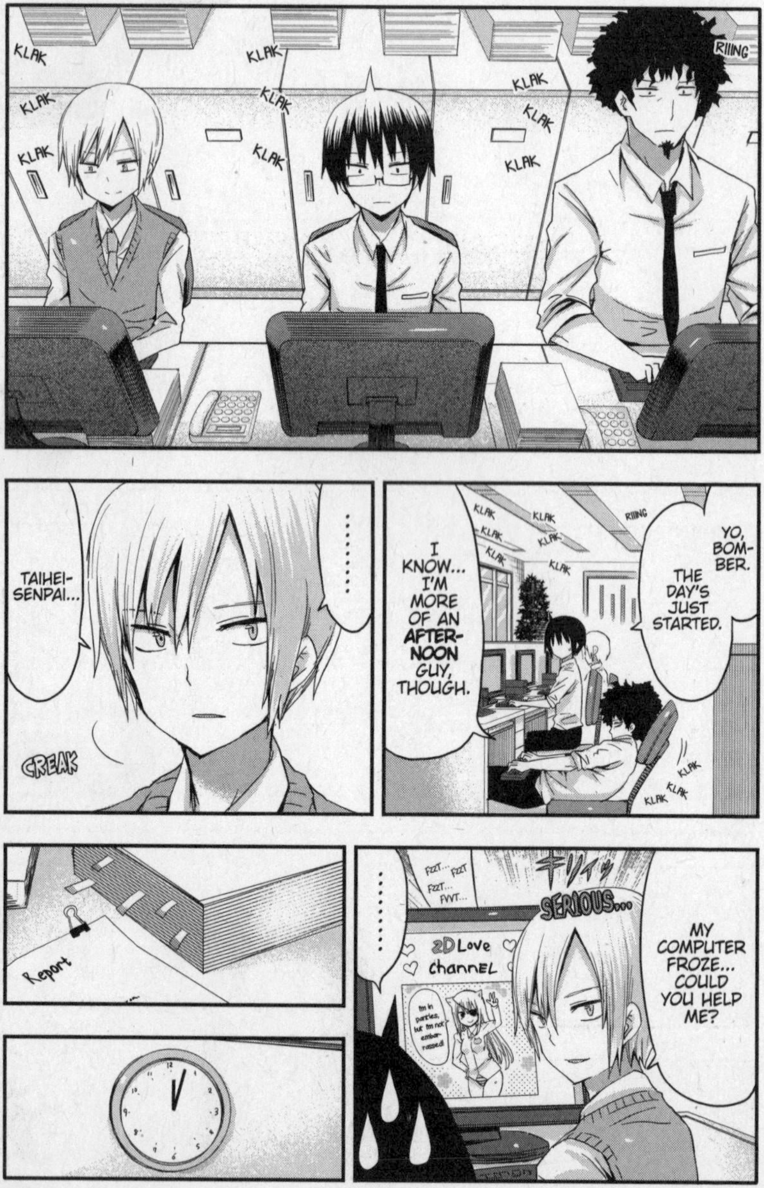
RIIING
KLAK
KLAK
KLAK
KLAK
KLAK
KLAK
KLAK
KLAK
KLAK
RIIING
YO, BOMBER. THE DAY'S JUST STARTED.
KLAK
KLAK
KLAK
KLAK
KLAK
I KNOW... I'M MORE OF AN AFTERNOON GUY, THOUGH.
KLAK
KLAK
KLAK
......
TAIHEI-SENPAI...
CREAK
MY COMPUTER FROZE... COULD YOU HELP ME?
SERIOUS...
FZZT... FZZT
FZZT... FVVT...
......
2D Love Channel
Report

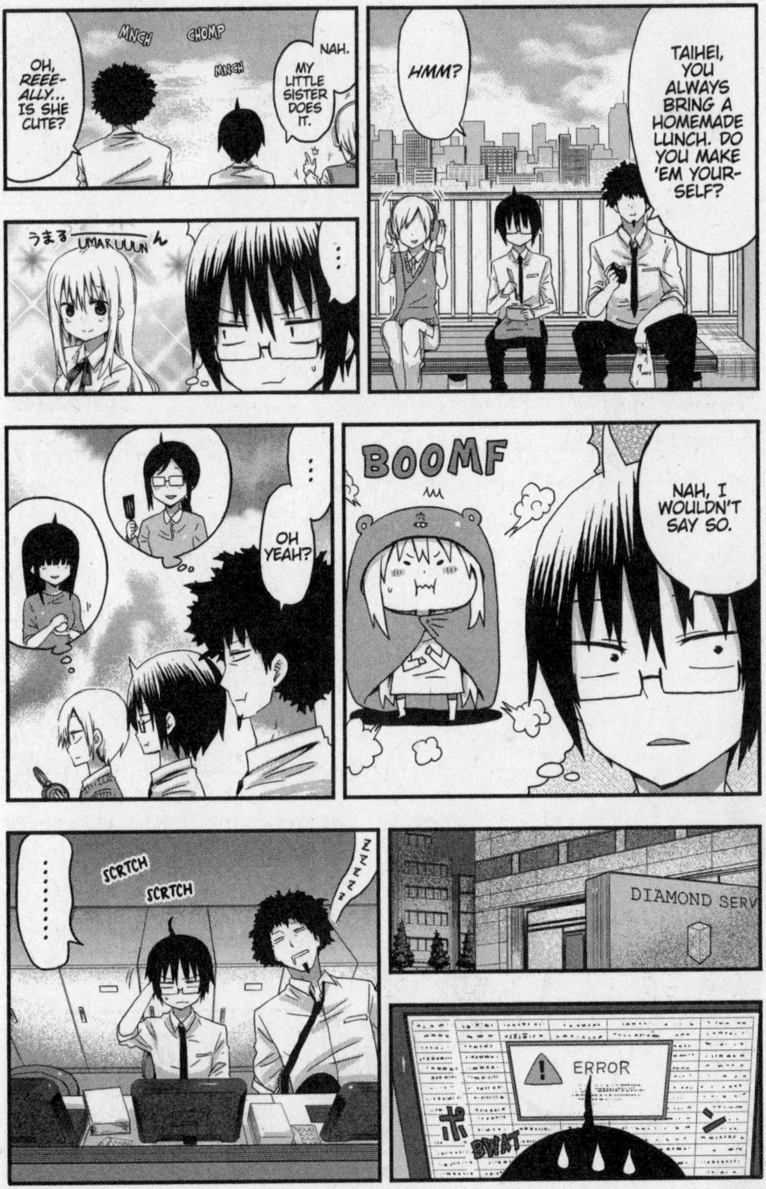
TAIHEI, YOU ALWAYS BRING A HOMEMADE LUNCH. DO YOU MAKE 'EM YOURSELF?
HMM?
NAH. MY LITTLE SISTER DOES IT.
CHOMP
MNCH
MNCH
OH, REEEALLY... IS SHE CUTE?
...
うまる UMARUUUN ん
NAH, I WOULDN'T SAY SO.
BOOMF
...
OH YEAH?
DIAMOND SERV
ERROR
ポ BWAT ン
ZZZZZZ
SCRTCH
SCRTCH
....

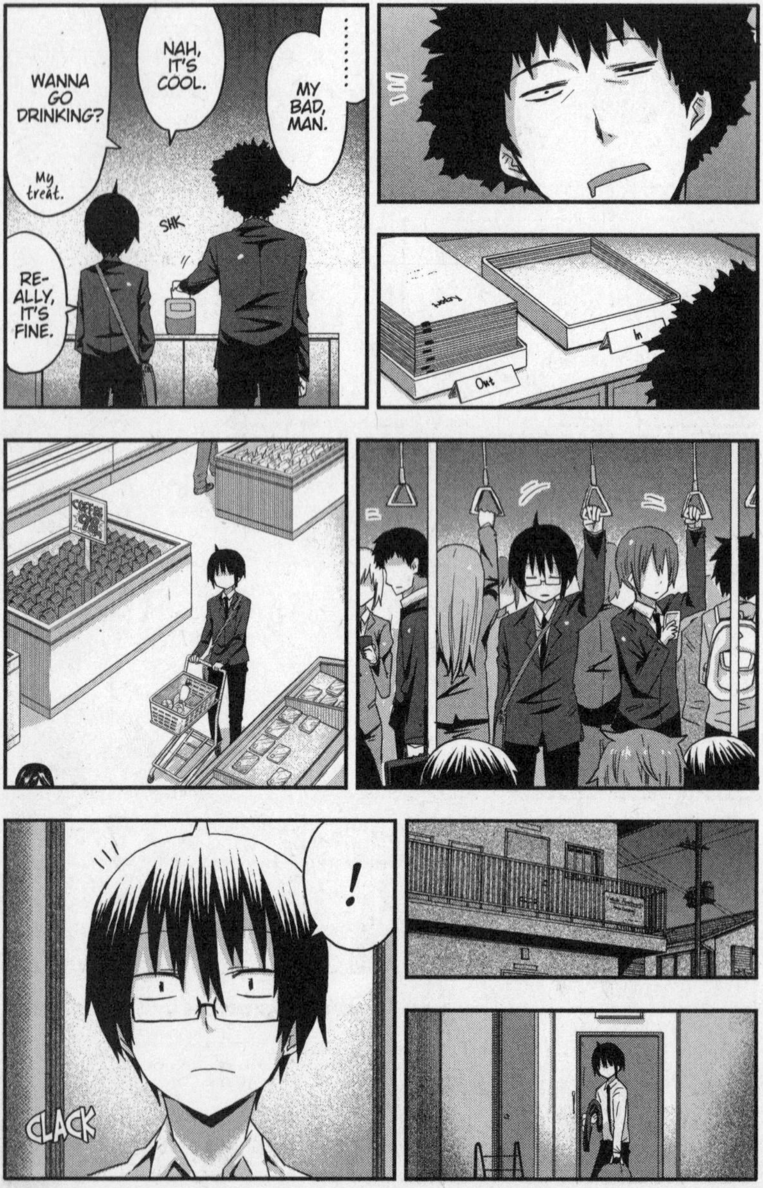
In
Out
......
MY BAD, MAN.
NAH, IT'S COOL.
WANNA GO DRINKING?
My treat.
SHK
RE-ALLY, IT'S FINE.
!
CLACK

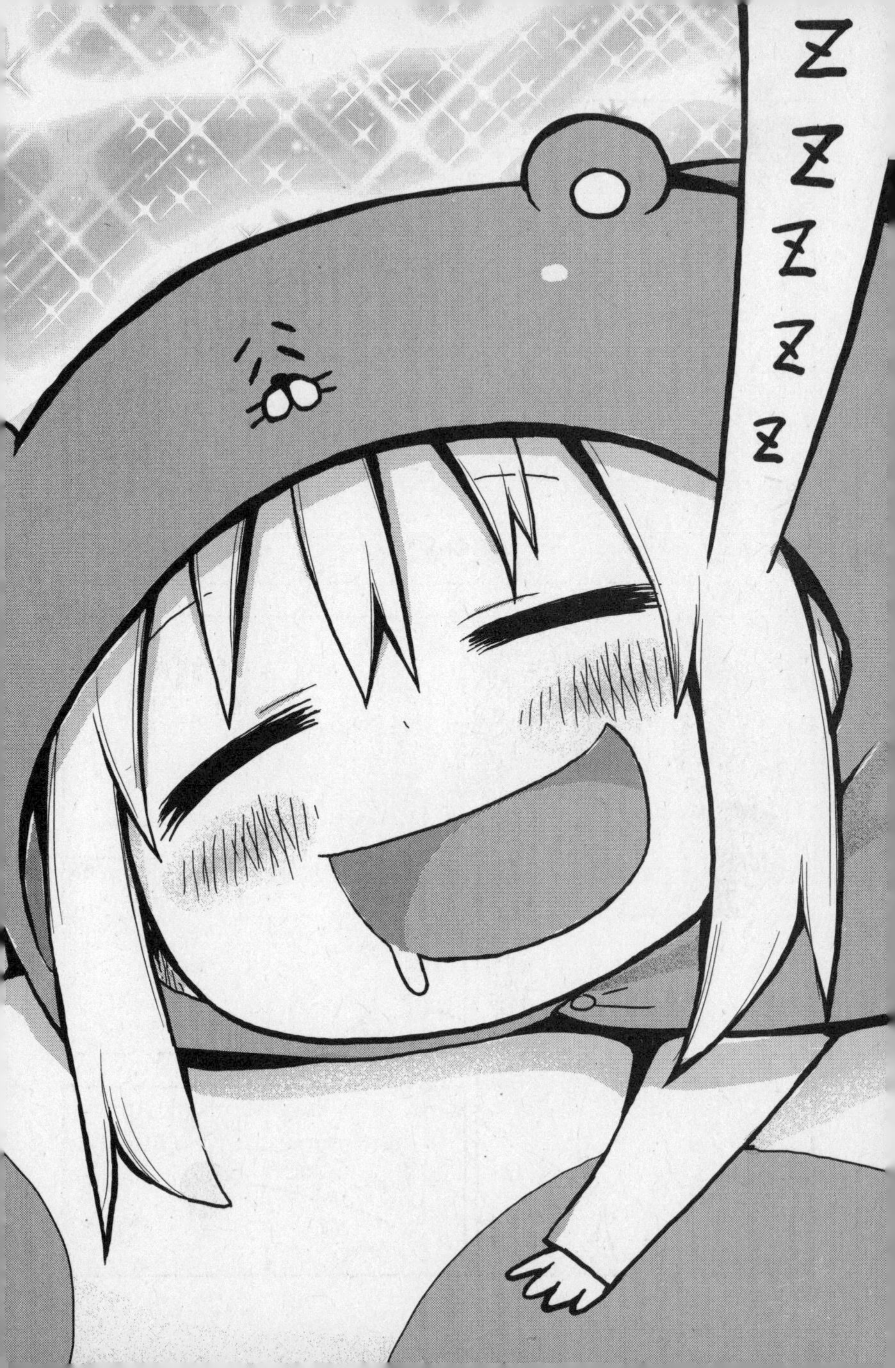
ZZZZZ

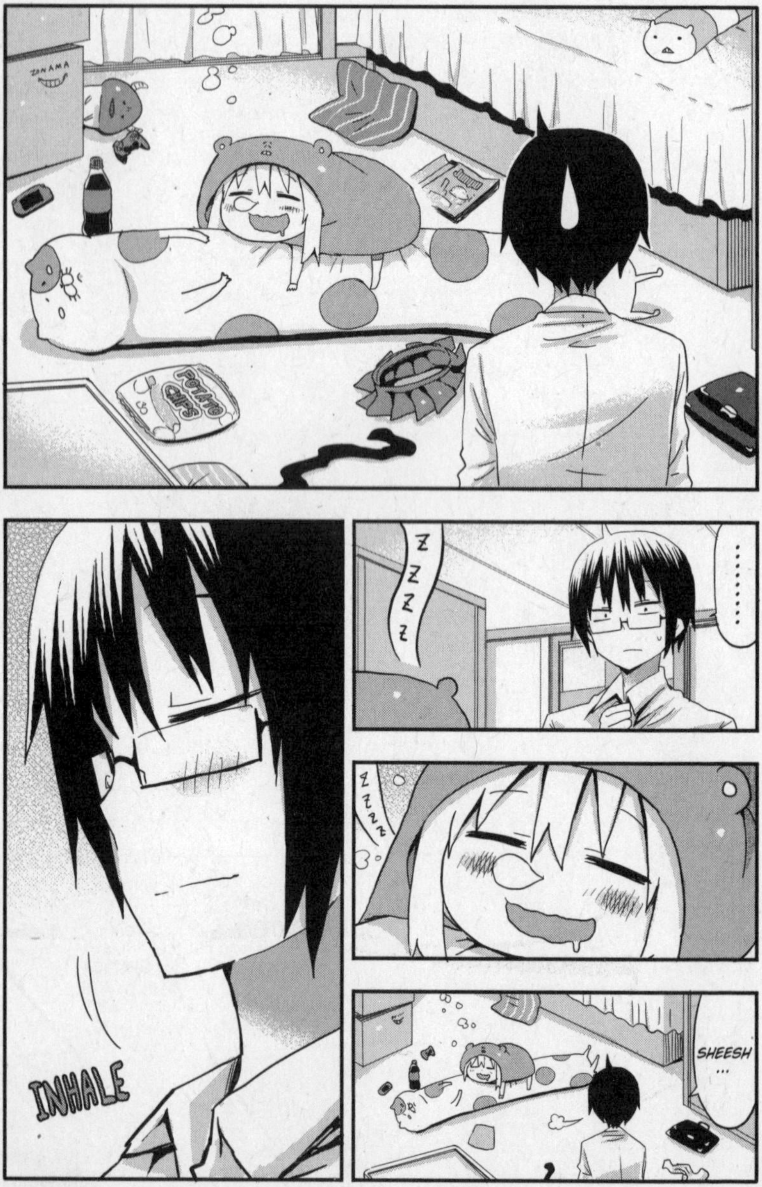

Z Z Z Z Z
......
Z Z Z Z Z
SHEESH ...
INHALE

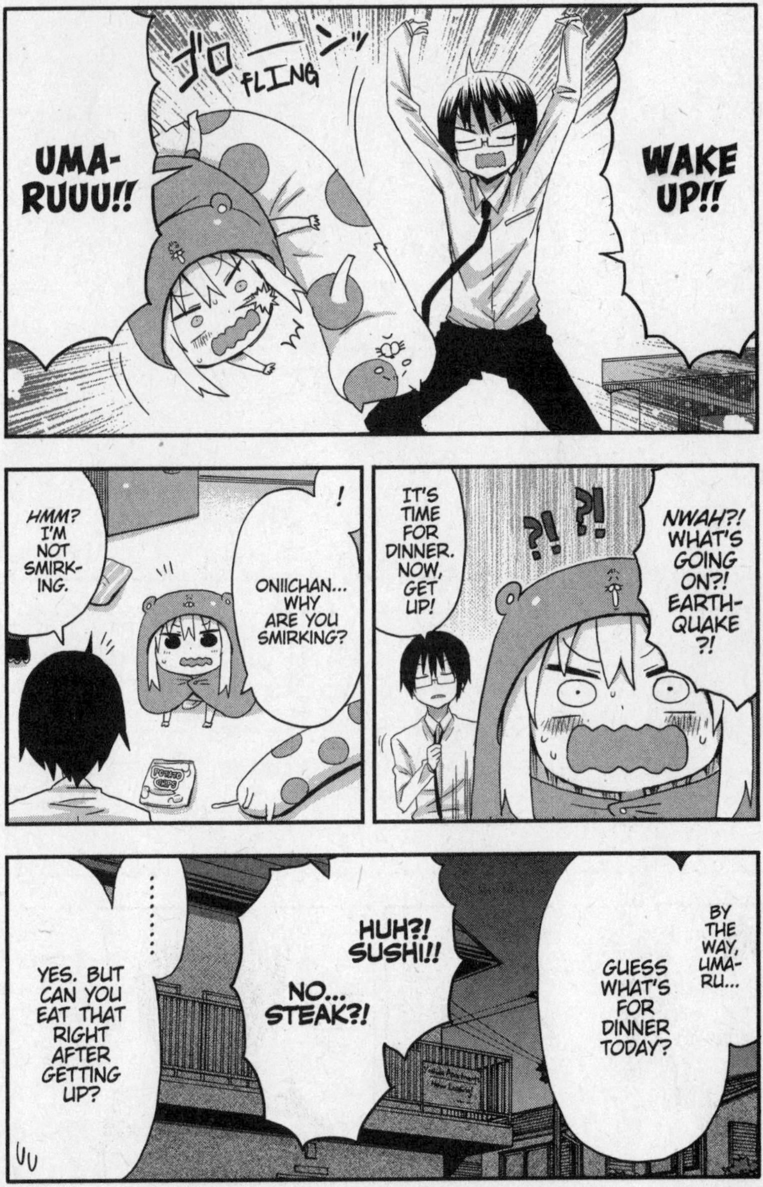
ゴローンッ
FLING
WAKE UP!!
UMA-RUUU!!
NWAH?! WHAT'S GOING ON?! EARTH-QUAKE ?!
?! ?!
IT'S TIME FOR DINNER. NOW, GET UP!
!
ONIICHAN... WHY ARE YOU SMIRKING?
HMM? I'M NOT SMIRK-ING.
POTATO CHIPS
BY THE WAY, UMA-RU...
GUESS WHAT'S FOR DINNER TODAY?
HUH?! SUSHI!!
NO... STEAK?!
......
YES. BUT CAN YOU EAT THAT RIGHT AFTER GETTING UP?
UU

No. 15 **Umaru & Repairs**

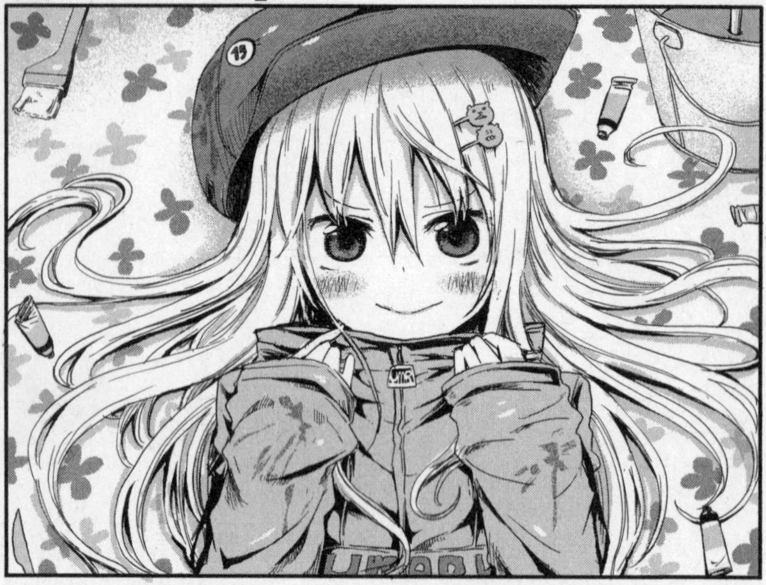

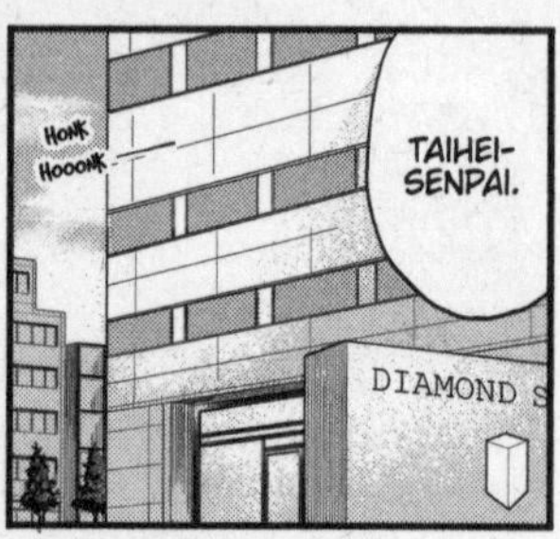
HONK
HOOOONK
TAIHEI-SENPAI.
DIAMOND S

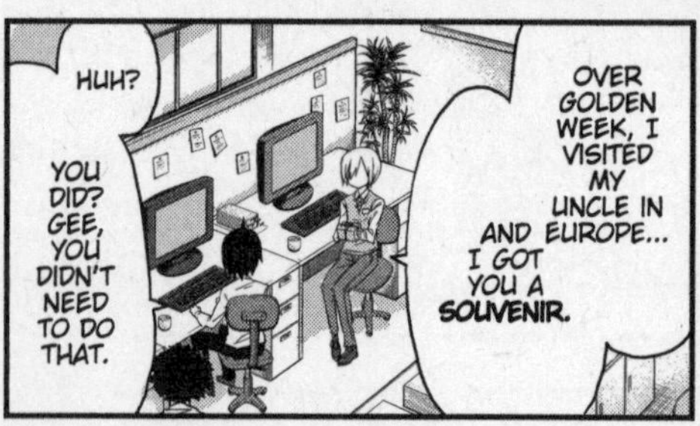
OVER GOLDEN WEEK, I VISITED MY UNCLE IN EUROPE... AND I GOT YOU A SOUVENIR.
HUH?
YOU DID? GEE, YOU DIDN'T NEED TO DO THAT.

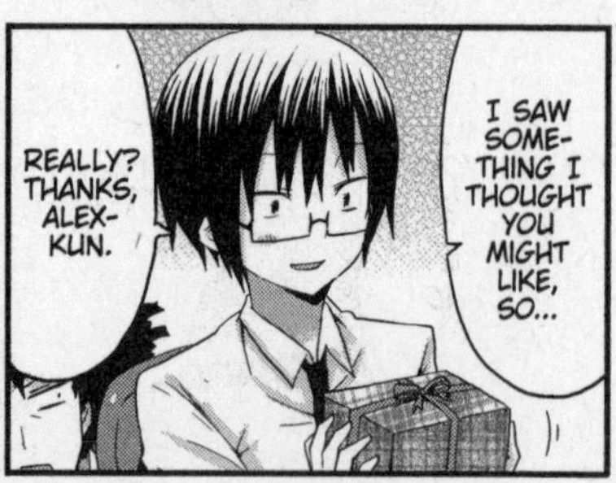
I SAW SOME-THING I THOUGHT YOU MIGHT LIKE, SO...
REALLY? THANKS, ALEX-KUN.

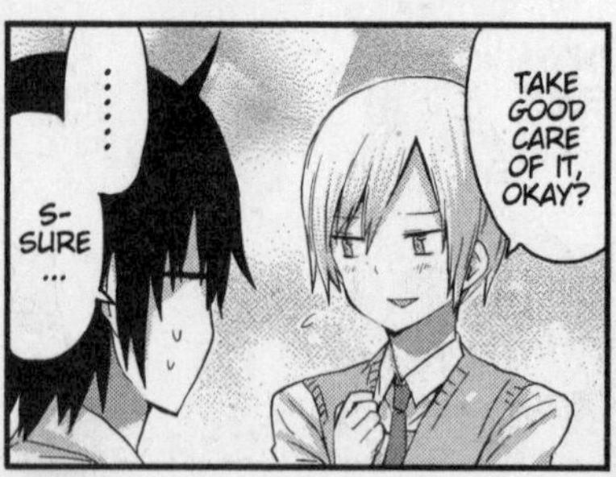
TAKE GOOD CARE OF IT, OKAY?
......
S-SURE...

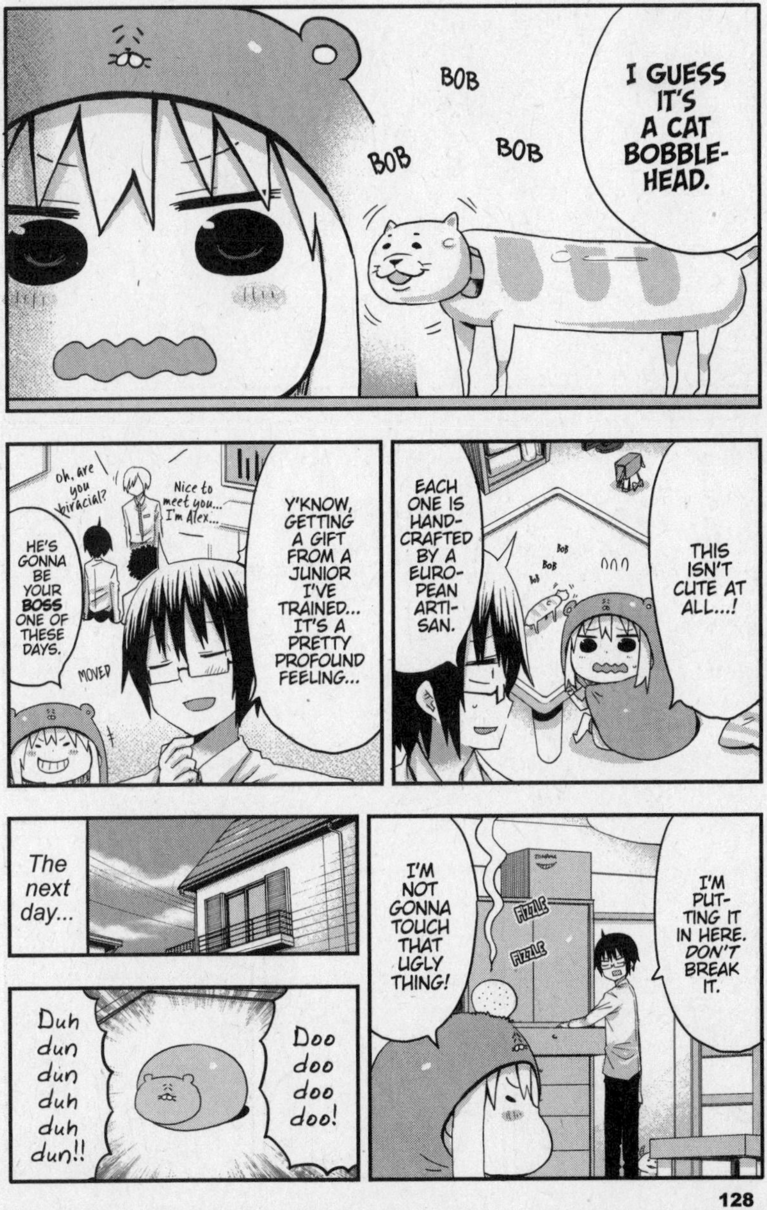

I GUESS IT'S A CAT BOBBLE-HEAD.
BOB
BOB
BOB
THIS ISN'T CUTE AT ALL...!
BOB
BOB
BOB
EACH ONE IS HAND-CRAFTED BY A EURO-PEAN ARTI-SAN.
Y'KNOW, GETTING A GIFT FROM A JUNIOR I'VE TRAINED... IT'S A PRETTY PROFOUND FEELING...
Nice to meet you... I'm Alex...
Oh, are you biracial?
HE'S GONNA BE YOUR BOSS ONE OF THESE DAYS.
MOVED
I'M PUT-TING IT IN HERE. DON'T BREAK IT.
FIZZLE
FIZZLE
I'M NOT GONNA TOUCH THAT UGLY THING!
The next day...
Doo doo doo doo!
Duh dun dun duh duh dun!!

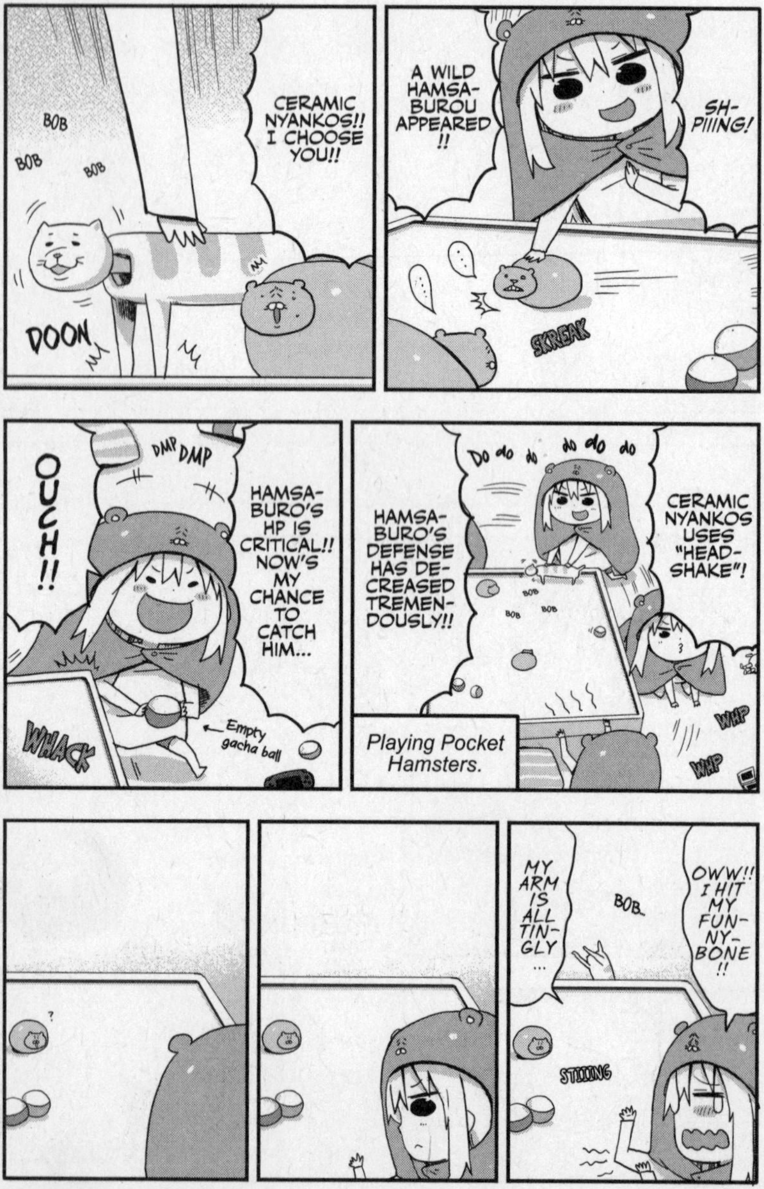
SH-PIIING!
A WILD HAMSA-BUROU APPEARED!!
SKREAK
CERAMIC NYANKOS!! I CHOOSE YOU!!
BOB
BOB
BOB
DOON
CERAMIC NYANKOS USES "HEAD-SHAKE"!
Do do do do do do
HAMSA-BURO'S DEFENSE HAS DE-CREASED TREMEN-DOUSLY!!
BOB
BOB
BOB
WHP
WHP
Playing Pocket Hamsters.
HAMSA-BURO'S HP IS CRITICAL!! NOW'S MY CHANCE TO CATCH HIM...
DMP DMP
OUCH!!
Empty gacha ball
WHACK
OWW!! I HIT MY FUN-NY-BONE!!
BOB
MY ARM IS ALL TIN-GLY...
STIIING
?

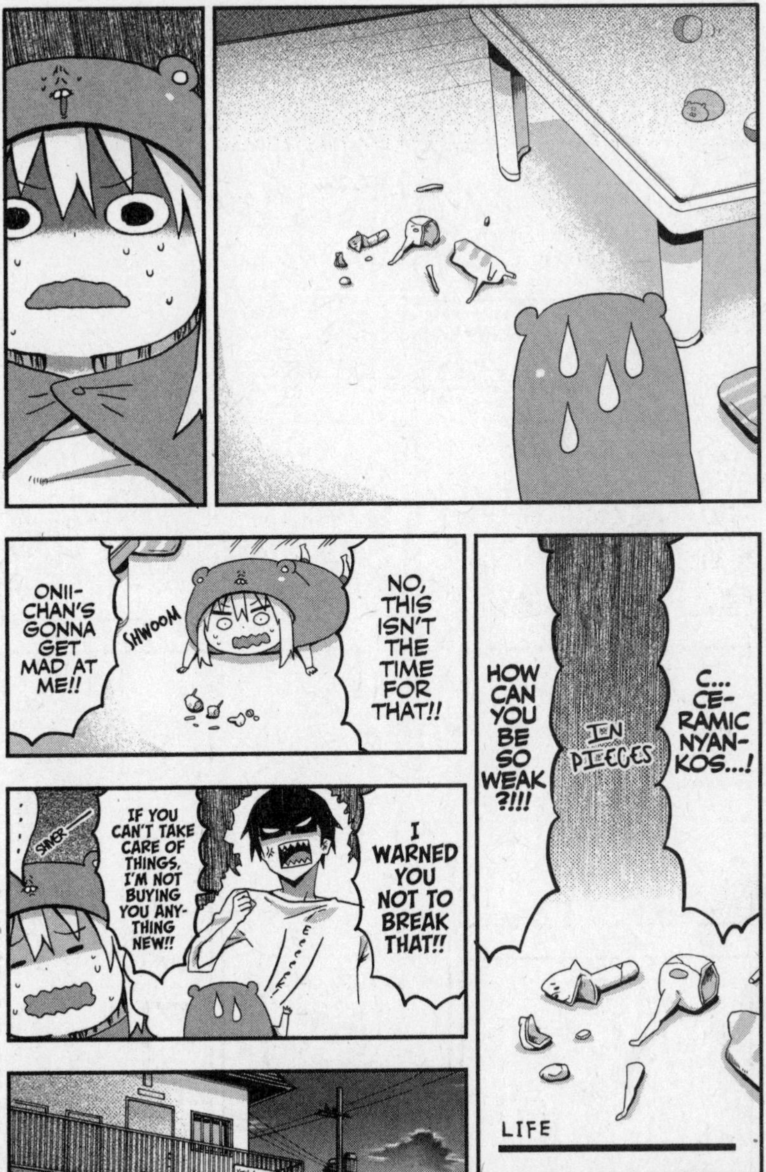
C... CERAMIC NYANKOS...!
IN PIECES
HOW CAN YOU BE SO WEAK?!!!
LIFE
NO, THIS ISN'T THE TIME FOR THAT!!
SHWOOM
ONII-CHAN'S GONNA GET MAD AT ME!!
I WARNED YOU NOT TO BREAK THAT!!
EEEEEK!
IF YOU CAN'T TAKE CARE OF THINGS, I'M NOT BUYING YOU ANYTHING NEW!!
SHIVER
...

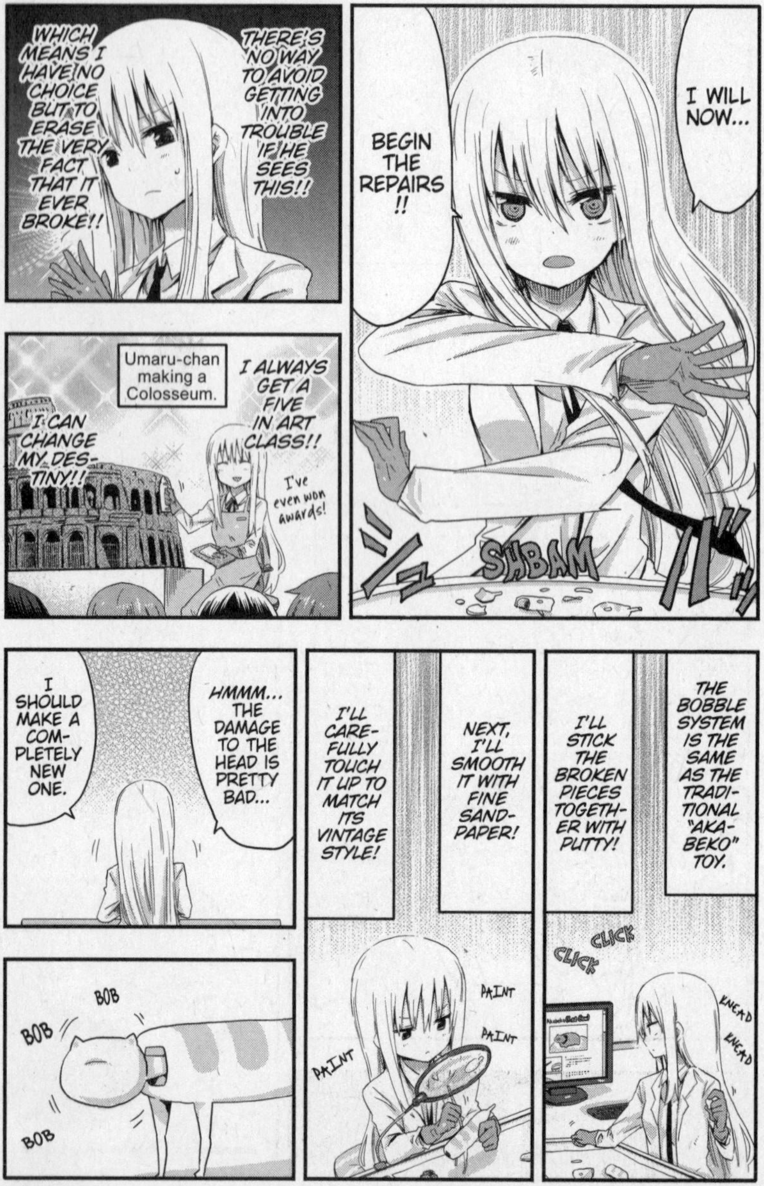

I WILL NOW...
BEGIN THE REPAIRS!!
SHBAM
THERE'S NO WAY TO AVOID GETTING INTO TROUBLE IF HE SEES THIS!!
WHICH MEANS I HAVE NO CHOICE BUT TO ERASE THE VERY FACT THAT IT EVER BROKE!!
I ALWAYS GET A FIVE IN ART CLASS!!
Umaru-chan making a Colosseum.
I've even won awards!
I CAN CHANGE MY DES-TINY!!
THE BOBBLE SYSTEM IS THE SAME AS THE TRADI-TIONAL "AKA-BEKO" TOY.
I'LL STICK THE BROKEN PIECES TOGETH-ER WITH PUTTY!
CLICK
CLICK
KNEAD
KNEAD
NEXT, I'LL SMOOTH IT WITH FINE SAND-PAPER!
I'LL CARE-FULLY TOUCH IT UP TO MATCH ITS VINTAGE STYLE!
PAINT
PAINT
PAINT
HMMM... THE DAMAGE TO THE HEAD IS PRETTY BAD...
I SHOULD MAKE A COM-PLETELY NEW ONE.
BOB
BOB
BOB

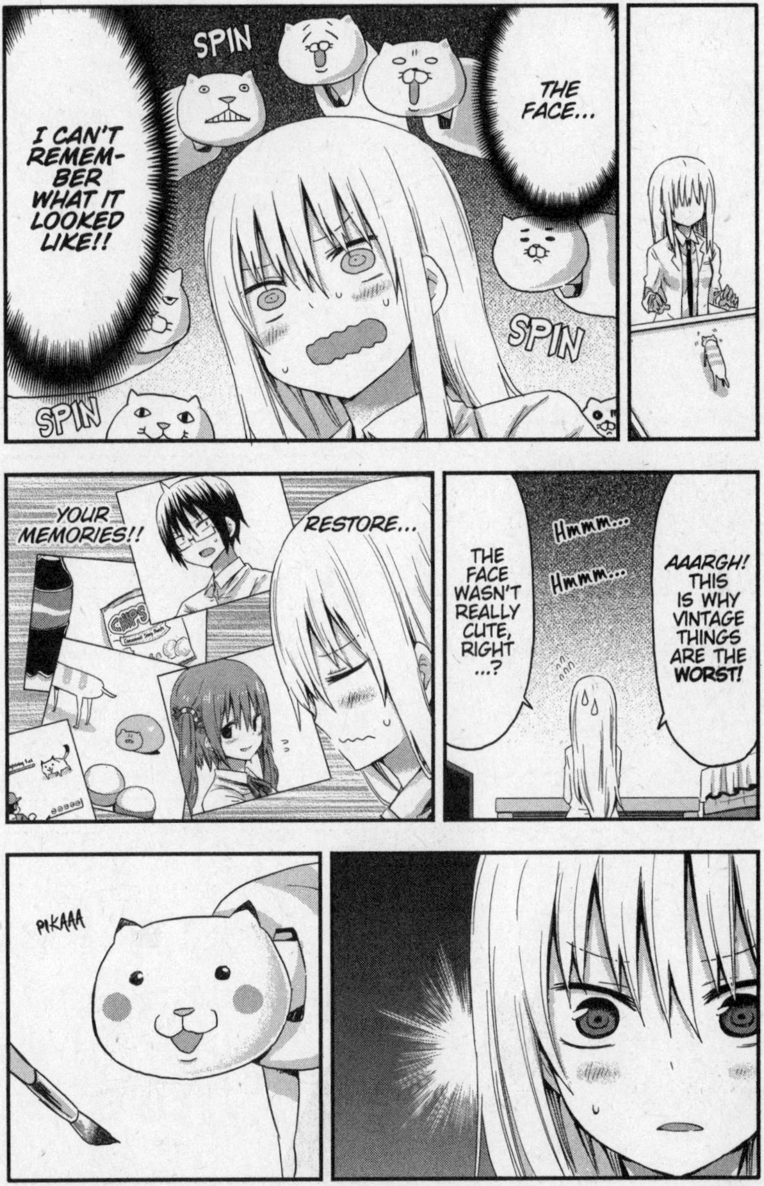
THE FACE...
SPIN
I CAN'T REMEMBER WHAT IT LOOKED LIKE!!
SPIN
SPIN
AAARGH! THIS IS WHY VINTAGE THINGS ARE THE **WORST!**
Hmmm...
Hmmm...
THE FACE WASN'T REALLY CUTE, RIGHT ...?
RESTORE...
YOUR MEMORIES!!
CHIPS
PIKAAA

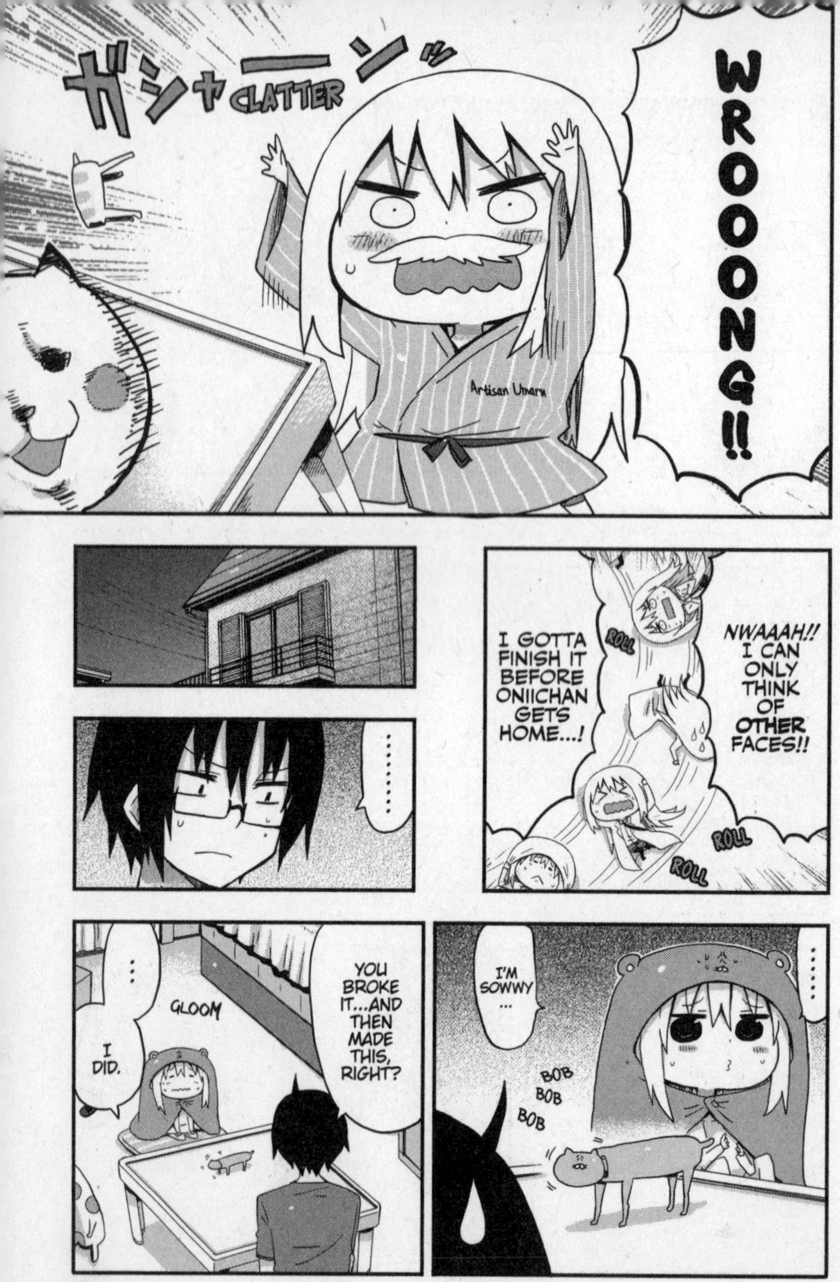
ガシャーーンッ
CLATTER
WROOOONG!!
Artisan Umaru
NWAAAH!! I CAN ONLY THINK OF OTHER FACES!!
ROLL
I GOTTA FINISH IT BEFORE ONIICHAN GETS HOME...!
ROLL
ROLL
......
......
I'M SOWWY ...
BOB
BOB
BOB
YOU BROKE IT...AND THEN MADE THIS, RIGHT?
GLOOM
...
I DID.

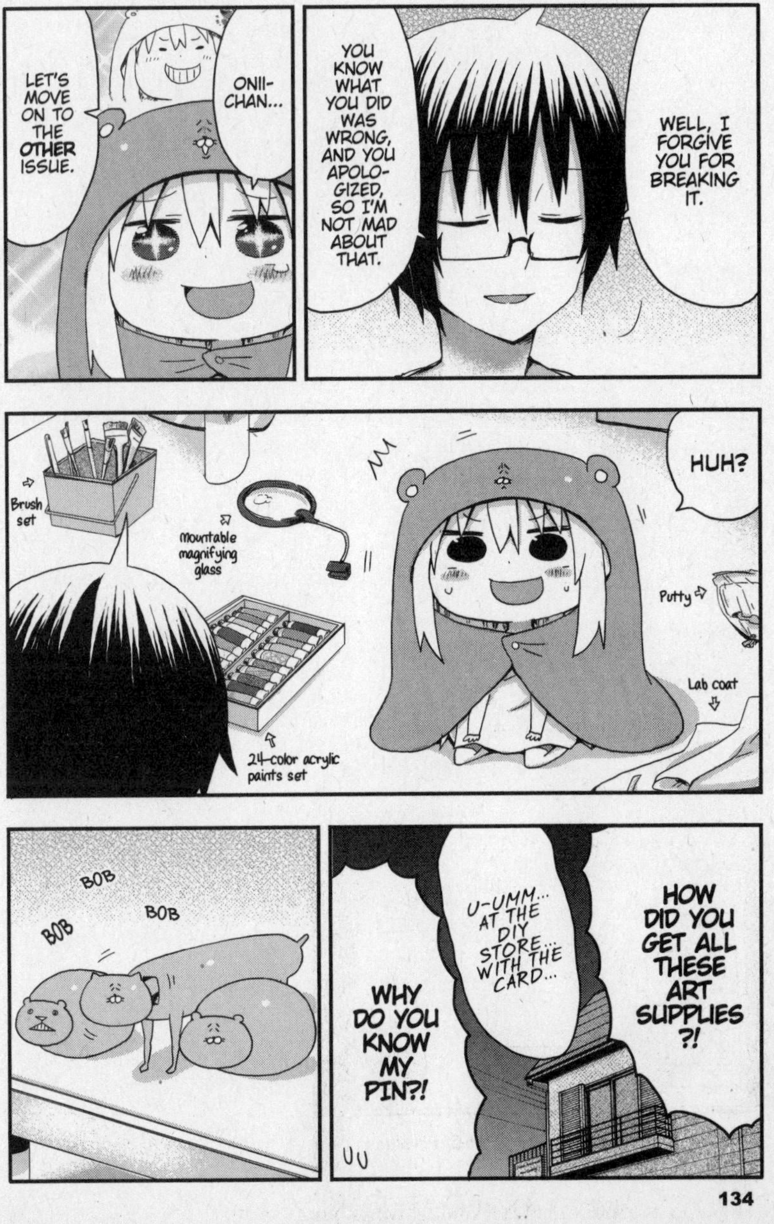
WELL, I FORGIVE YOU FOR BREAKING IT.
YOU KNOW WHAT YOU DID WAS WRONG, AND YOU APOLOGIZED, SO I'M NOT MAD ABOUT THAT.
ONII-CHAN...
LET'S MOVE ON TO THE OTHER ISSUE.
HUH?
Putty
Lab coat
Brush set
Mountable magnifying glass
24-color acrylic paints set
HOW DID YOU GET ALL THESE ART SUPPLIES?!
U-UMM... AT THE DIY STORE... WITH THE CARD...
WHY DO YOU KNOW MY PIN?!
BOB
BOB
BOB

Pocket Hamster

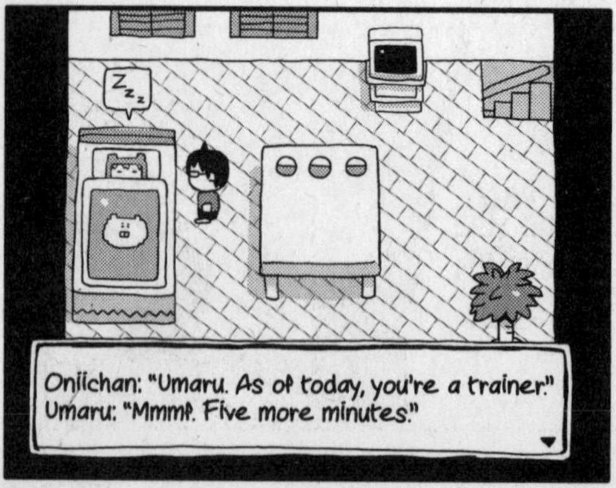
Z z z
Oniichan: "Umaru. As of today, you're a trainer."
Umaru: "Mmmf. Five more minutes."

HIMOUTO! UMARU-CHAN

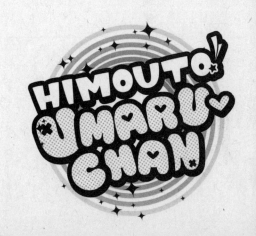

No. 16 Umaru & Studying

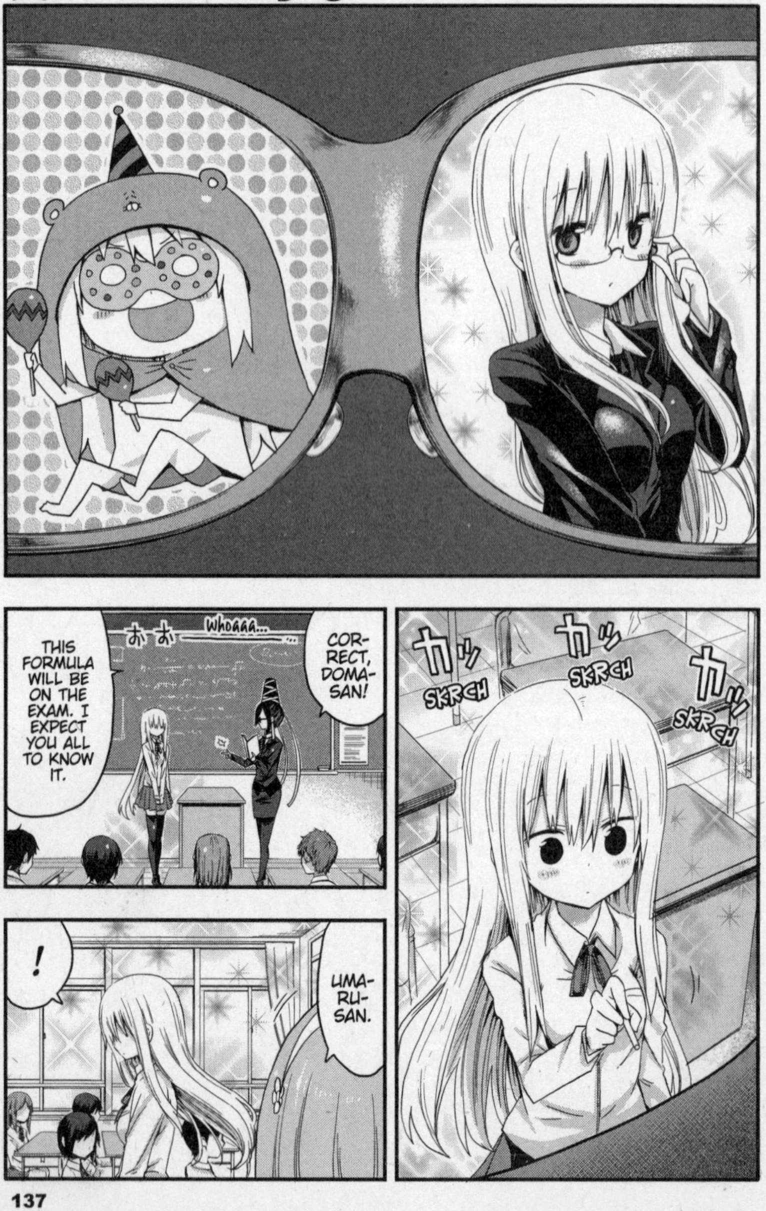

カッ
SKRCH
カッ
SKRCH
カッ
SKRCH
CORRECT, DOMA-SAN!
WHOAAA...
おお
THIS FORMULA WILL BE ON THE EXAM. I EXPECT YOU ALL TO KNOW IT.
UMARU-SAN.
!

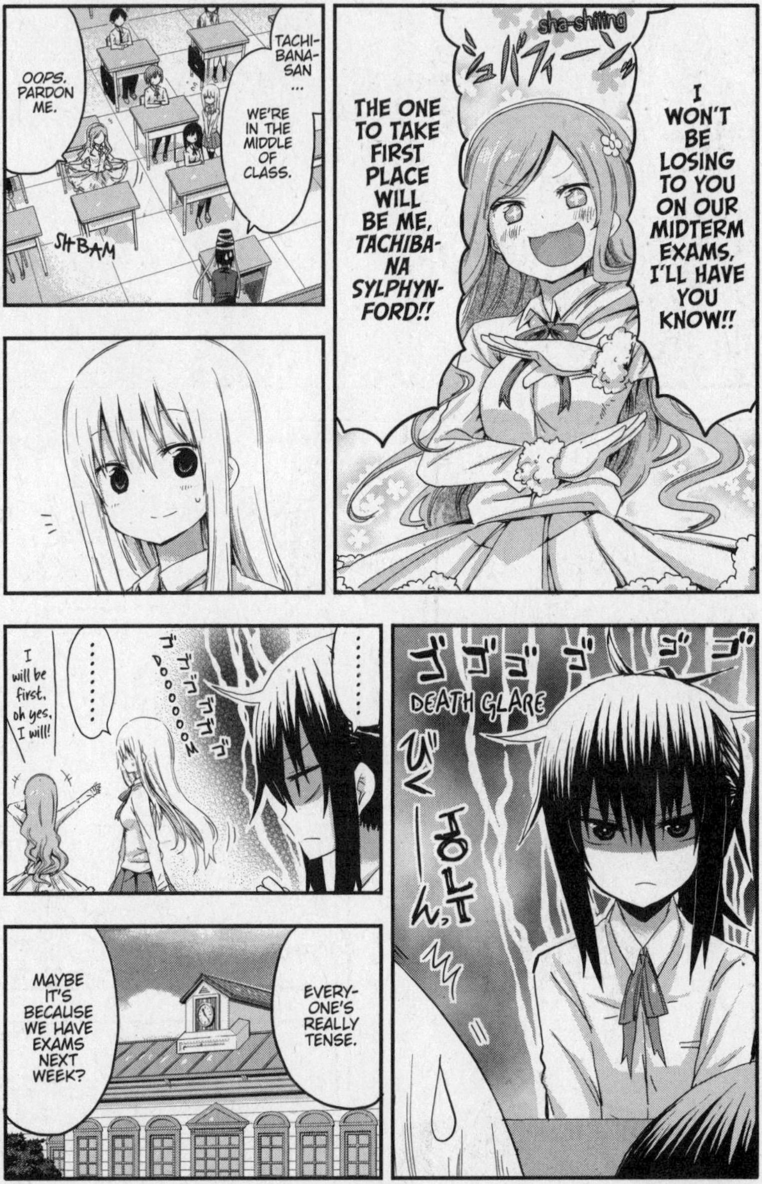
sha-shiiing
シュバフィーン
I WON'T BE LOSING TO YOU ON OUR MIDTERM EXAMS, I'LL HAVE YOU KNOW!!
THE ONE TO TAKE FIRST PLACE WILL BE ME, TACHIBANA SYLPHYNFORD!!
TACHIBANA-SAN ... WE'RE IN THE MIDDLE OF CLASS.
OOPS. PARDON ME.
SHBAM
ゴゴゴゴゴゴ
DEATH GLARE
びくーん
JOLT
......
......
DOOOOOOOM
I will be first, oh yes, I will!
EVERYONE'S REALLY TENSE.
MAYBE IT'S BECAUSE WE HAVE EXAMS NEXT WEEK?

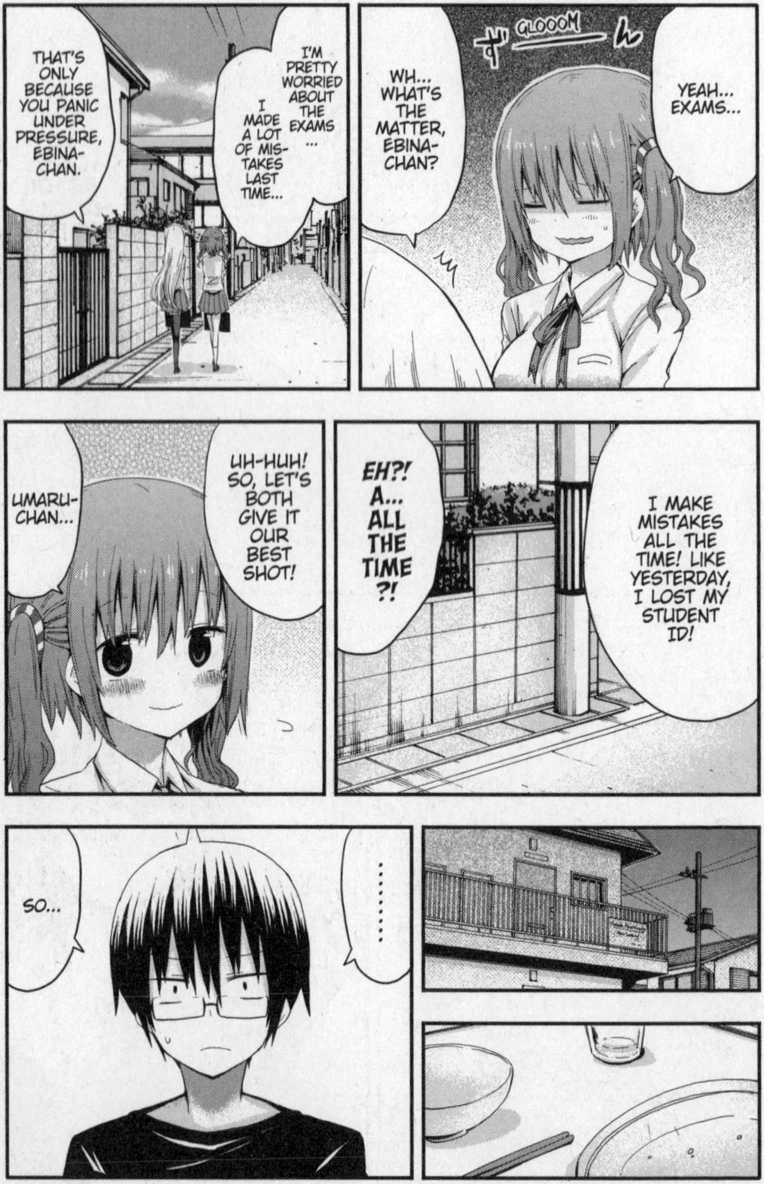
YEAH... EXAMS...
GLOOOM
WH... WHAT'S THE MATTER, EBINA-CHAN?
I'M PRETTY WORRIED ABOUT THE EXAMS ...
I MADE A LOT OF MIS-TAKES LAST TIME...
THAT'S ONLY BECAUSE YOU PANIC UNDER PRESSURE, EBINA-CHAN.
I MAKE MISTAKES ALL THE TIME! LIKE YESTERDAY, I LOST MY STUDENT ID!
EH?! A... ALL THE TIME?!
UH-HUH! SO, LET'S BOTH GIVE IT OUR BEST SHOT!
UMARU-CHAN...
....
SO...

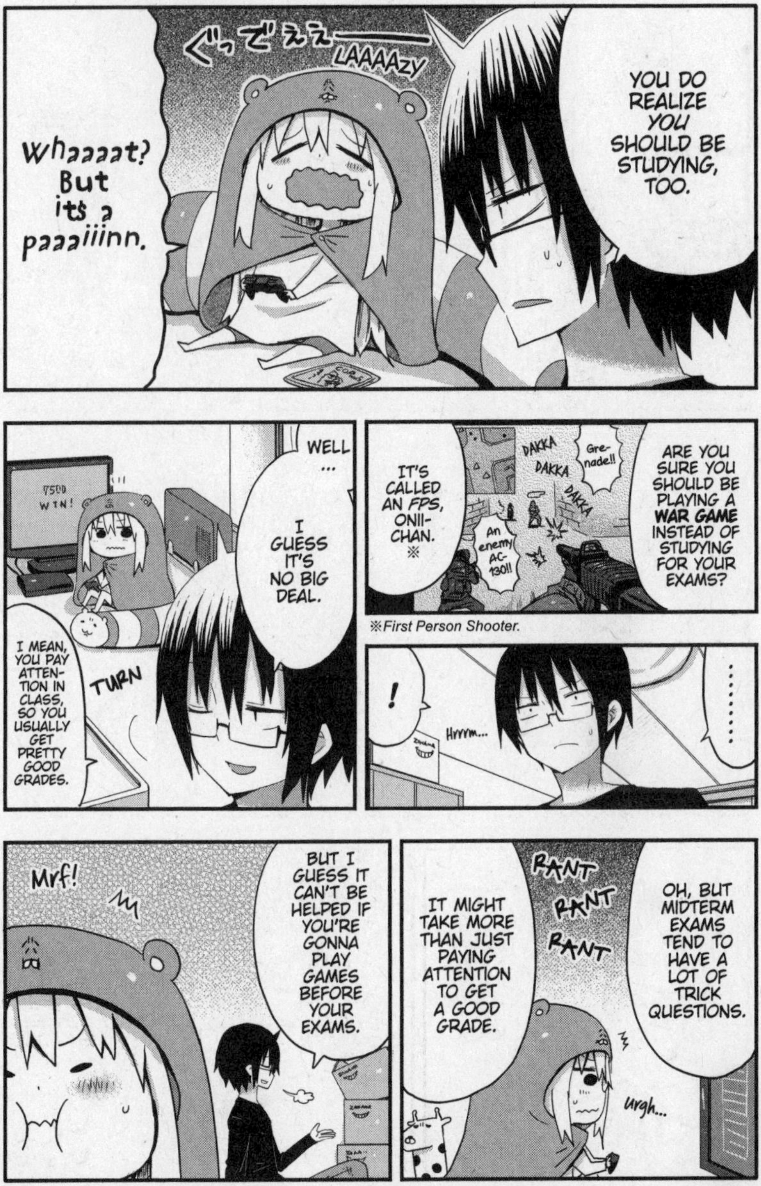
YOU DO REALIZE *YOU* SHOULD BE STUDYING, TOO.
ぐってぇぇ――
LAAAAzy
Whaaaat? But its a paaaiiinn.
ARE YOU SURE YOU SHOULD BE PLAYING A **WAR GAME** INSTEAD OF STUDYING FOR YOUR EXAMS?
Gre-nade!!
DAKKA DAKKA DAKKA
An enemy AC-130!!
IT'S CALLED AN *FPS*, ONII-CHAN. ※
......
Hrrrm...
!
WELL ...
I GUESS IT'S NO BIG DEAL.
TURN
I MEAN, YOU PAY ATTEN-TION IN CLASS, SO YOU USUALLY GET PRETTY GOOD GRADES.
OH, BUT MIDTERM EXAMS TEND TO HAVE A LOT OF TRICK QUESTIONS.
RANT RANT RANT
IT MIGHT TAKE MORE THAN JUST PAYING ATTENTION TO GET A GOOD GRADE.
Urgh...
BUT I GUESS IT CAN'T BE HELPED IF YOU'RE GONNA PLAY GAMES BEFORE YOUR EXAMS.
Mrf!

※First Person Shooter.

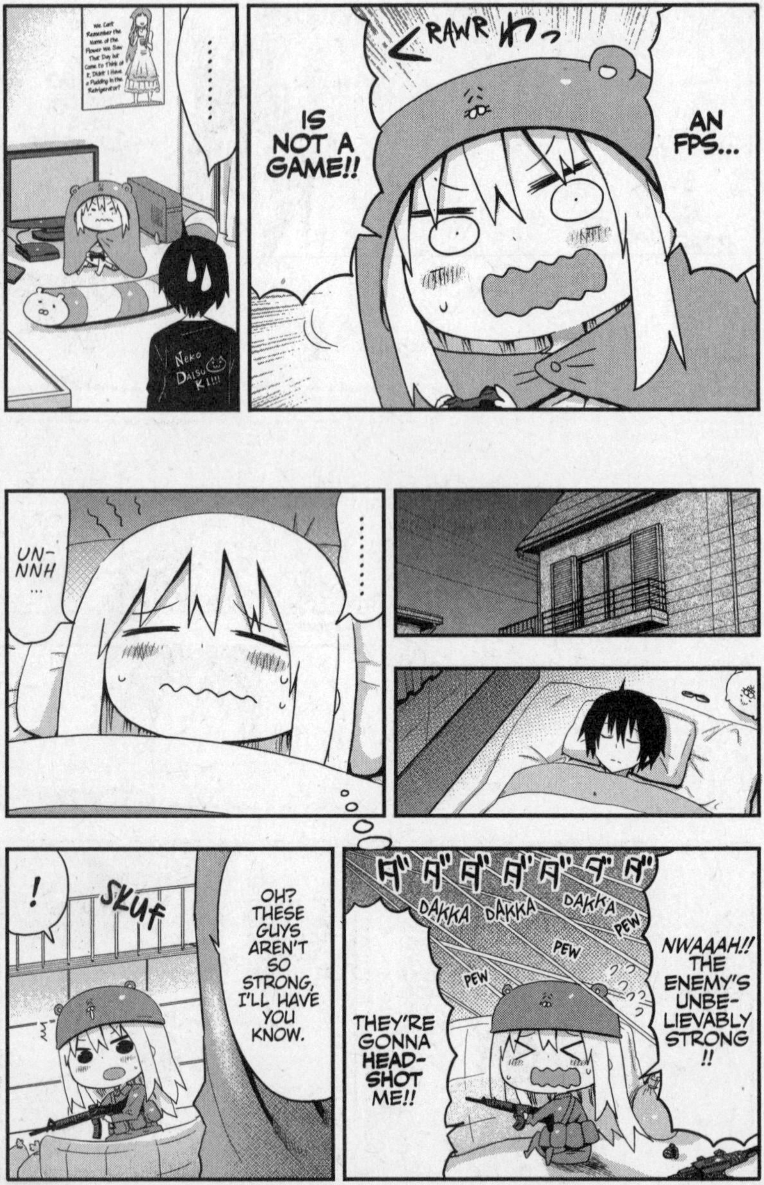
RAWR わっ
AN FPS...
IS NOT A GAME!!
We Can't Remember the Name of the Flower We Saw That Day but Come to Think of It, Didn't I Have a Pudding in the Refrigerator?
......
NEKO DAISUKI!!!
UN-NNH...
......
ダダダダダダダ
DAKKA DAKKA DAKKA
PEW
PEW
PEW
NWAAAH!! THE ENEMY'S UNBELIEVABLY STRONG!!
THEY'RE GONNA HEADSHOT ME!!
OH? THESE GUYS AREN'T SO STRONG, I'LL HAVE YOU KNOW.
SKUF
!

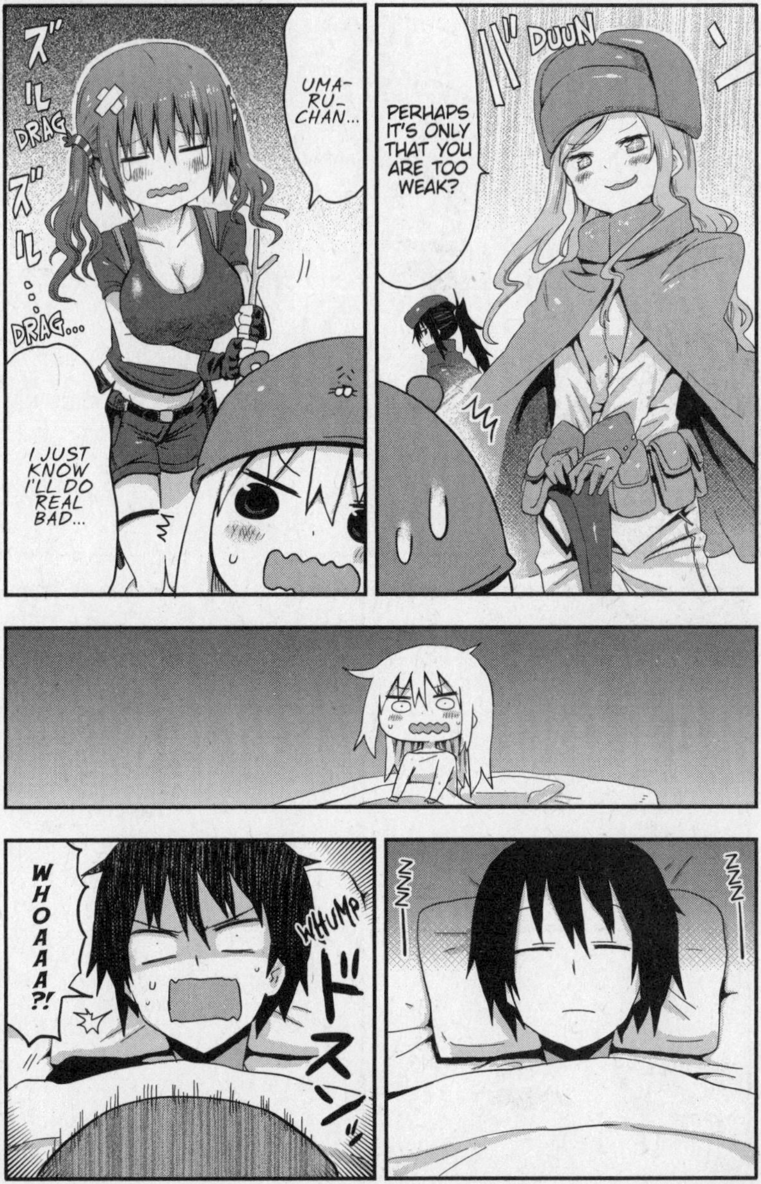
DUUN
PERHAPS IT'S ONLY THAT YOU ARE TOO WEAK?
UMA-RU-CHAÑ...
DRAG
DRAG...
I JUST KNOW I'LL DO REAL BAD...
ZZZ—
ZZZ—
WHUMP
WHOAAAA?!

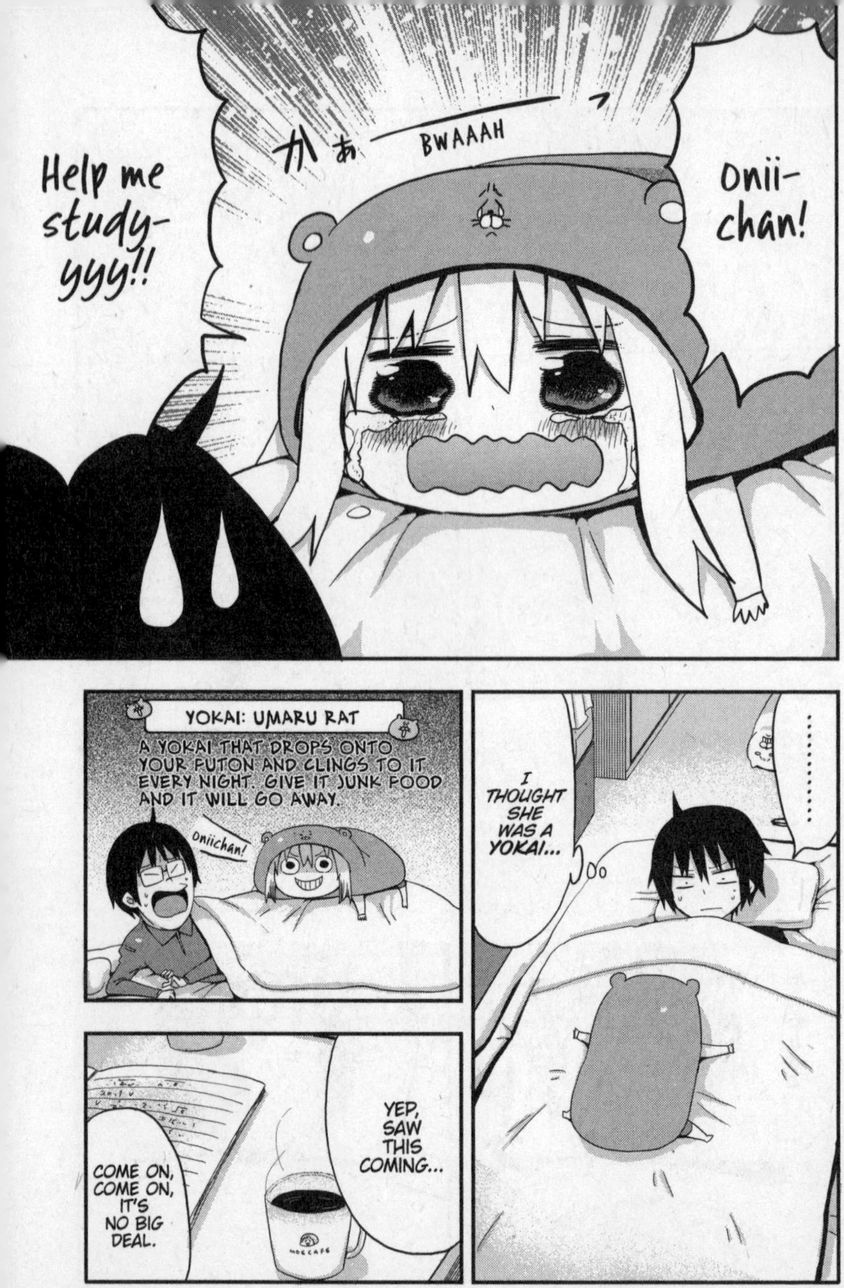

Onii-chan!
かぁ BWAAAH
Help me study-yyy!!
......
I THOUGHT SHE WAS A YOKAI...
YOKAI: UMARU RAT
A YOKAI THAT DROPS ONTO YOUR FUTON AND CLINGS TO IT EVERY NIGHT. GIVE IT JUNK FOOD AND IT WILL GO AWAY.
Oniichan!
YEP, SAW THIS COMING...
COME ON, COME ON, IT'S NO BIG DEAL.

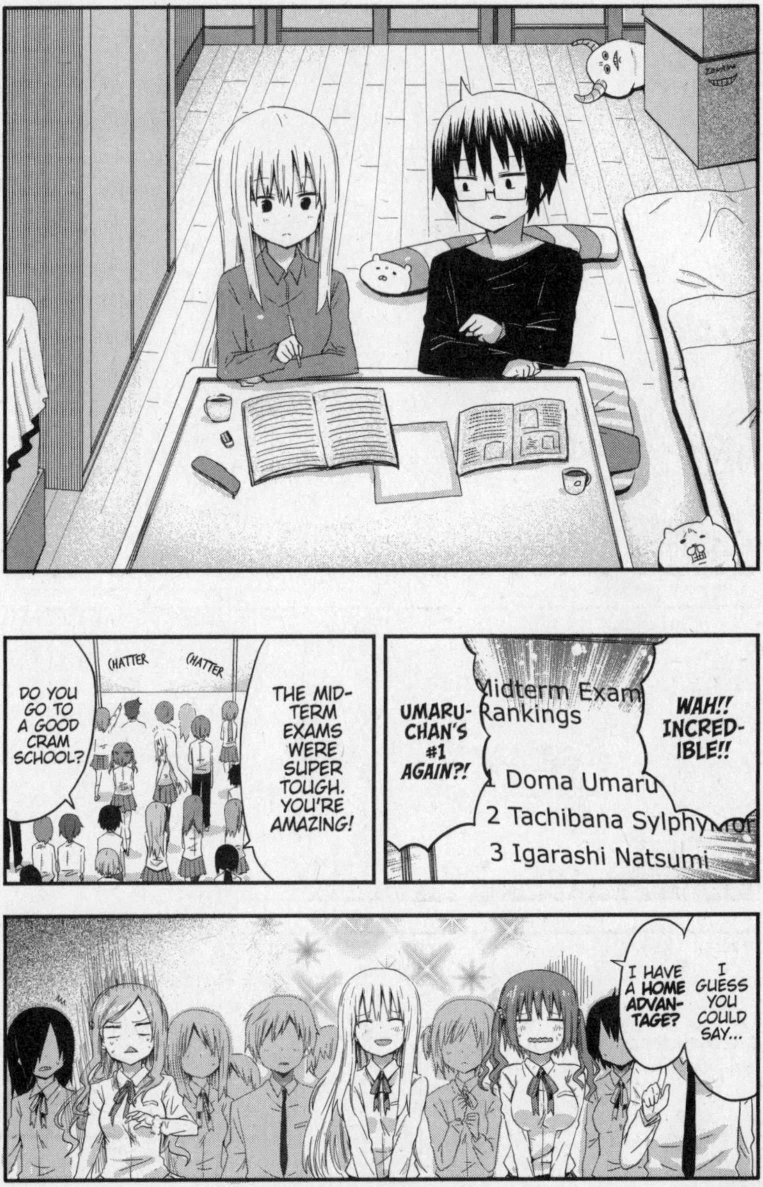
WAH!! INCREDIBLE!!
UMARU-CHAN'S #1 AGAIN?!
Midterm Exam Rankings
1 Doma Umaru
2 Tachibana Sylphyn
3 Igarashi Natsumi
THE MID-TERM EXAMS WERE SUPER TOUGH. YOU'RE AMAZING!
CHATTER
CHATTER
DO YOU GO TO A GOOD CRAM SCHOOL?
I GUESS YOU COULD SAY...
I HAVE A **HOME** ADVANTAGE?

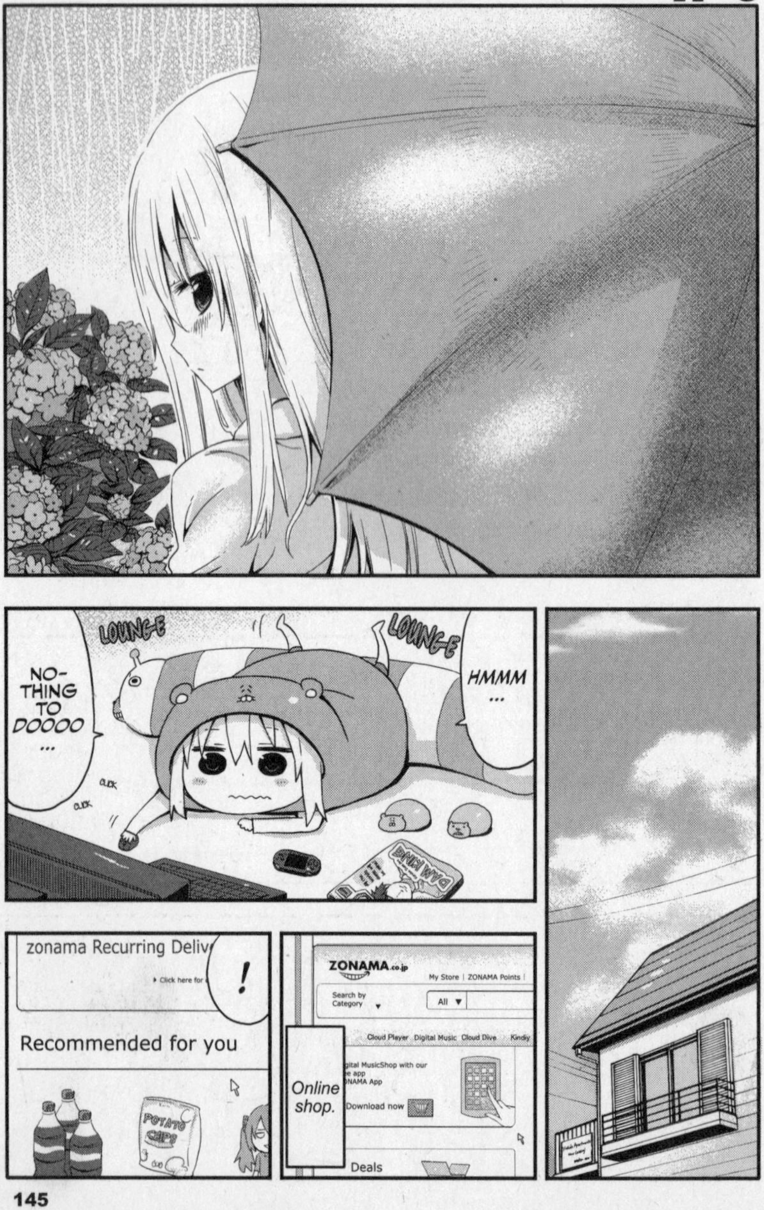
HMMM ...
LOUNGE
LOUNGE
NO-THING TO DOOOO ...
CLICK
CLICK
Online shop.
ZONAMA.co.jp
My Store | ZONAMA Points |
Search by Category
All
Cloud Player Digital Music Cloud Dive Kindiy
Download now
Deals
!
Recommended for you
POTATO CHIPS

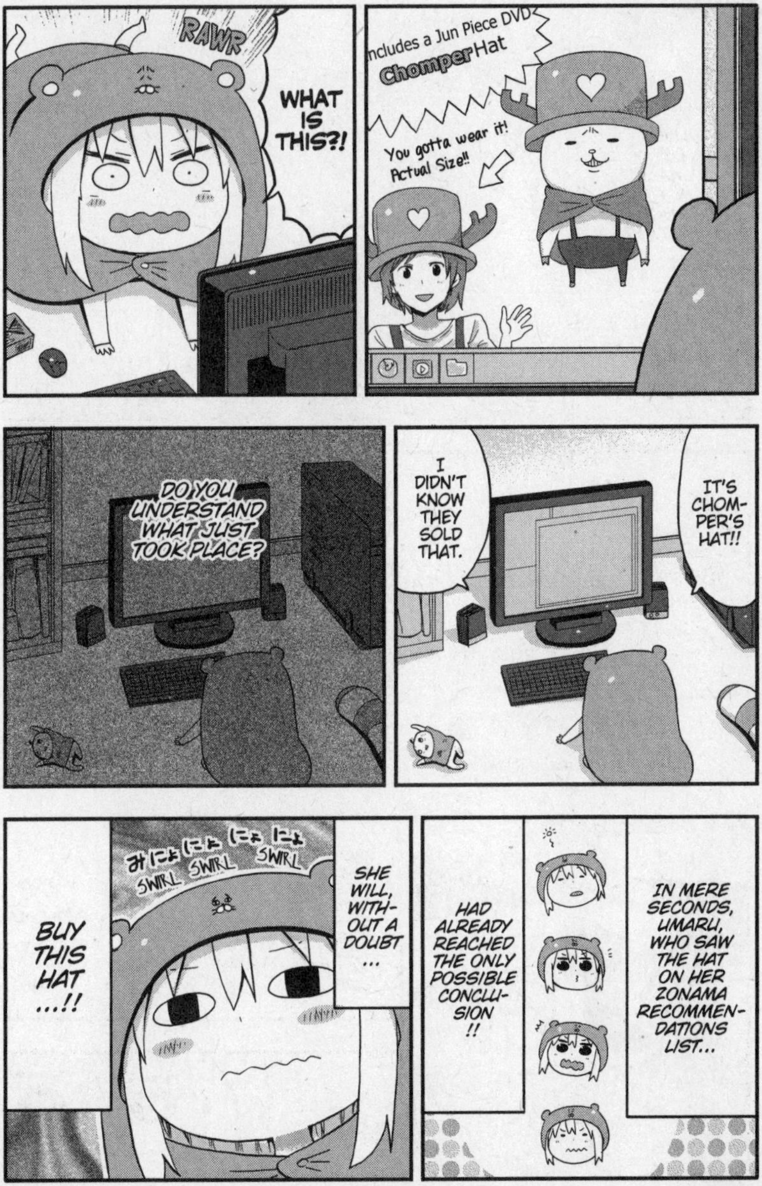

ncludes a Jun Piece DVD
Chomper Hat
You gotta wear it! Actual Size!!
RAWR
WHAT IS THIS?!
IT'S CHOMPER'S HAT!!
I DIDN'T KNOW THEY SOLD THAT.
DO YOU UNDERSTAND WHAT JUST TOOK PLACE?
IN MERE SECONDS, UMARU, WHO SAW THE HAT ON HER ZONAMA RECOMMENDATIONS LIST...
HAD ALREADY REACHED THE ONLY POSSIBLE CONCLUSION!!
みにょ にょ にょ にょ
SWIRL SWIRL SWIRL
SHE WILL, WITHOUT A DOUBT...
BUY THIS HAT...!!

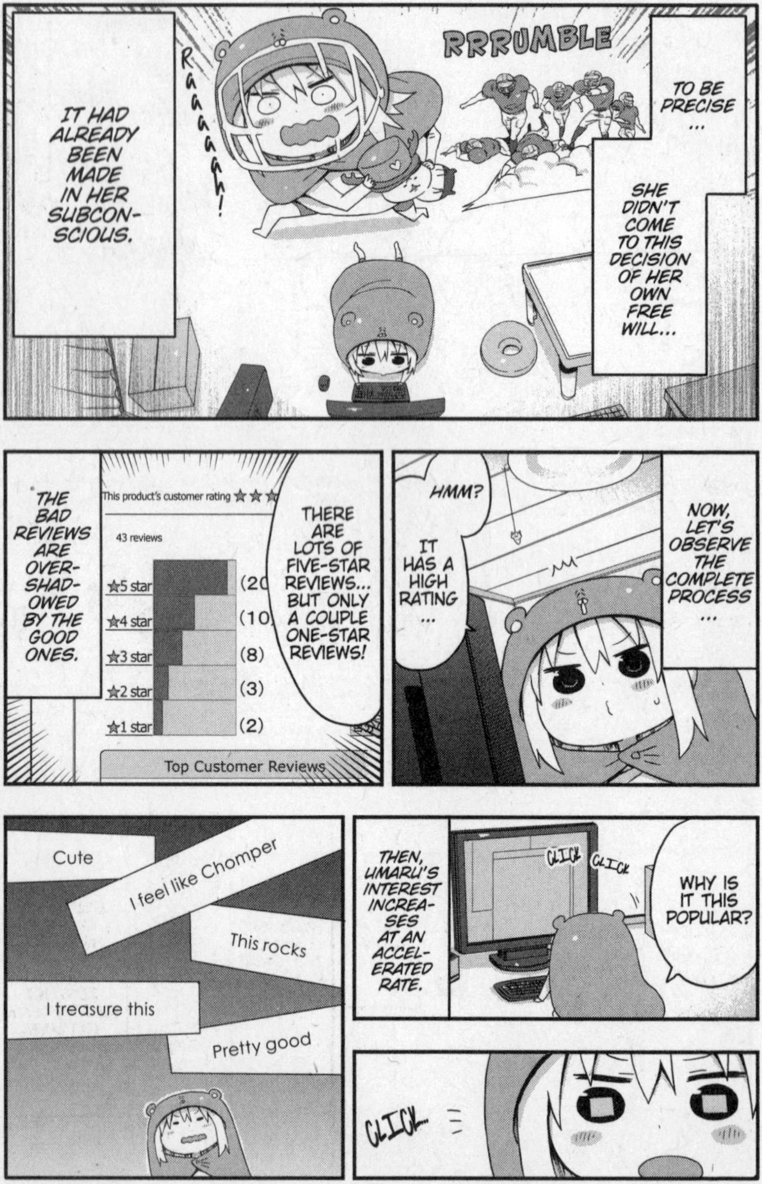
TO BE PRECISE ...
SHE DIDN'T COME TO THIS DECISION OF HER OWN FREE WILL...
RRRUMBLE
Raaaaaah!
IT HAD ALREADY BEEN MADE IN HER SUBCONSCIOUS.
NOW, LET'S OBSERVE THE COMPLETE PROCESS ...
HMM?
IT HAS A HIGH RATING ...
THERE ARE LOTS OF FIVE-STAR REVIEWS... BUT ONLY A COUPLE ONE-STAR REVIEWS!
This product's customer rating
43 reviews
☆5 star (20
☆4 star (10)
☆3 star (8)
☆2 star (3)
☆1 star (2)
Top Customer Reviews
THE BAD REVIEWS ARE OVER-SHAD-OWED BY THE GOOD ONES.
WHY IS IT THIS POPULAR?
CLICK CLICK
THEN, UMARU'S INTEREST INCREA-SES AT AN ACCEL-ERATED RATE.
CLICK...
Cute
I feel like Chomper
This rocks
I treasure this
Pretty good

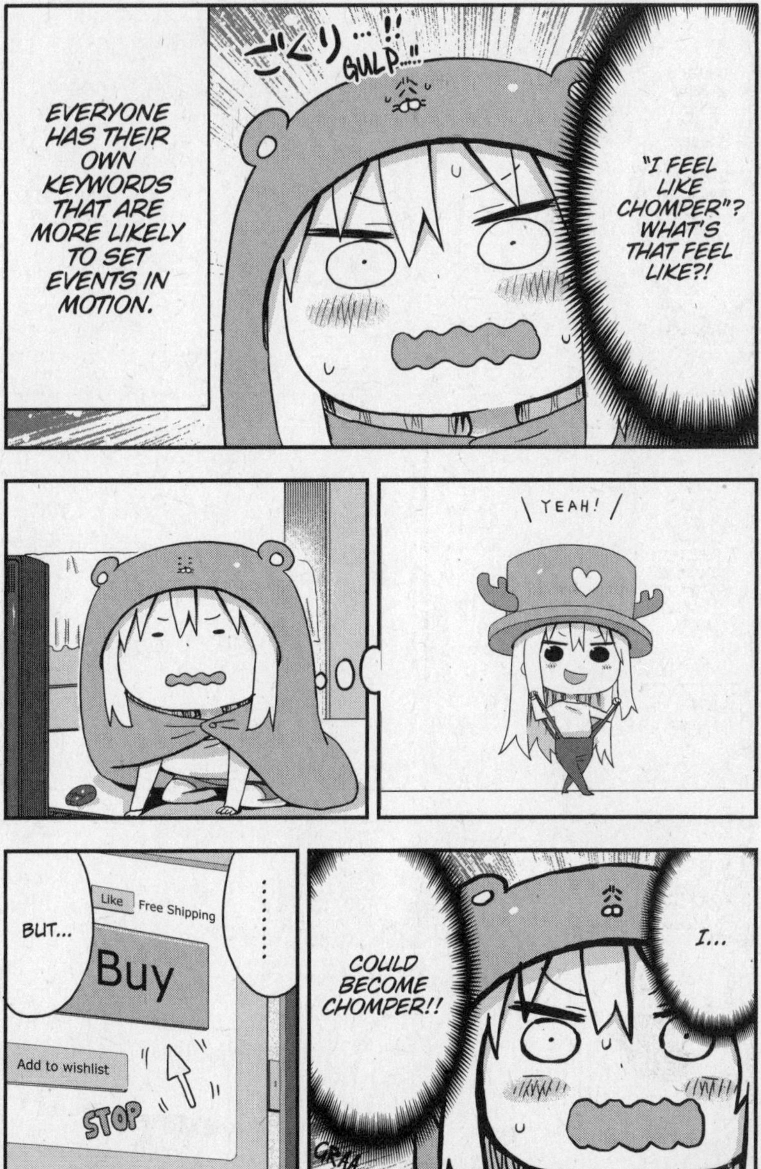
ごくり…!!
GULP...!!
"I FEEL LIKE CHOMPER"? WHAT'S THAT FEEL LIKE?!
EVERYONE HAS THEIR OWN KEYWORDS THAT ARE MORE LIKELY TO SET EVENTS IN MOTION.
YEAH!
I...
COULD BECOME CHOMPER!!
GRAA
......
Like
Free Shipping
BUT...
Buy
Add to wishlist
STOP

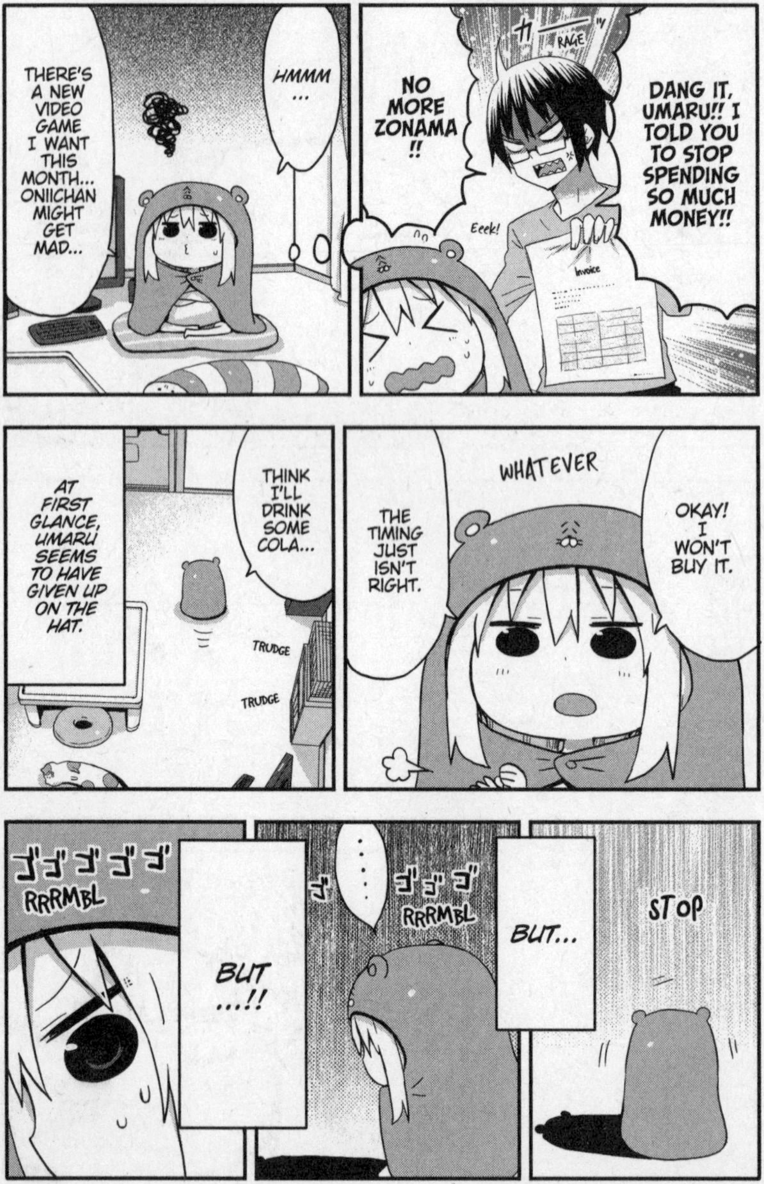
カーッ
RAGE
DANG IT, UMARU!! I TOLD YOU TO STOP SPENDING SO MUCH MONEY!!
NO MORE ZONAMA !!
Eeek!
Invoice
HMMM ...
THERE'S A NEW VIDEO GAME I WANT THIS MONTH... ONIICHAN MIGHT GET MAD...
OKAY! I WON'T BUY IT.
WHATEVER
THE TIMING JUST ISN'T RIGHT.
THINK I'LL DRINK SOME COLA...
TRUDGE
TRUDGE
AT FIRST GLANCE, UMARU SEEMS TO HAVE GIVEN UP ON THE HAT.
STOP
BUT...
ゴゴゴ
RRRMBL
ゴ
....
BUT ...!!
ゴゴゴゴゴ
RRRMBL

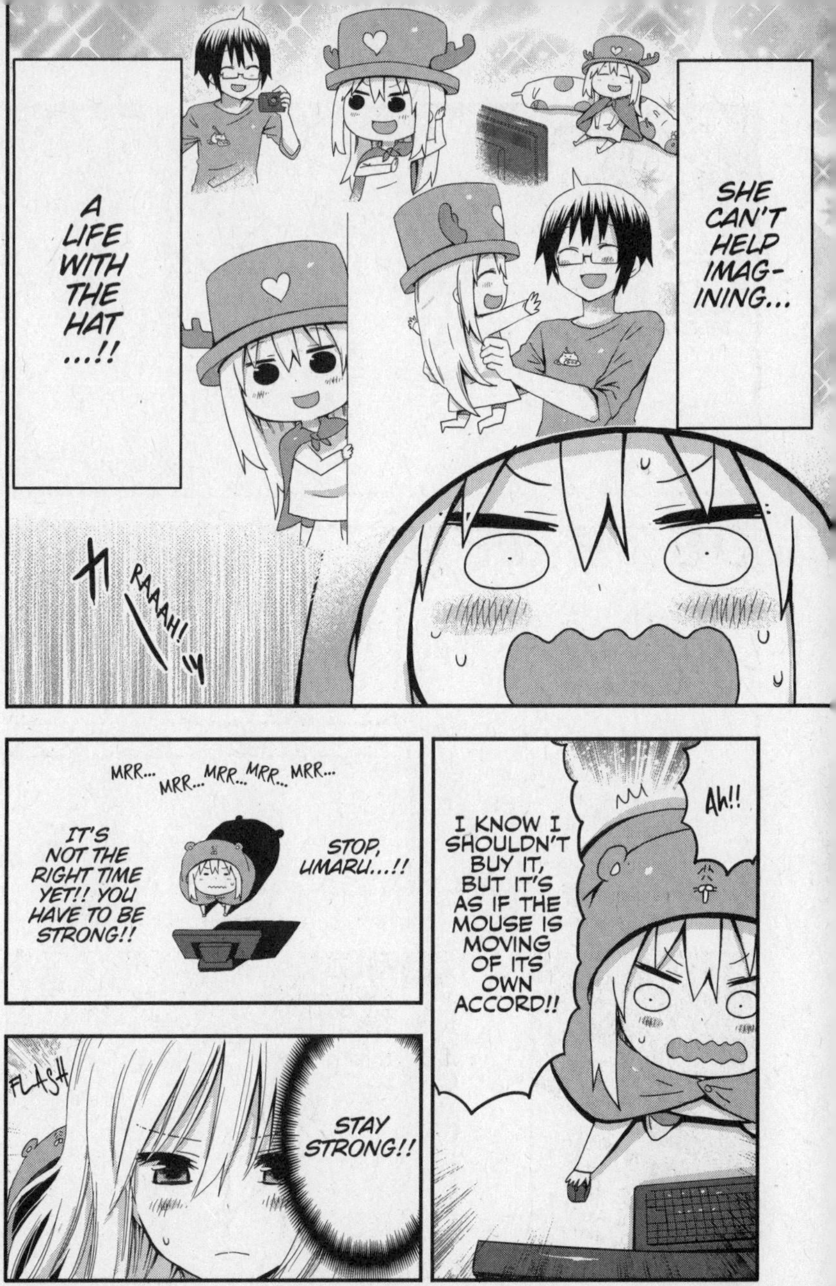
SHE CAN'T HELP IMAGINING...
A LIFE WITH THE HAT...!!
RAAAAH!!
AH!!
I KNOW I SHOULDN'T BUY IT, BUT IT'S AS IF THE MOUSE IS MOVING OF ITS OWN ACCORD!!
MRR... MRR... MRR... MRR... MRR...
STOP, UMARU...!!
IT'S NOT THE RIGHT TIME YET!! YOU HAVE TO BE STRONG!!
STAY STRONG!!
FLASH

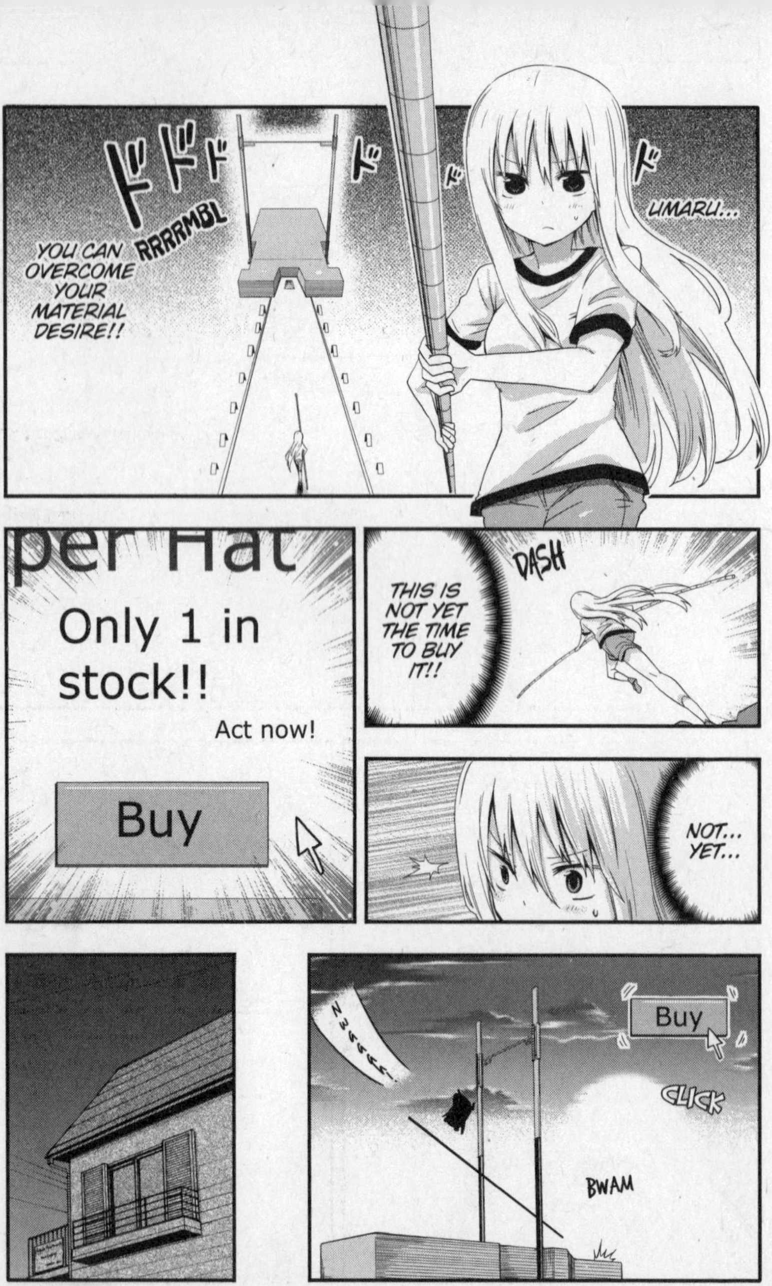
UMARU...
ドドド
ドドド
RRRRMBL
YOU CAN OVERCOME YOUR MATERIAL DESIRE!!
DASH
THIS IS NOT YET THE TIME TO BUY IT!!
NOT... YET...
per Hat
Only 1 in stock!!
Act now!
Buy
Buy
CLICK
BWAM

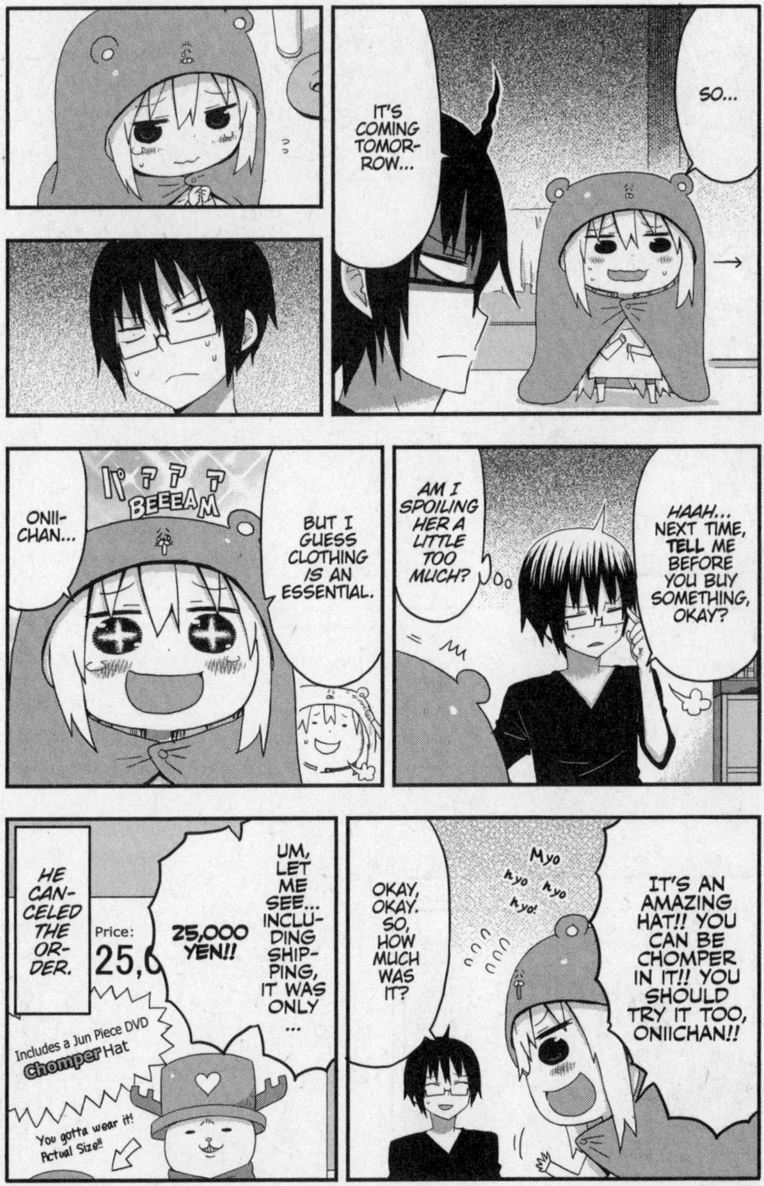

SO...
IT'S COMING TOMORROW...
HAAH... NEXT TIME, TELL ME BEFORE YOU BUY SOMETHING, OKAY?
AM I SPOILING HER A LITTLE TOO MUCH?
BUT I GUESS CLOTHING IS AN ESSENTIAL.
パァァァ
BEEEAM
ONII-CHAN...
IT'S AN AMAZING HAT!! YOU CAN BE CHOMPER IN IT!! YOU SHOULD TRY IT TOO, ONIICHAN!!
Myo hyo hyo hyo!
OKAY, OKAY. SO, HOW MUCH WAS IT?
UM, LET ME SEE... INCLUDING SHIPPING, IT WAS ONLY ...
25,000 YEN!!
Price: 25,0
HE CANCELED THE ORDER.
Includes a Jun Piece DVD
Chomper Hat
You gotta wear it! Actual Size!!

No. 18 Umaru & Kirie: Part 1

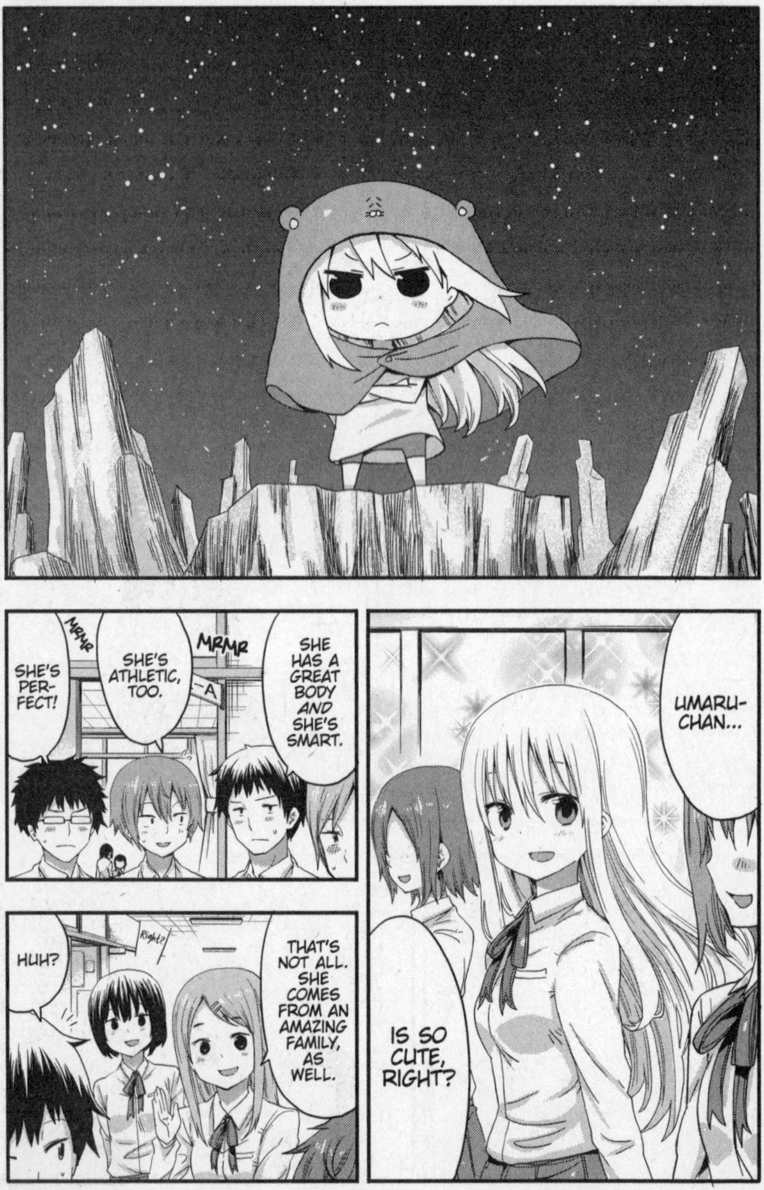
UMARU-CHAN...
IS SO CUTE, RIGHT?
SHE HAS A GREAT BODY AND SHE'S SMART.
MRMR
SHE'S ATHLETIC, TOO.
MRMR
SHE'S PERFECT!
THAT'S NOT ALL. SHE COMES FROM AN AMAZING FAMILY, AS WELL.
Right?
HUH?

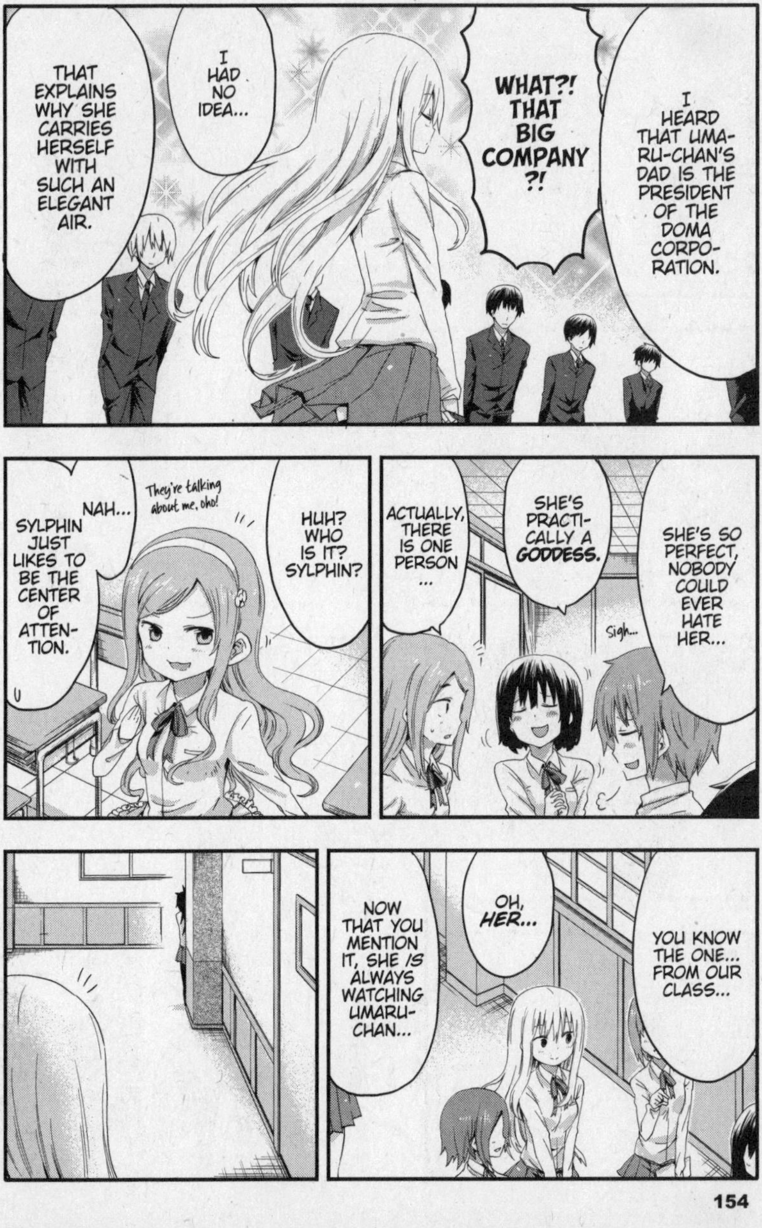
I HEARD THAT UMARU-CHAN'S DAD IS THE PRESIDENT OF THE DOMA CORPORATION.
WHAT?! THAT BIG COMPANY?!
I HAD NO IDEA...
THAT EXPLAINS WHY SHE CARRIES HERSELF WITH SUCH AN ELEGANT AIR.
SHE'S SO PERFECT, NOBODY COULD EVER HATE HER...
Sigh...
SHE'S PRACTICALLY A GODDESS.
ACTUALLY, THERE IS ONE PERSON...
HUH? WHO IS IT? SYLPHIN?
They're talking about me, oho!
NAH... SYLPHIN JUST LIKES TO BE THE CENTER OF ATTENTION.
YOU KNOW THE ONE... FROM OUR CLASS...
OH, HER...
NOW THAT YOU MENTION IT, SHE IS ALWAYS WATCHING UMARU-CHAN...

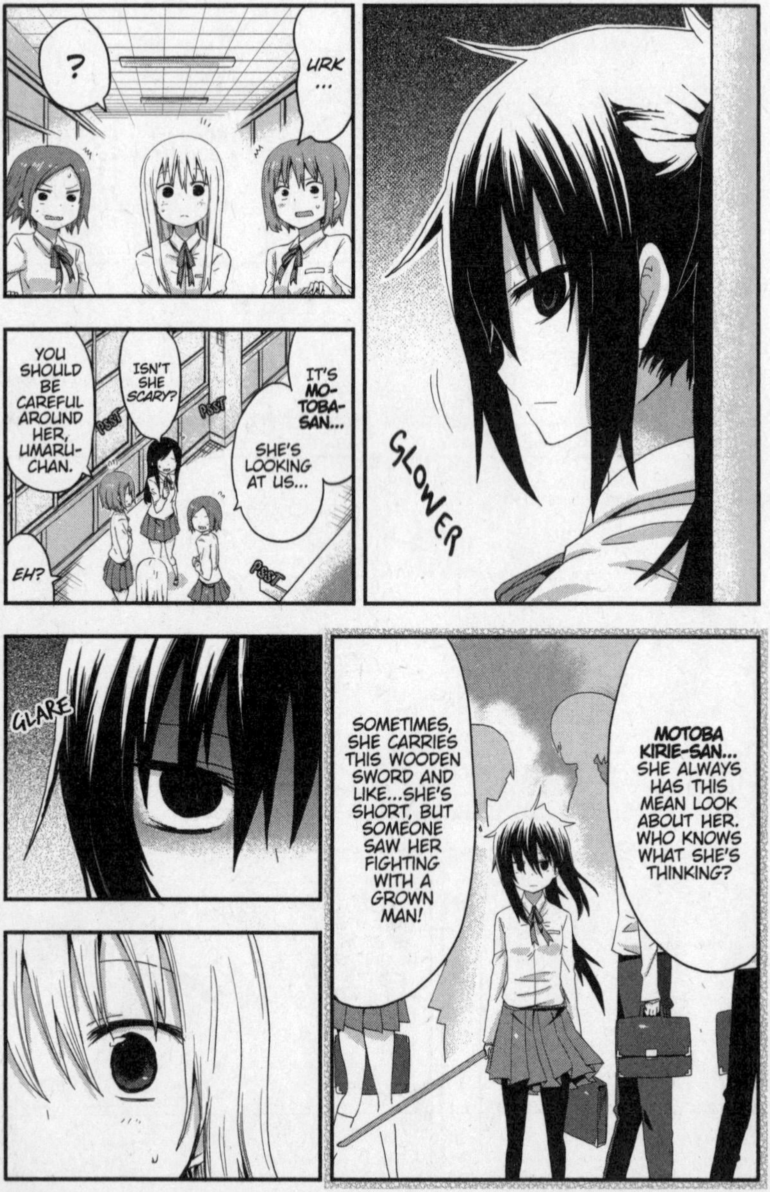
GLOWER
URK ...
?
IT'S MOTOBA-SAN...
SHE'S LOOKING AT US...
PSSST
ISN'T SHE SCARY?
PSSST
YOU SHOULD BE CAREFUL AROUND HER, UMARU-CHAN.
EH?
MOTOBA KIRIE-SAN... SHE ALWAYS HAS THIS MEAN LOOK ABOUT HER. WHO KNOWS WHAT SHE'S THINKING?
SOMETIMES, SHE CARRIES THIS WOODEN SWORD AND LIKE...SHE'S SHORT, BUT SOMEONE SAW HER FIGHTING WITH A GROWN MAN!
GLARE

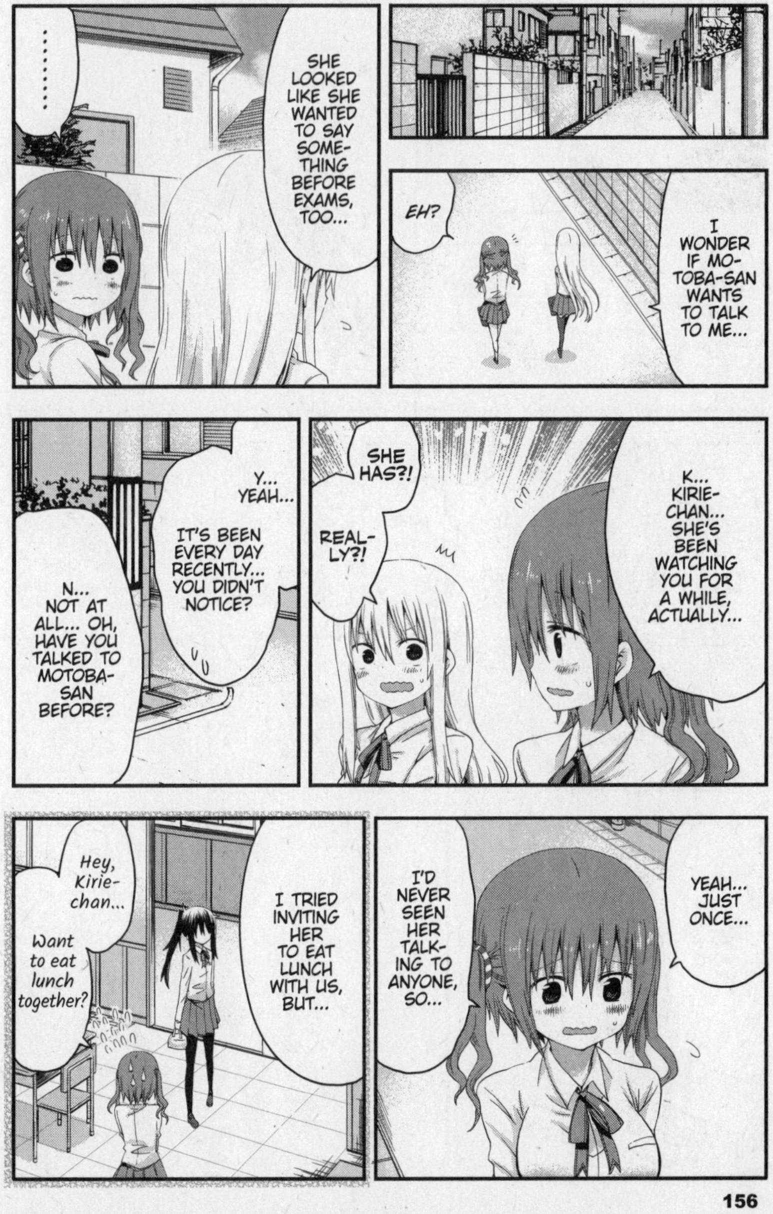
I WONDER IF MOTOBA-SAN WANTS TO TALK TO ME...
EH?
SHE LOOKED LIKE SHE WANTED TO SAY SOMETHING BEFORE EXAMS, TOO...
......
K... KIRIE-CHAN... SHE'S BEEN WATCHING YOU FOR A WHILE, ACTUALLY...
SHE HAS?!
REALLY?!
Y... YEAH...
IT'S BEEN EVERY DAY RECENTLY... YOU DIDN'T NOTICE?
N... NOT AT ALL... OH, HAVE YOU TALKED TO MOTOBA-SAN BEFORE?
YEAH... JUST ONCE...
I'D NEVER SEEN HER TALKING TO ANYONE, SO...
I TRIED INVITING HER TO EAT LUNCH WITH US, BUT...
Hey, Kirie-chan...
Want to eat lunch together?

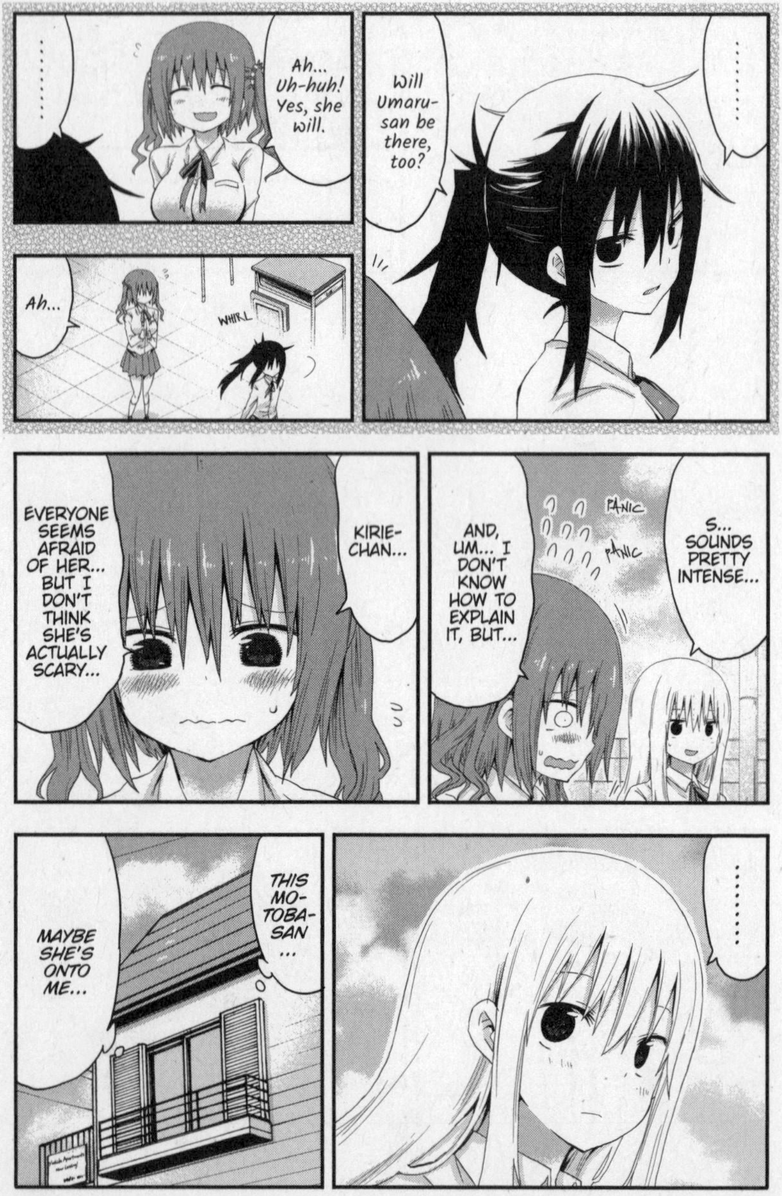
......
Will Umaru-san be there, too?
Ah... Uh-huh! Yes, she will.
......
Ah...
WHIRL
S... SOUNDS PRETTY INTENSE...
PANIC
PANIC
AND, UM... I DON'T KNOW HOW TO EXPLAIN IT, BUT...
KIRIE-CHAN...
EVERYONE SEEMS AFRAID OF HER... BUT I DON'T THINK SHE'S ACTUALLY SCARY...
....
THIS MOTOBA-SAN ...
MAYBE SHE'S ONTO ME...

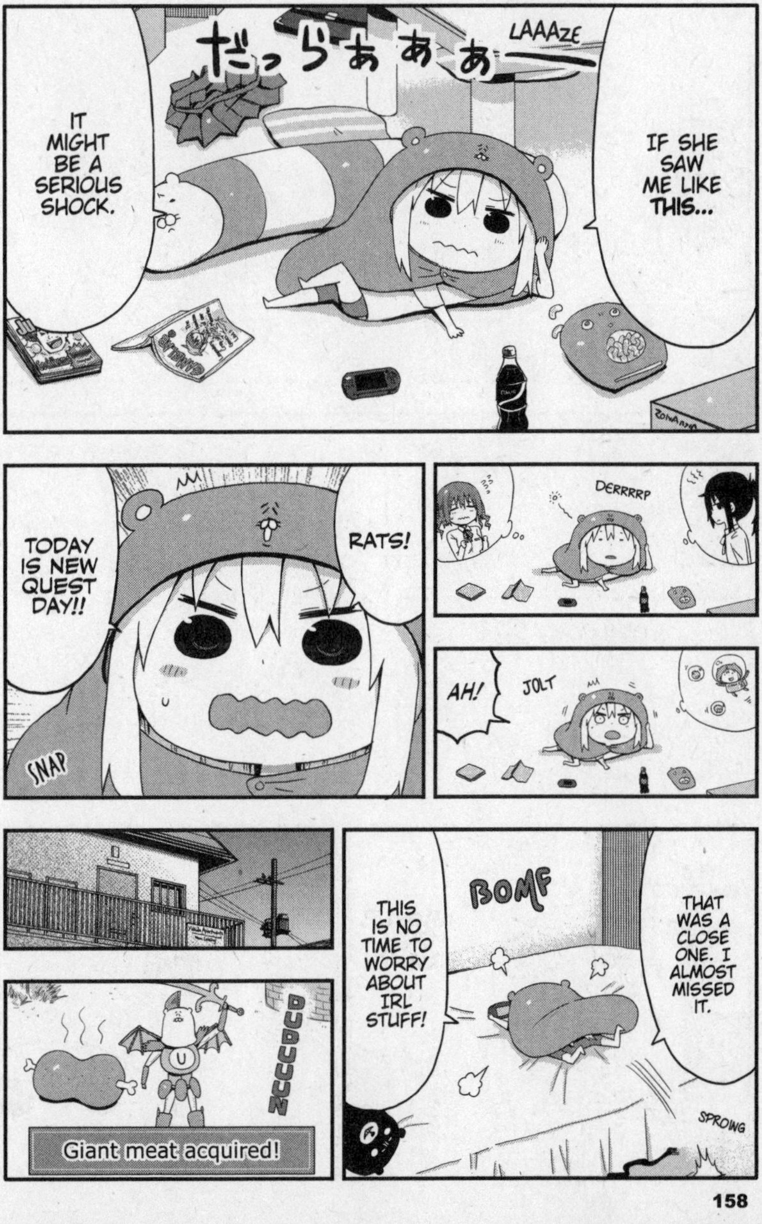
IF SHE SAW ME LIKE THIS...
だっらぁぁぁ—
LAAAZE
IT MIGHT BE A SERIOUS SHOCK.
DERRRRP
AH!
JOLT
RATS!
TODAY IS NEW QUEST DAY!!
SNAP
THAT WAS A CLOSE ONE. I ALMOST MISSED IT.
BOMF
THIS IS NO TIME TO WORRY ABOUT IRL STUFF!
SPROING
DUDUUUN
Giant meat acquired!

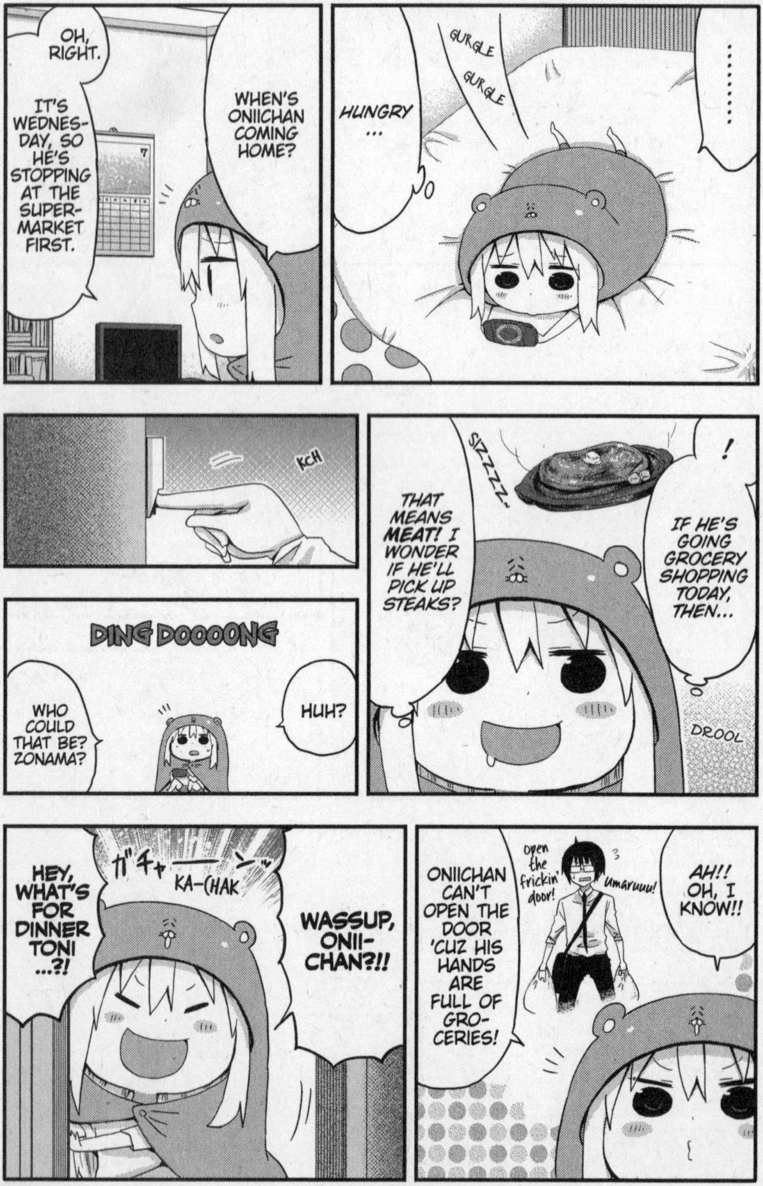

......
GURGLE
GURGLE
HUNGRY ...
WHEN'S ONIICHAN COMING HOME?
OH, RIGHT.
IT'S WEDNES-DAY, SO HE'S STOPPING AT THE SUPER-MARKET FIRST.
!
IF HE'S GOING GROCERY SHOPPING TODAY, THEN...
SIZZZZ
THAT MEANS MEAT! I WONDER IF HE'LL PICK UP STEAKS?
DROOL
KCH
DING DOOOONG
HUH?
WHO COULD THAT BE? ZONAMA?
AH!! OH, I KNOW!!
Umaruuu!
open the frickin' door!
ONIICHAN CAN'T OPEN THE DOOR 'CUZ HIS HANDS ARE FULL OF GRO-CERIES!
WASSUP, ONII-CHAN?!!
ガチャーーン
KA-CHAK
HEY, WHAT'S FOR DINNER TONI ...?!

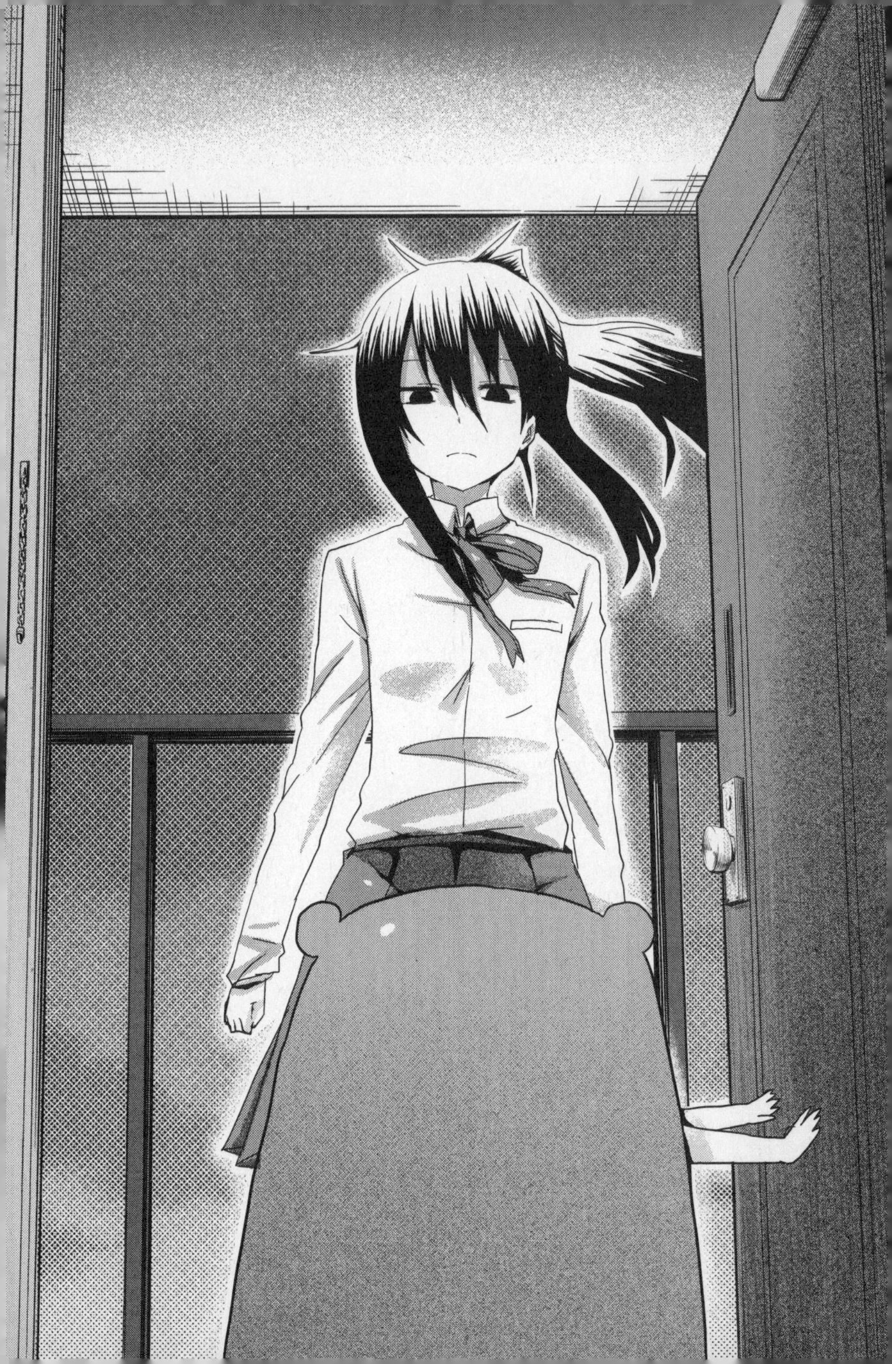

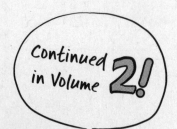

Continued in Volume 2!

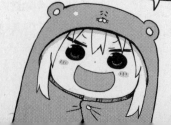

HIMOUTO! UMARU-CHAN

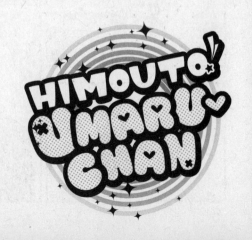

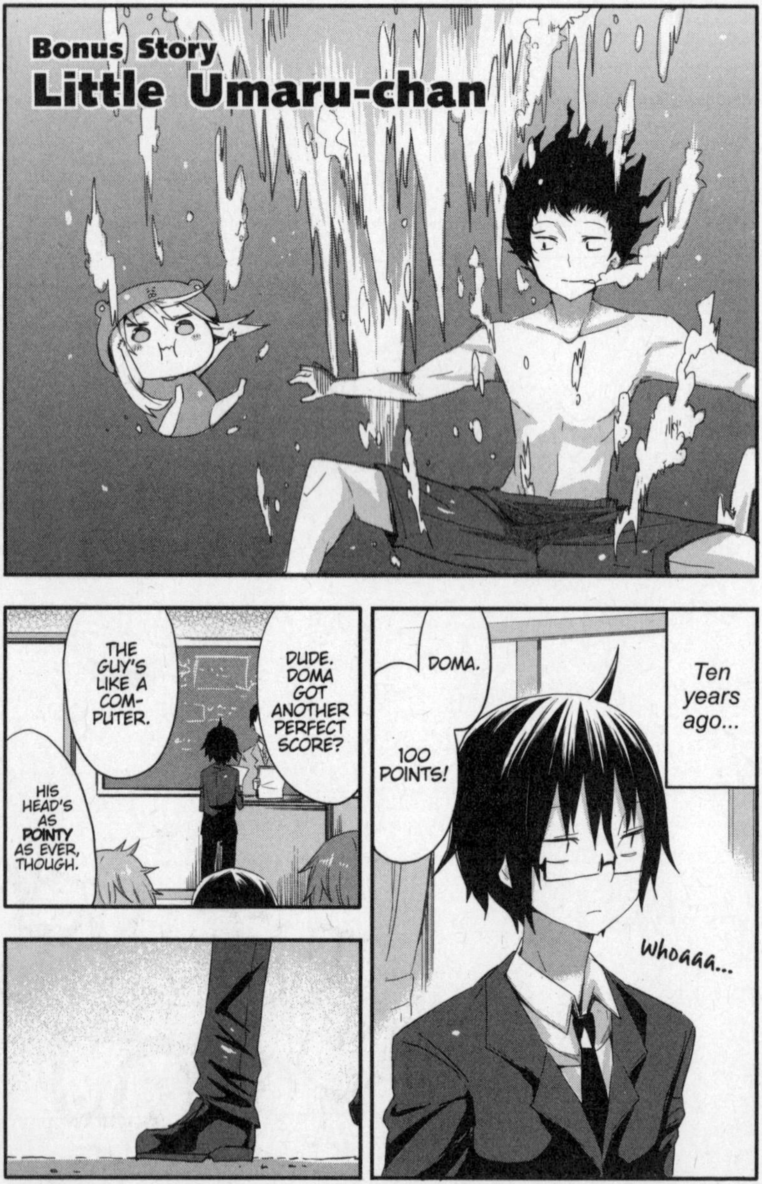
Bonus Story
Little Umaru-chan
Ten years ago...
DOMA.
100 POINTS!
Whoaaa...
DUDE. DOMA GOT ANOTHER PERFECT SCORE?
THE GUY'S LIKE A COMPUTER.
HIS HEAD'S AS POINTY AS EVER, THOUGH.

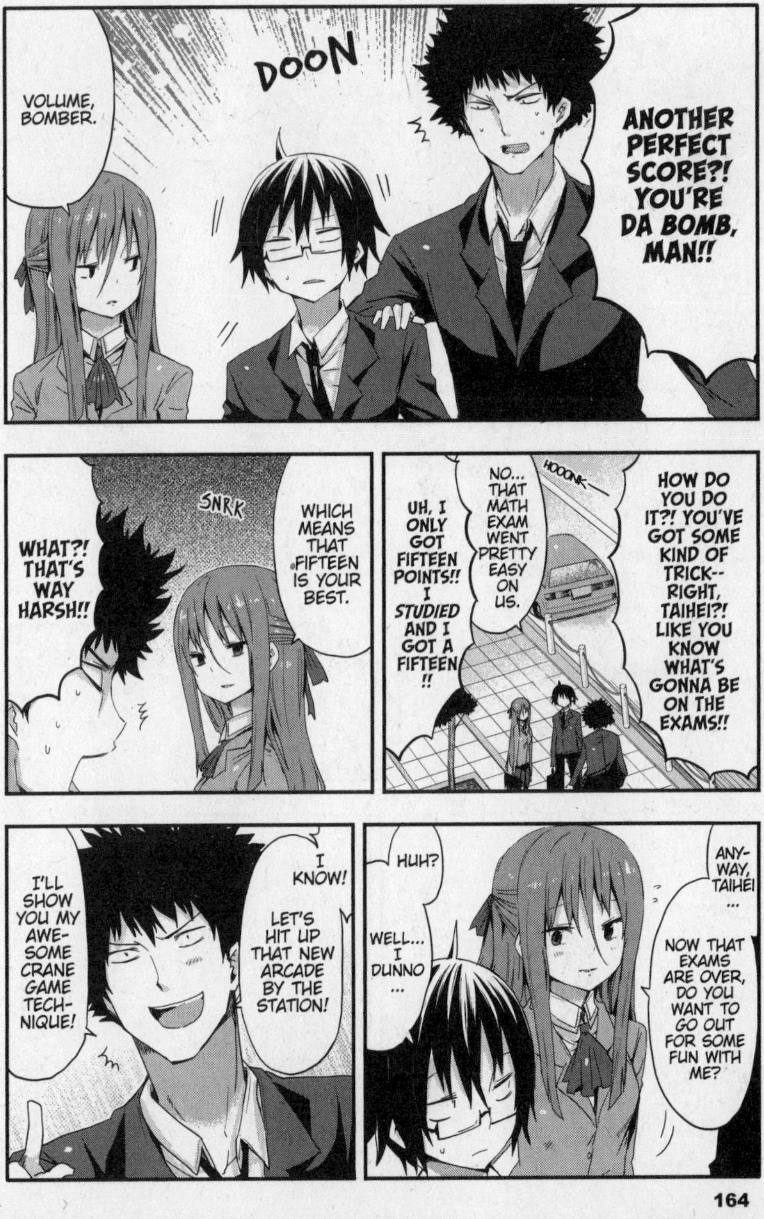
ANOTHER PERFECT SCORE?! YOU'RE DA *BOMB*, MAN!!
DOON
VOLUME, BOMBER.
HOW DO YOU DO IT?! YOU'VE GOT SOME KIND OF TRICK-- RIGHT, TAIHEI?! LIKE YOU KNOW WHAT'S GONNA BE ON THE EXAMS!!
HOOONK
NO... THAT MATH EXAM WENT PRETTY EASY ON US.
UH, I ONLY GOT FIFTEEN POINTS!! I *STUDIED* AND I GOT A FIFTEEN!!
WHICH MEANS THAT FIFTEEN IS YOUR BEST.
SNRK
WHAT?! THAT'S WAY HARSH!!
ANYWAY, TAIHEI...
NOW THAT EXAMS ARE OVER, DO YOU WANT TO GO OUT FOR SOME FUN WITH ME?
HUH?
WELL... I DUNNO...
I KNOW!
LET'S HIT UP THAT NEW ARCADE BY THE STATION!
I'LL SHOW YOU MY AWESOME CRANE GAME TECHNIQUE!

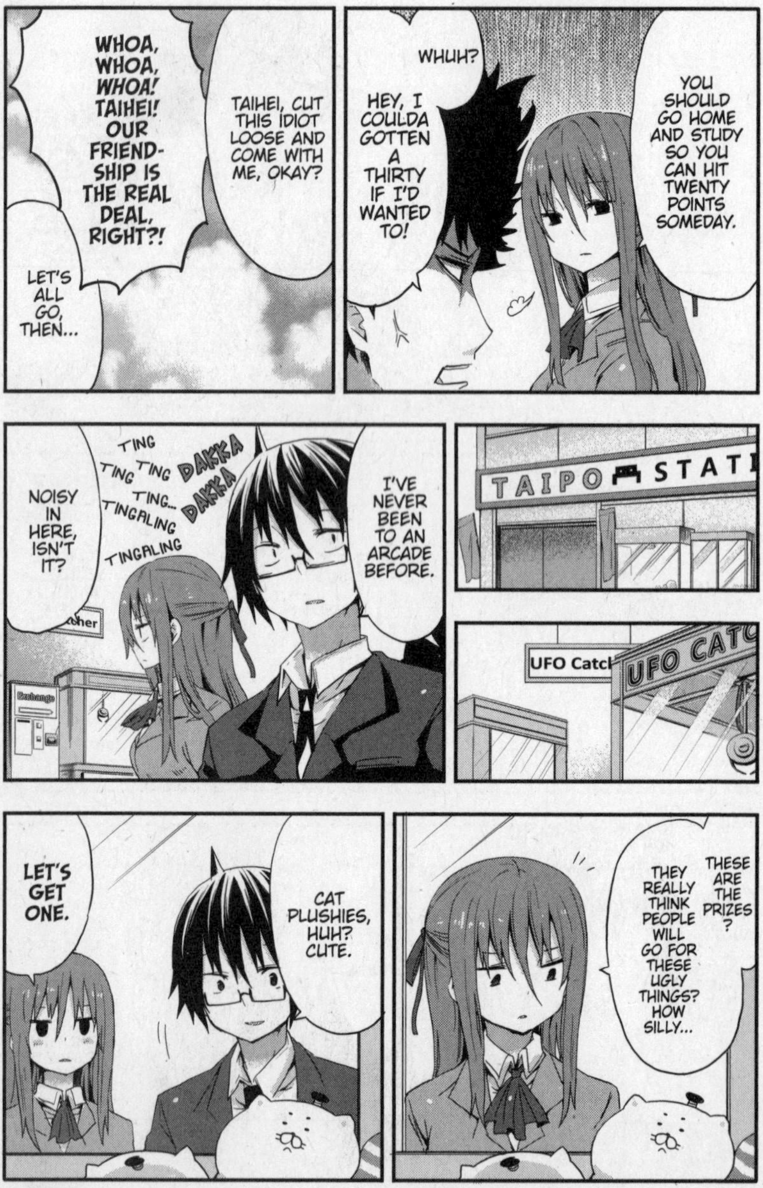
YOU SHOULD GO HOME AND STUDY SO YOU CAN HIT TWENTY POINTS SOMEDAY.
WHUH?
HEY, I COULDA GOTTEN A THIRTY IF I'D WANTED TO!
TAIHEI, CUT THIS IDIOT LOOSE AND COME WITH ME, OKAY?
WHOA, WHOA, WHOA! TAIHEI! OUR FRIEND-SHIP IS THE REAL DEAL, RIGHT?!
LET'S ALL GO, THEN...
TAIPO STATI
UFO Catc
UFO Catcl
I'VE NEVER BEEN TO AN ARCADE BEFORE.
DAKKA DAKKA
TING TING TING TING... TINGALING TINGALING
NOISY IN HERE, ISN'T IT?
Exchange
THESE ARE THE PRIZES?
THEY REALLY THINK PEOPLE WILL GO FOR THESE UGLY THINGS? HOW SILLY...
CAT PLUSHIES, HUH? CUTE.
LET'S GET ONE.

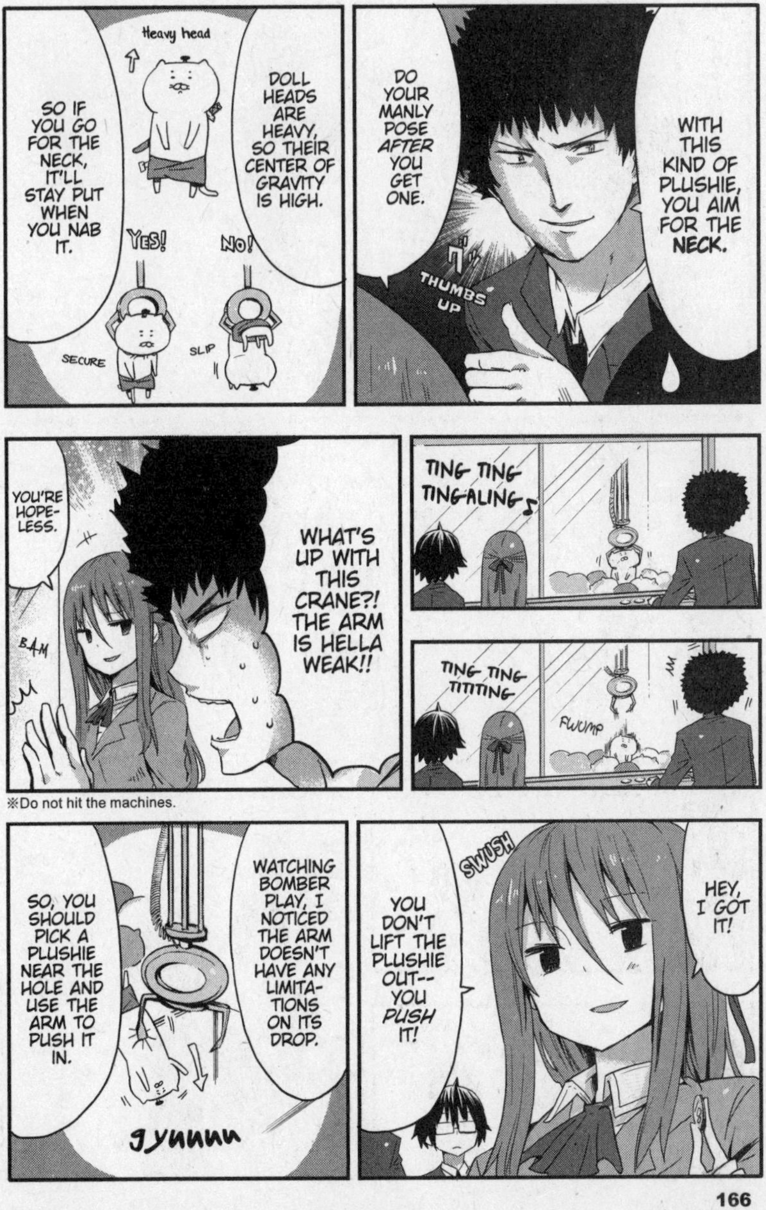
WITH THIS KIND OF PLUSHIE, YOU AIM FOR THE NECK.
THUMBS UP
DO YOUR MANLY POSE AFTER YOU GET ONE.
DOLL HEADS ARE HEAVY, SO THEIR CENTER OF GRAVITY IS HIGH.
Heavy head
SO IF YOU GO FOR THE NECK, IT'LL STAY PUT WHEN YOU NAB IT.
NO!
YES!
SLIP
SECURE
TING TING TINGALING
TING TING TITITING
FWUMP
WHAT'S UP WITH THIS CRANE?! THE ARM IS HELLA WEAK!!
YOU'RE HOPELESS.
BAM
※Do not hit the machines.
HEY, I GOT IT!
SWUSH
YOU DON'T LIFT THE PLUSHIE OUT-- YOU PUSH IT!
WATCHING BOMBER PLAY, I NOTICED THE ARM DOESN'T HAVE ANY LIMITATIONS ON ITS DROP.
SO, YOU SHOULD PICK A PLUSHIE NEAR THE HOLE AND USE THE ARM TO PUSH IT IN.
gyunnn

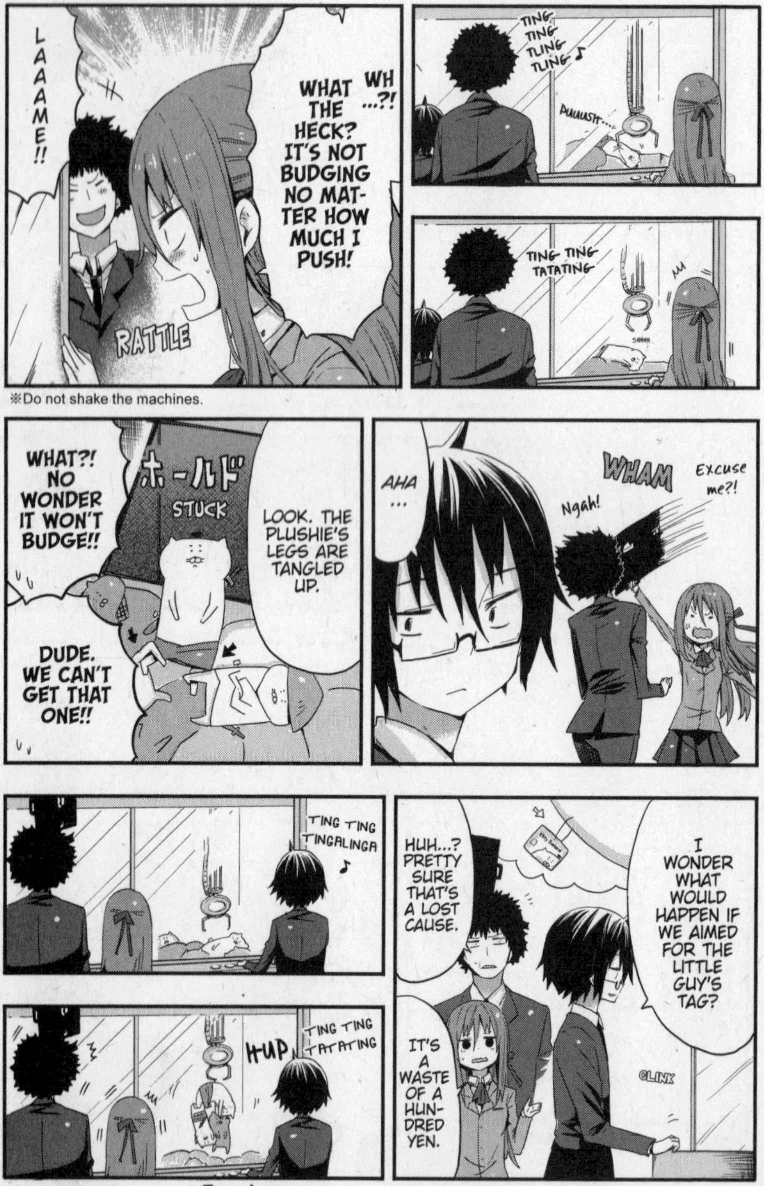
TING, TING TLING TLING ♪
PUUUSH...
TING TING TATATING
WH ...?!
WHAT THE HECK? IT'S NOT BUDGING NO MATTER HOW MUCH I PUSH!
LAAAAME!!
RATTLE
Excuse me?!
WHAM
Ngah!
AHA ...
LOOK. THE PLUSHIE'S LEGS ARE TANGLED UP.
ホールド
STUCK
WHAT?! NO WONDER IT WON'T BUDGE!!
DUDE. WE CAN'T GET THAT ONE!!
I WONDER WHAT WOULD HAPPEN IF WE AIMED FOR THE LITTLE GUY'S TAG?
HUH...? PRETTY SURE THAT'S A LOST CAUSE.
IT'S A WASTE OF A HUNDRED YEN.
CLINK
TING TING TINGALINGA ♪
HUP
TING TING TATATING

※Do not shake the machines.

↑ Three-in-one

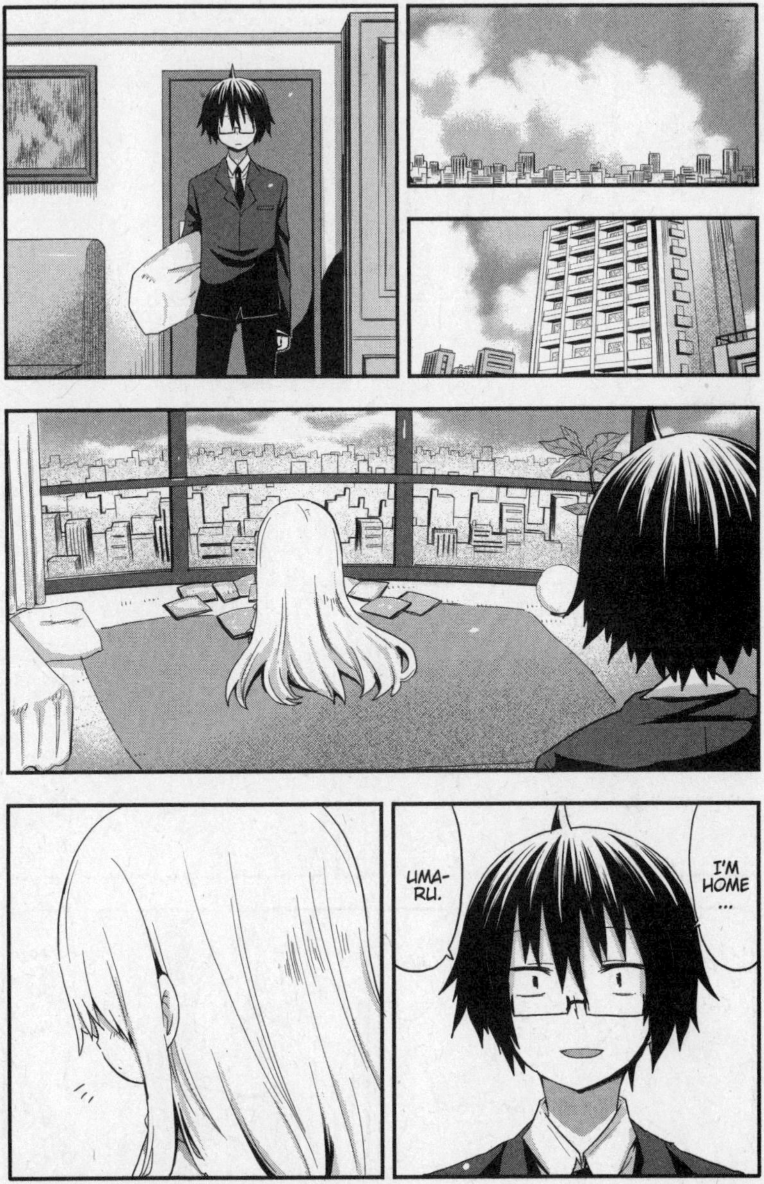
I'M HOME ...
UMA-RU.

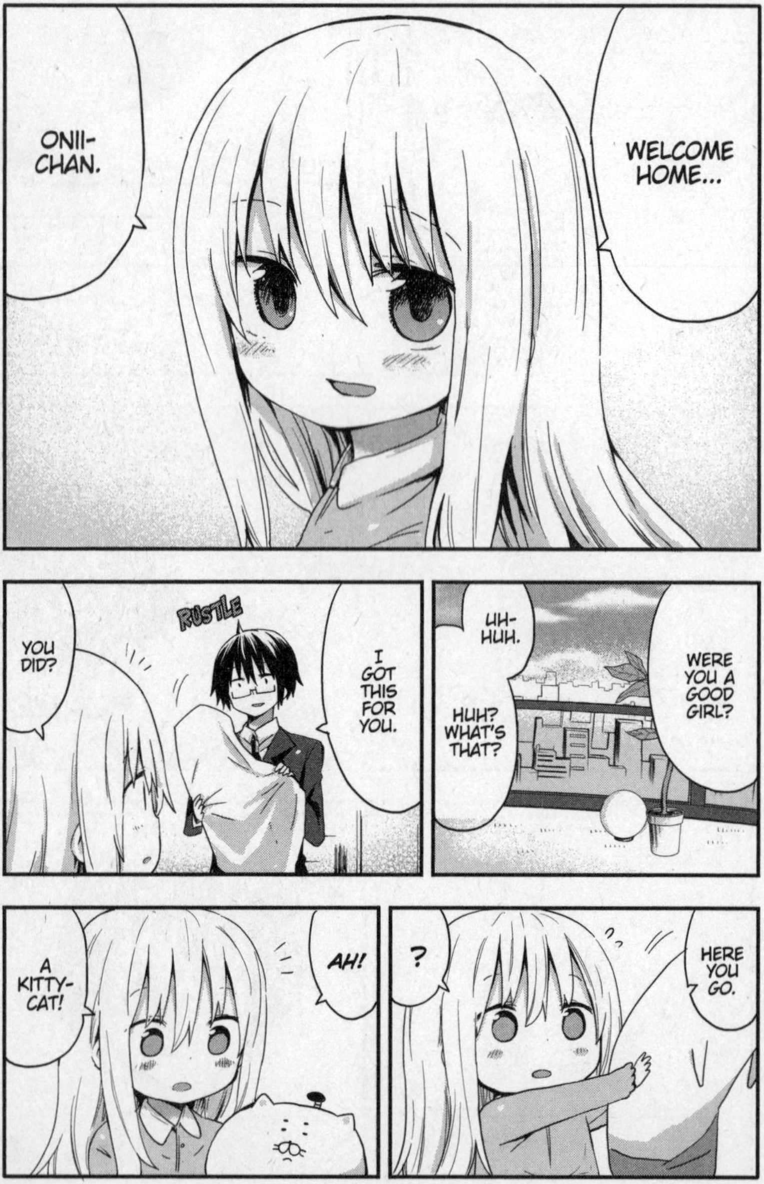
WELCOME HOME...
ONII-CHAN.
WERE YOU A GOOD GIRL?
UH-HUH.
HUH? WHAT'S THAT?
I GOT THIS FOR YOU.
RUSTLE
YOU DID?
HERE YOU GO.
?
AH!
A KITTY-CAT!

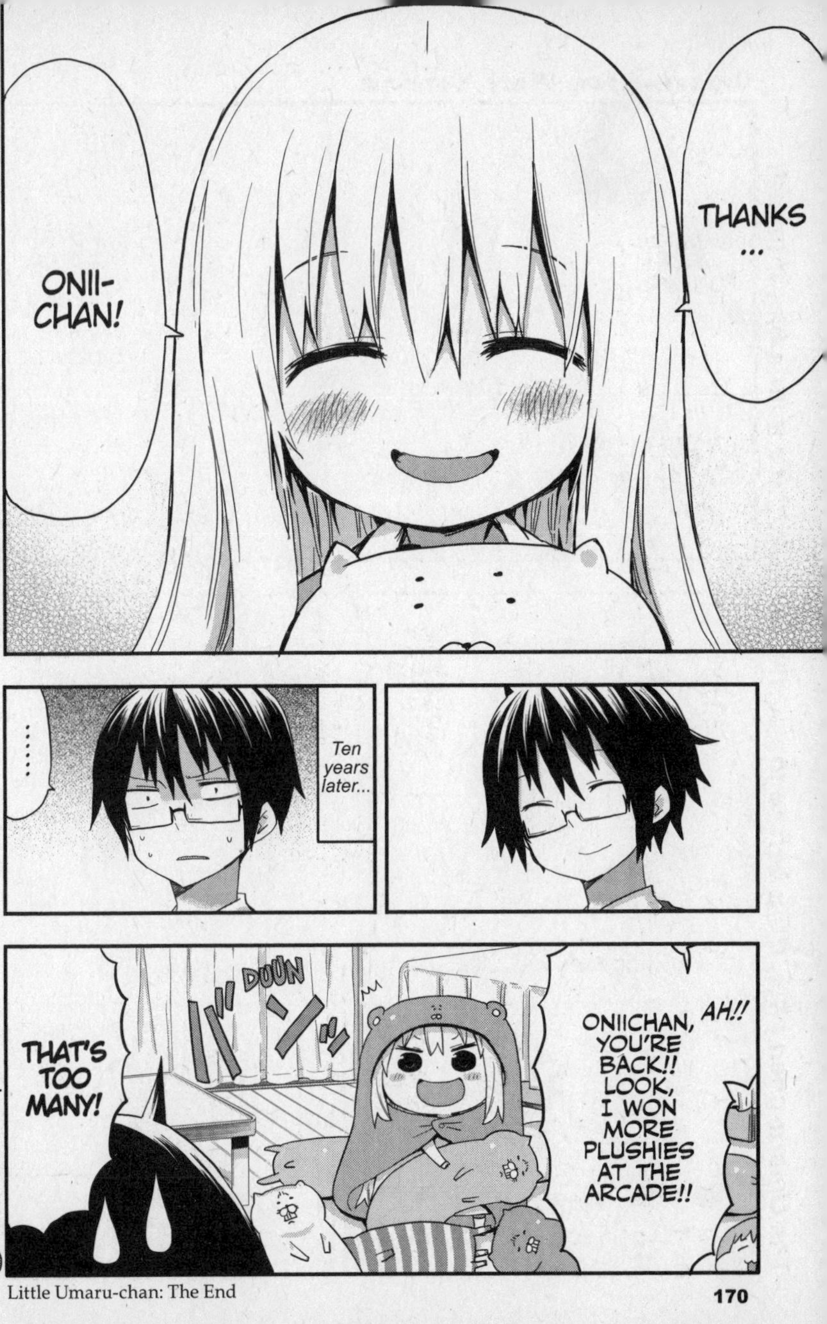
THANKS ...
ONII-CHAN!
Ten years later...
......
AH!!
ONIICHAN, YOU'RE BACK!! LOOK, I WON MORE PLUSHIES AT THE ARCADE!!
DUUN
THAT'S TOO MANY!

Connects to Chapter 12

Little Umaru-chan: The End

Umaru-chan Pilot Version

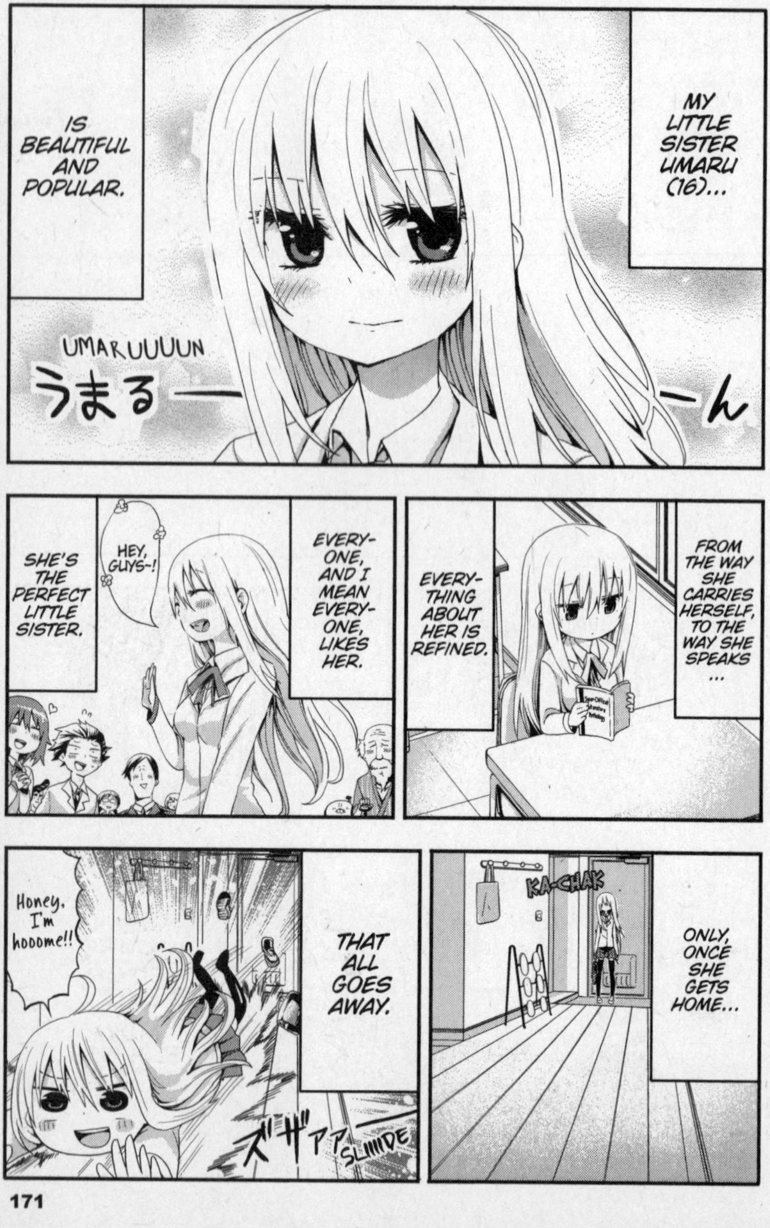
MY LITTLE SISTER UMARU (16)...
IS BEAUTIFUL AND POPULAR.
UMARUUUUN
うまる——ーん
FROM THE WAY SHE CARRIES HERSELF, TO THE WAY SHE SPEAKS...
EVERYTHING ABOUT HER IS REFINED.
EVERYONE, AND I MEAN EVERYONE, LIKES HER.
HEY, GUYS~!
SHE'S THE PERFECT LITTLE SISTER.
ONLY, ONCE SHE GETS HOME...
KA-CHAK
THAT ALL GOES AWAY.
Honey, I'm hooome!!
ズザァァ
SLIIIDE

The Umaru-chan pilot, from before the series ran in YJ!! It's a little bit different!!

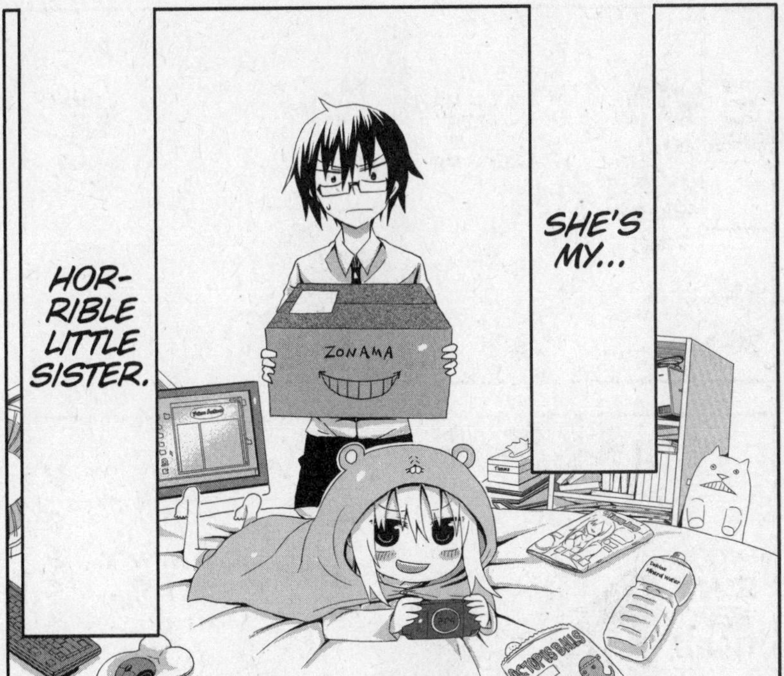
SHE'S MY...
HOR-RIBLE LITTLE SISTER.
ZONAMA
OCTOPUS BALLS
Umaru-chan (Pilot)
No Soliciting

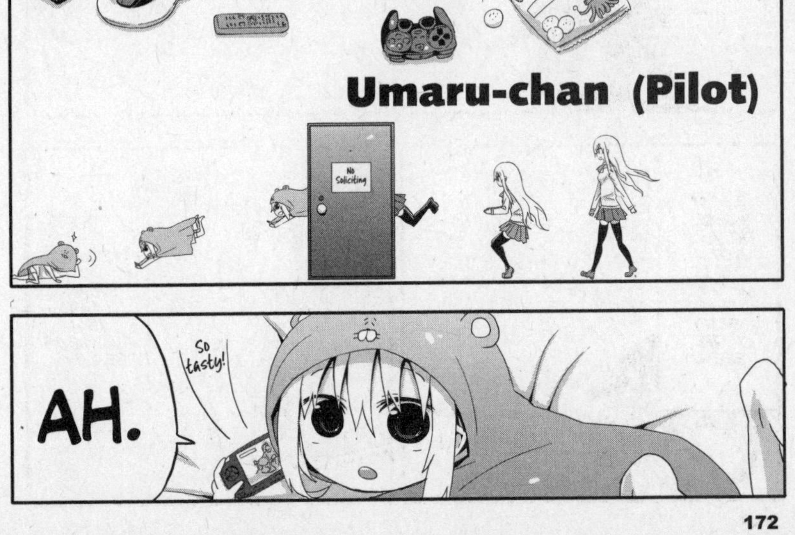
So tasty!
AH.

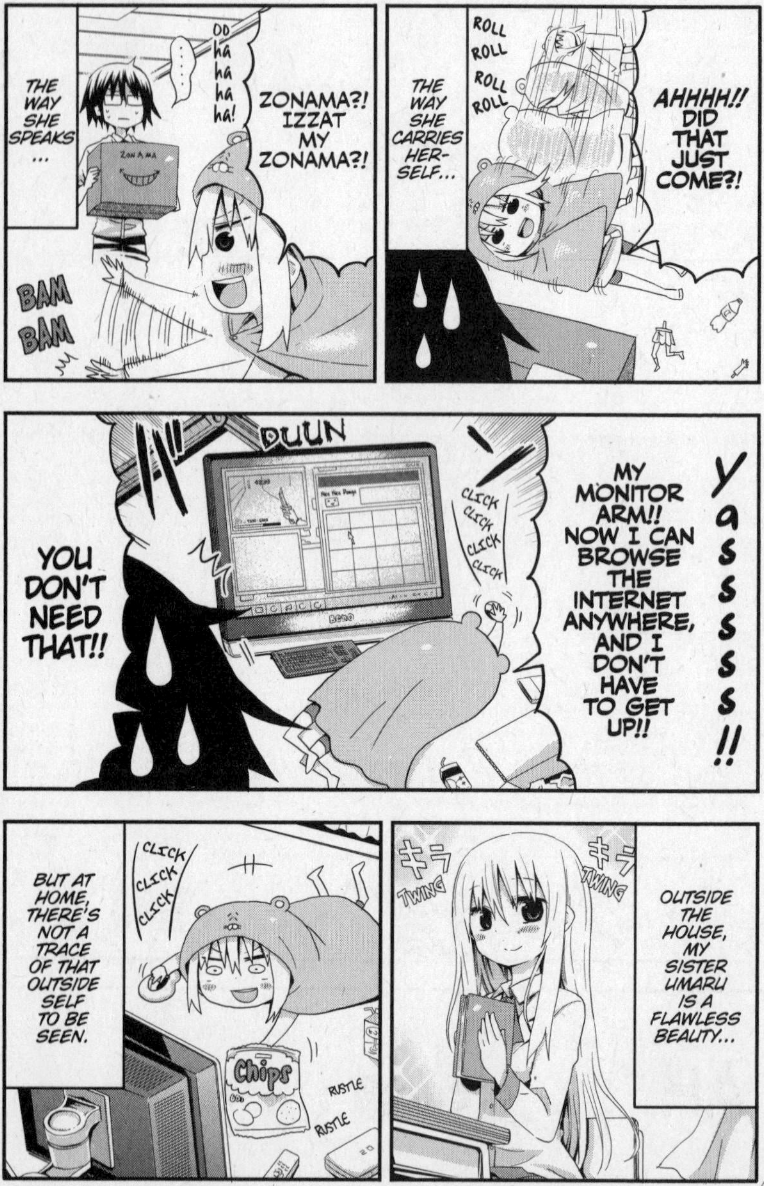
AHHHH!! DID THAT JUST COME?!
ROLL
ROLL
ROLL
ROLL
THE WAY SHE CARRIES HER-SELF...
ZONAMA?! IZZAT MY ZONAMA?!
OO ha ha ha ha ha!
......
THE WAY SHE SPEAKS...
ZONAMA
BAM BAM
Yassss!!
MY MONITOR ARM!! NOW I CAN BROWSE THE INTERNET ANYWHERE, AND I DON'T HAVE TO GET UP!!
CLICK CLICK CLICK CLICK
DUUN
YOU DON'T NEED THAT!!
キラ TWING
キラ TWING
OUTSIDE THE HOUSE, MY SISTER UMARU IS A FLAWLESS BEAUTY...
BUT AT HOME, THERE'S NOT A TRACE OF THAT OUTSIDE SELF TO BE SEEN.
CLICK CLICK CLICK
Chips
RUSTLE
RUSTLE

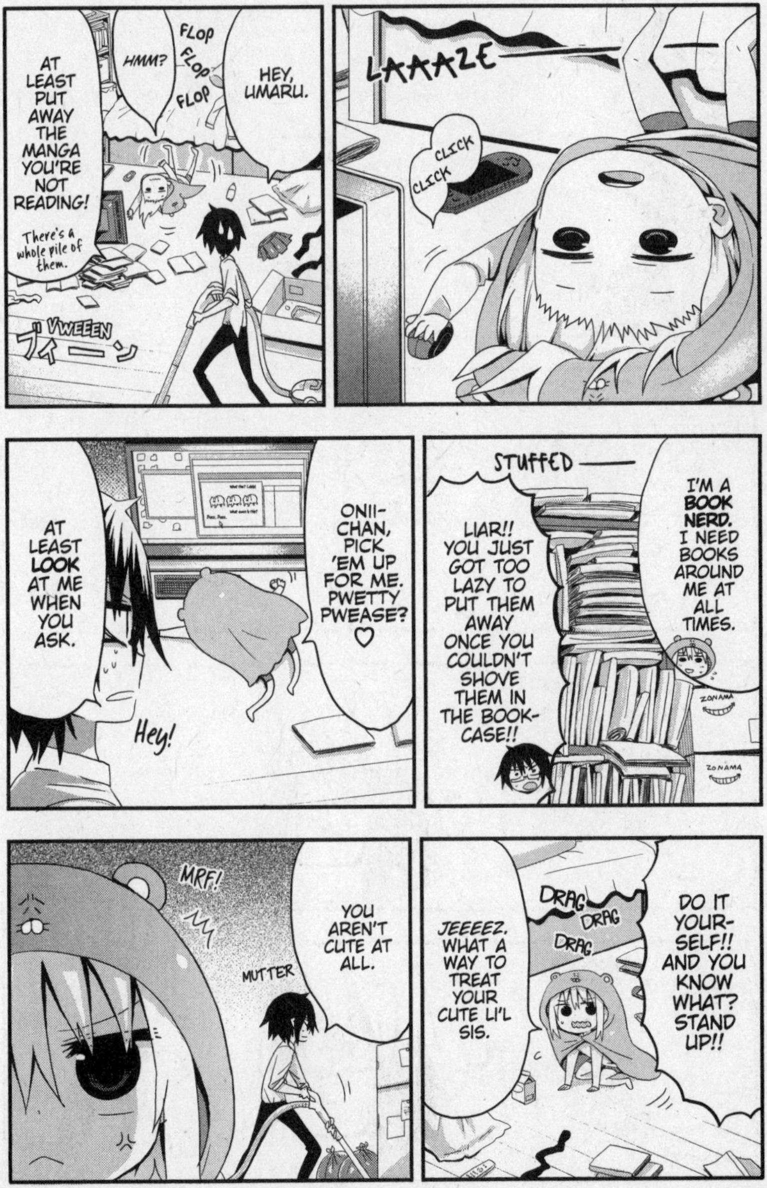

LAAAZE
CLICK CLICK
HEY, UMARU.
FLOP FLOP FLOP
HMM?
AT LEAST PUT AWAY THE MANGA YOU'RE NOT READING!
There's a whole pile of them.
VWEEEN
ヴィーン
STUFFED
I'M A BOOK NERD. I NEED BOOKS AROUND ME AT ALL TIMES.
LIAR!! YOU JUST GOT TOO LAZY TO PUT THEM AWAY ONCE YOU COULDN'T SHOVE THEM IN THE BOOK-CASE!!
ZONAMA
ZONAMA
ONII-CHAN, PICK 'EM UP FOR ME. PWETTY PWEASE? ♡
AT LEAST LOOK AT ME WHEN YOU ASK.
Hey!
DO IT YOURSELF!! AND YOU KNOW WHAT? STAND UP!!
DRAG DRAG DRAG
JEEEEZ. WHAT A WAY TO TREAT YOUR CUTE LI'L SIS.
YOU AREN'T CUTE AT ALL.
MUTTER
MRF!

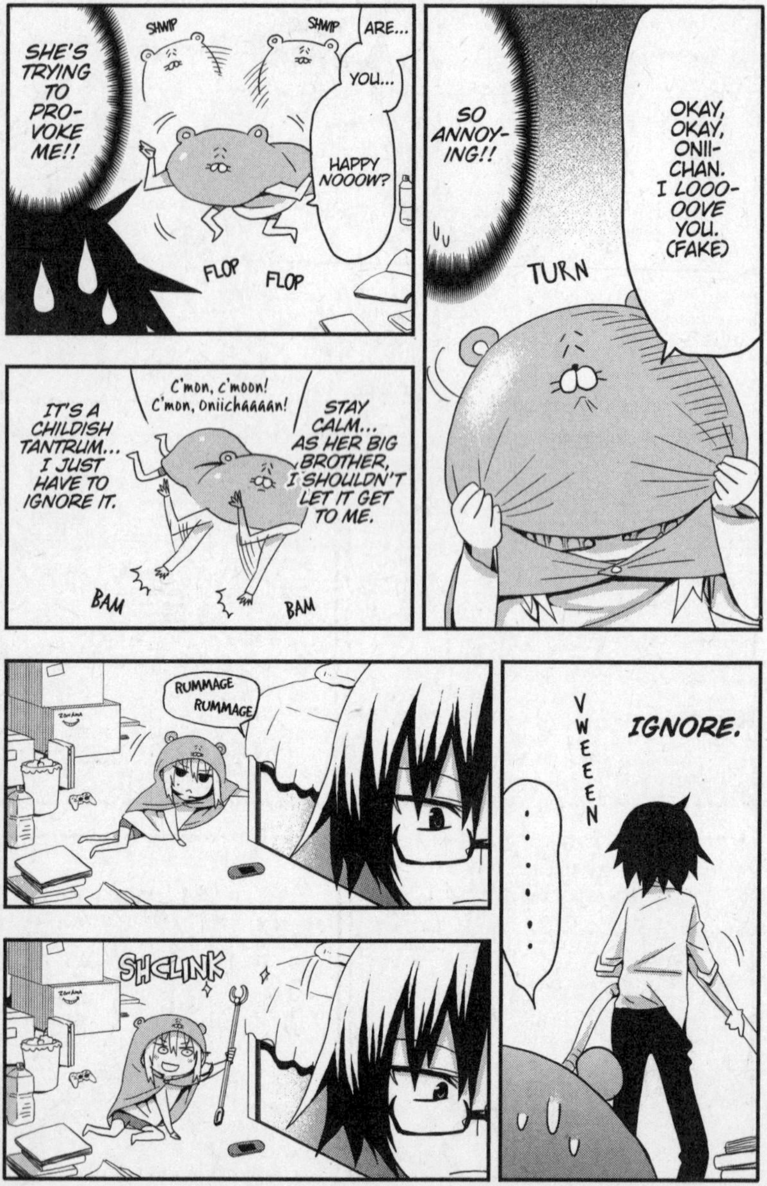

OKAY, OKAY, ONII-CHAN. I LOOO-OOVE YOU. (FAKE)
SO ANNOY-ING!!
TURN
ARE...
YOU...
HAPPY NOOOW?
SHWIP
SHWIP
SHE'S TRYING TO PRO-VOKE ME!!
FLOP
FLOP
STAY CALM... AS HER BIG BROTHER, I SHOULDN'T LET IT GET TO ME.
C'mon, c'moon! C'mon, Oniichaaaan!
IT'S A CHILDISH TANTRUM... I JUST HAVE TO IGNORE IT.
BAM
BAM
IGNORE.
VWEEEN
......
RUMMAGE RUMMAGE
SHCLINK

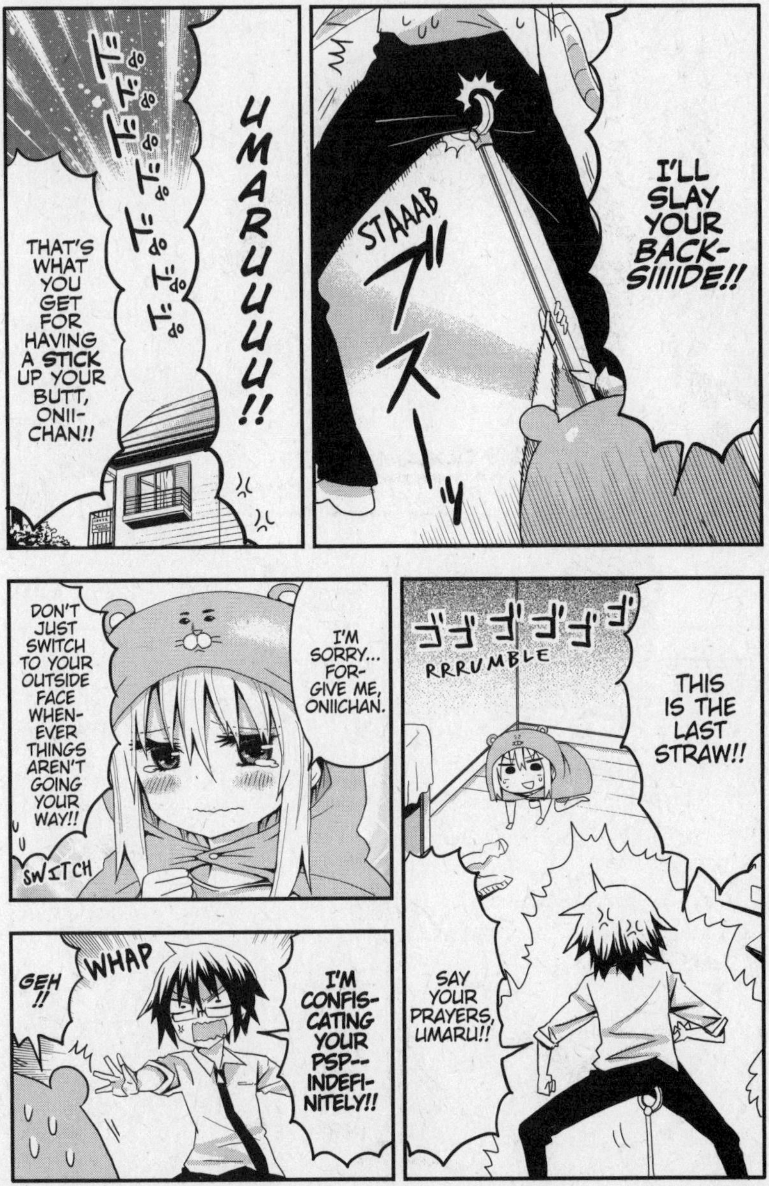
I'LL SLAY YOUR BACK-SIIIIDE!!
STAAAB
ブスーッ
UMARUUUUU!!
THAT'S WHAT YOU GET FOR HAVING A STICK UP YOUR BUTT, ONII-CHAN!!
ゴゴゴゴゴ
RRRUMBLE
THIS IS THE LAST STRAW!!
SAY YOUR PRAYERS, UMARU!!
I'M SORRY... FOR-GIVE ME, ONIICHAN.
DON'T JUST SWITCH TO YOUR OUTSIDE FACE WHEN-EVER THINGS AREN'T GOING YOUR WAY!!
SWITCH
I'M CONFIS-CATING YOUR PSP-- INDEFI-NITELY!!
WHAP
GEH!!

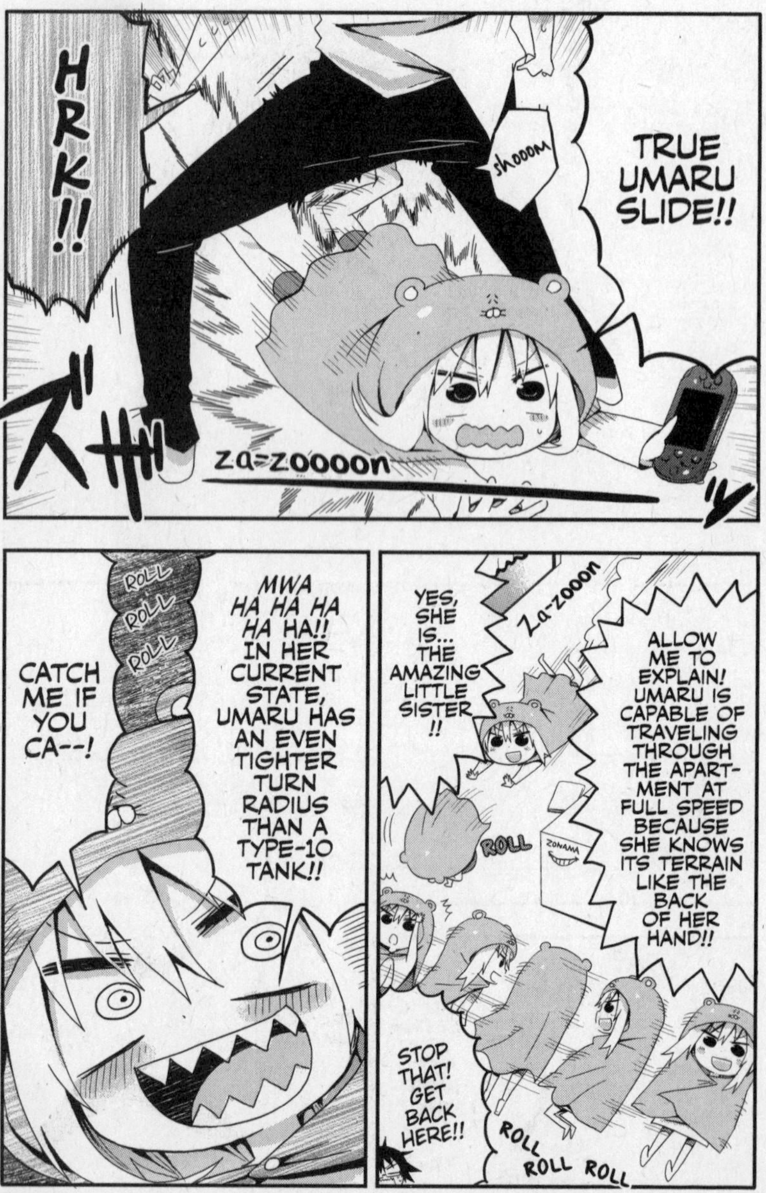
TRUE UMARU SLIDE!!
shooom
HRK!!
za-zoooon
ALLOW ME TO EXPLAIN! UMARU IS CAPABLE OF TRAVELING THROUGH THE APARTMENT AT FULL SPEED BECAUSE SHE KNOWS ITS TERRAIN LIKE THE BACK OF HER HAND!!
Za-zooon
YES, SHE IS... THE AMAZING LITTLE SISTER!!
ROLL
ZONAMA
STOP THAT! GET BACK HERE!!
ROLL ROLL ROLL
MWA HA HA HA HA HA!! IN HER CURRENT STATE, UMARU HAS AN EVEN TIGHTER TURN RADIUS THAN A TYPE-10 TANK!!
ROLL ROLL ROLL
CATCH ME IF YOU CA--!

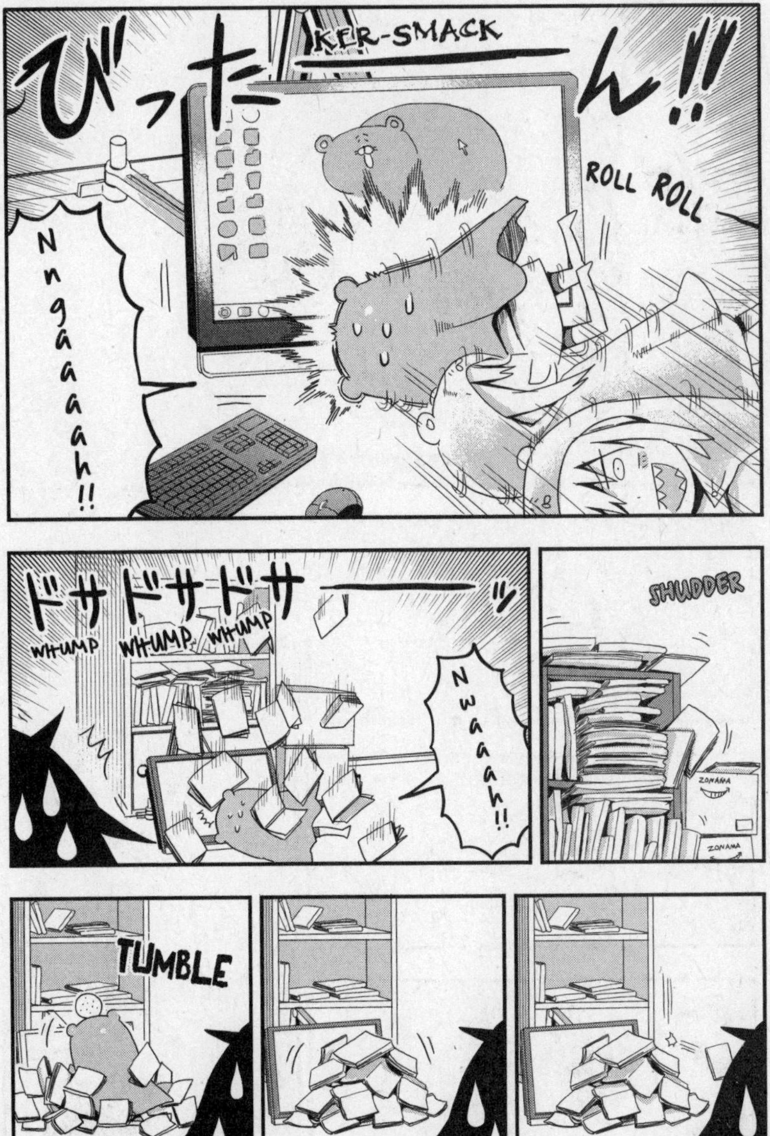

びったーーん!!
KER-SMACK
ROLL ROLL
Nngaaaaaah!!
SHUDDER
ZONAMA
ZONAMA
ドサドサドサーーーッ
WHUMP WHUMP WHUMP
Nwaaaah!!
TUMBLE

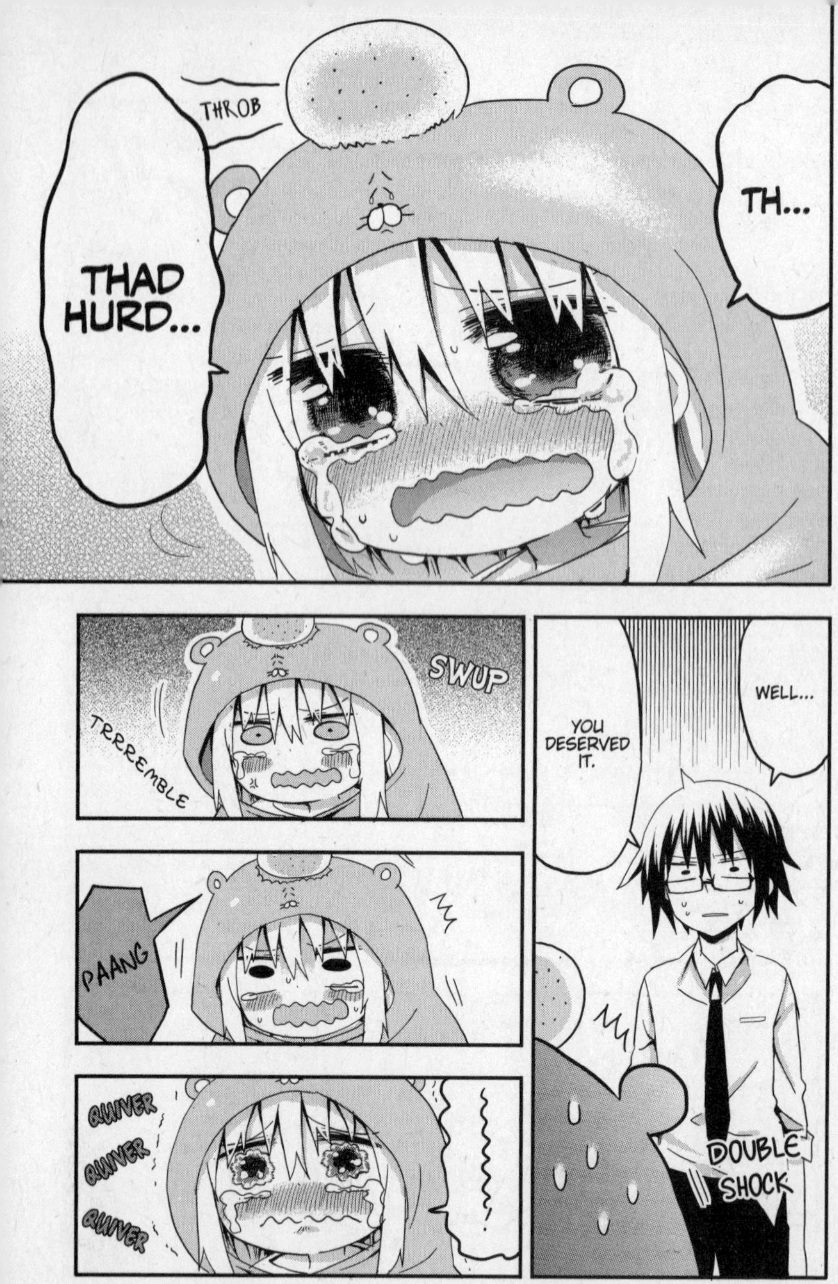
TH...
THROB
THAD HURD...
WELL...
YOU DESERVED IT.
DOUBLE SHOCK
SWUP
TRRREMBLE
PAANG
QUIVER
QUIVER
QUIVER

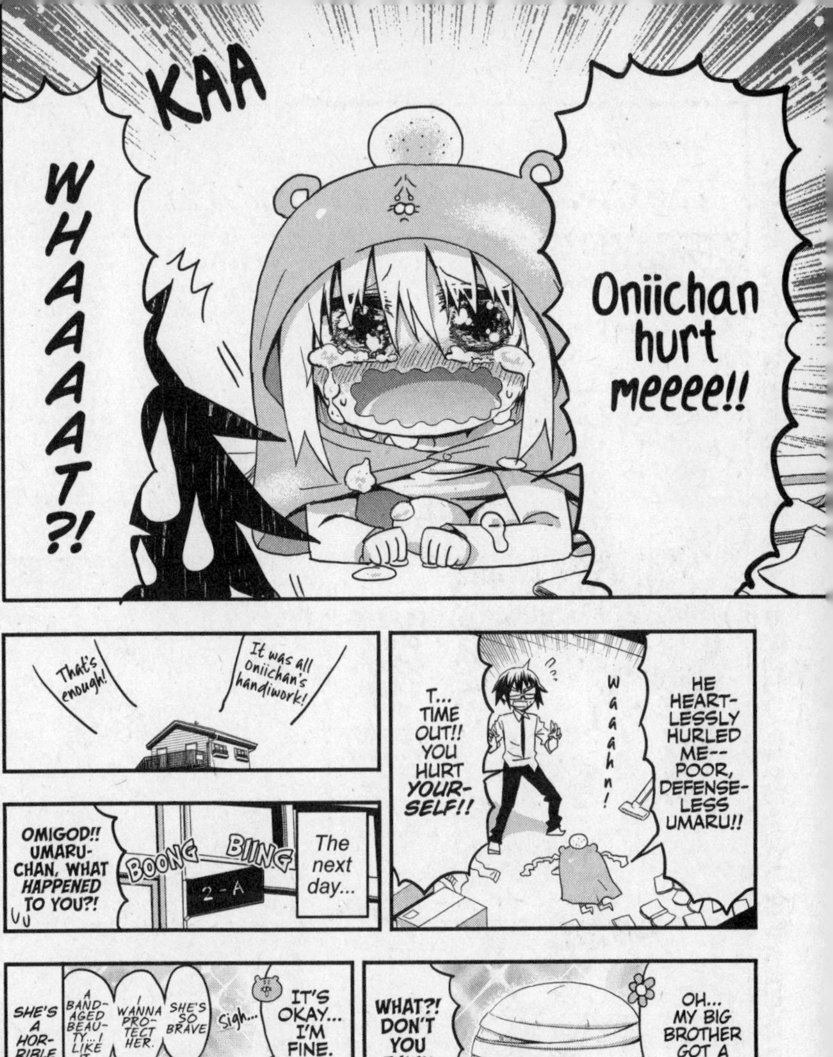

Oniichan hurt meeee!!
KAA
WHAAAAAT?!
HE HEARTLESSLY HURLED ME-- POOR, DEFENSELESS UMARU!!
Waaahn!
T... TIME OUT!! YOU HURT YOURSELF!!
It was all Oniichan's handiwork!
That's enough!
The next day...
2-A
BIING
BOONG
OMIGOD!! UMARU-CHAN, WHAT HAPPENED TO YOU?!
OH... MY BIG BROTHER GOT A LITTLE MAD AT ME...
FIDGET
WHAT?! DON'T YOU THINK HE WENT A BIT FAR?!
FIDGET
IT'S OKAY... I'M FINE.
Sigh...
SHE'S SO BRAVE
I WANNA PROTECT HER.
A BANDAGED BEAUTY... I LIKE IT...
SHE'S A HORRIBLE LITTLE SISTER.
BA-DUMP BA-DUMP

Umaru-chan (Pilot) The End

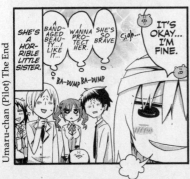

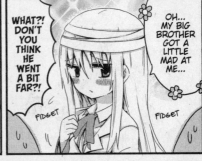

Afterword

The Creation of *Umaru-chan*: Part 1

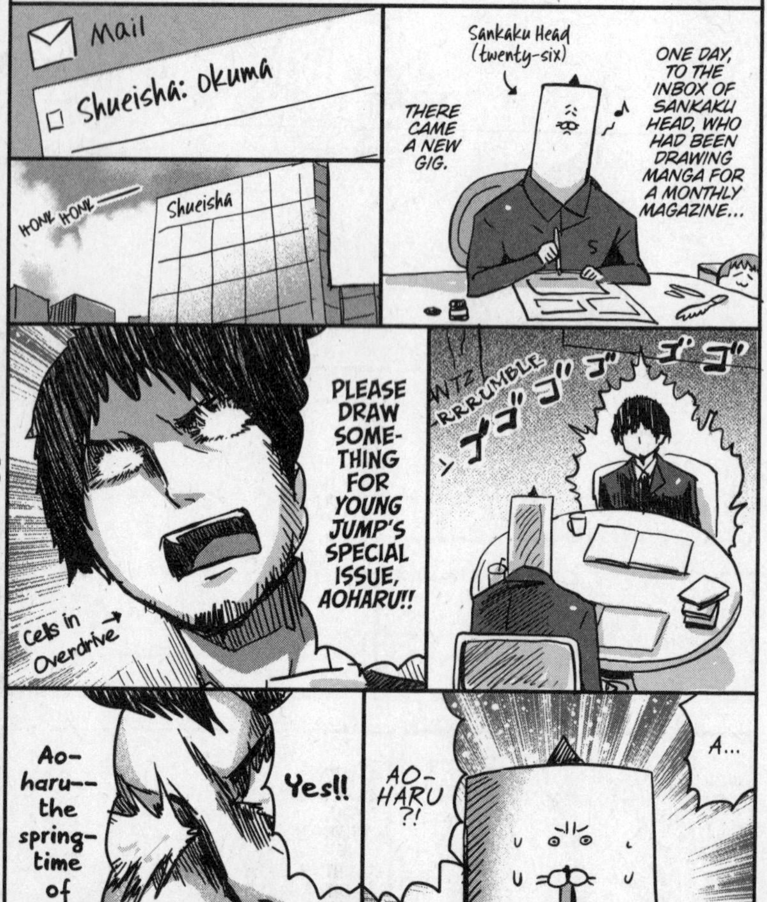

ONE DAY, TO THE INBOX OF SANKAKU HEAD, WHO HAD BEEN DRAWING MANGA FOR A MONTHLY MAGAZINE...
Sankaku Head (twenty-six)
THERE CAME A NEW GIG.
Mail
Shueisha: okuma
Shueisha
HONK HONK
RRRUMBLE
ゴゴゴゴゴゴ
PLEASE DRAW SOME-THING FOR YOUNG JUMP'S SPECIAL ISSUE, AOHARU!!
Cells in Overdrive
A...
AO-HARU?!
Yes!!
Ao-haru--the spring-time of youth!!

This is a long, long afterword detailing the struggle that led to the creation of Umaru-chan!!

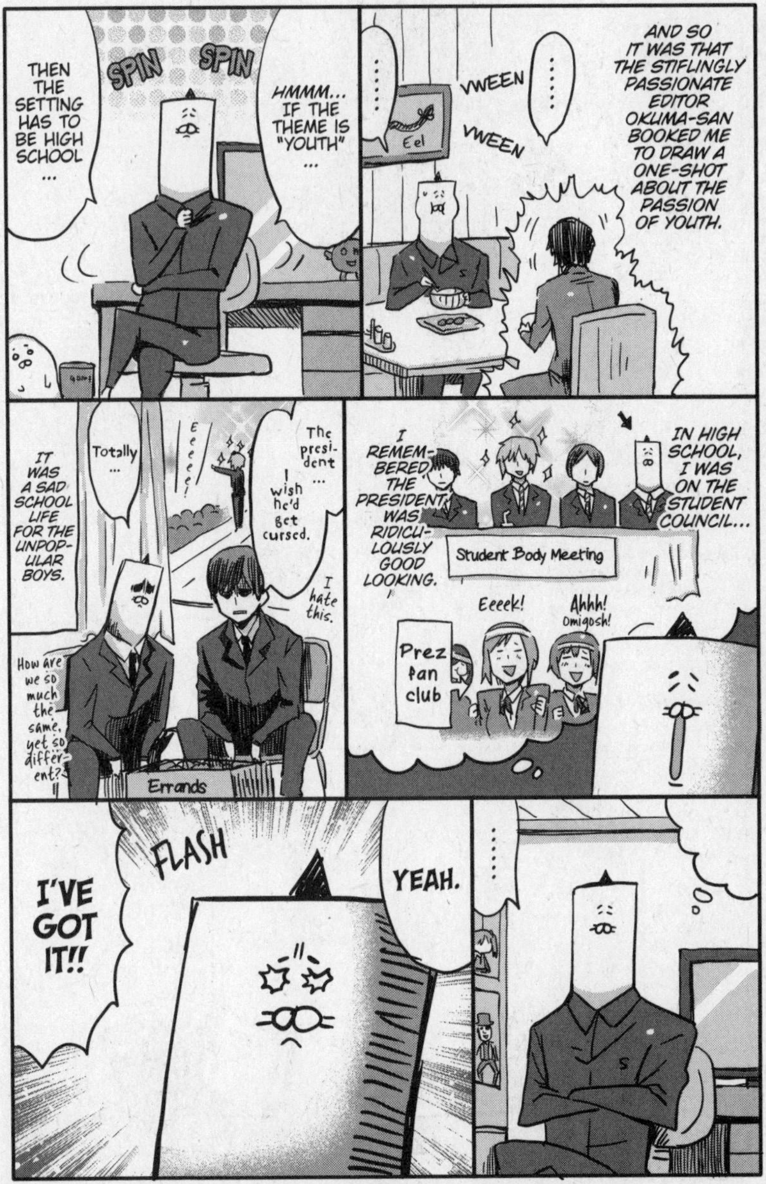
AND SO IT WAS THAT THE STIFLINGLY PASSIONATE EDITOR OKUMA-SAN BOOKED ME TO DRAW A ONE-SHOT ABOUT THE PASSION OF YOUTH.
......
VWEEN
VWEEN
......
Eel
HMMM... IF THE THEME IS "YOUTH" ...
SPIN
SPIN
THEN THE SETTING HAS TO BE HIGH SCHOOL ...
IN HIGH SCHOOL, I WAS ON THE STUDENT COUNCIL...
I REMEMBERED THE PRESIDENT WAS RIDICULOUSLY GOOD LOOKING.
Student Body Meeting
Ahhh! Omigosh!
Eeeek!
Prez fan club
The president ...
I wish he'd get cursed.
Eeeee!
Totally ...
IT WAS A SAD SCHOOL LIFE FOR THE UNPOPULAR BOYS.
I hate this.
How are we so much the same, yet so different?
Errands
......
YEAH.
FLASH
I'VE GOT IT!!

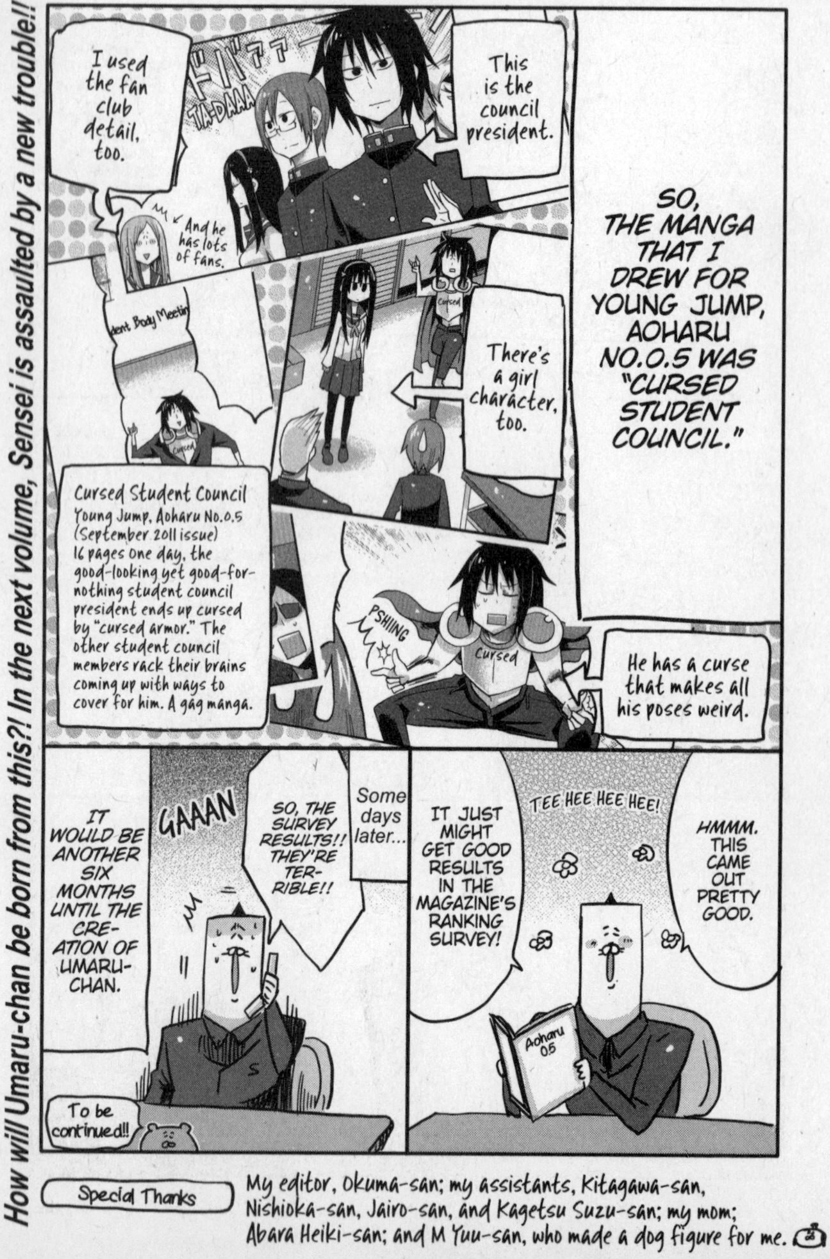
SO, THE MANGA THAT I DREW FOR YOUNG JUMP, AOHARU NO.0.5 WAS "CURSED STUDENT COUNCIL."
This is the council president.
TA-DAAA
I used the fan club detail, too.
And he has lots of fans.
There's a girl character, too.
Cursed
Cursed Student Council
Young Jump, Aoharu No.0.5 (September 2011 issue) 16 pages One day, the good-looking yet good-for-nothing student council president ends up cursed by "cursed armor." The other student council members rack their brains coming up with ways to cover for him. A gag manga.
He has a curse that makes all his poses weird.
PSHING
Cursed
HMMM. THIS CAME OUT PRETTY GOOD.
TEE HEE HEE HEE!
IT JUST MIGHT GET GOOD RESULTS IN THE MAGAZINE'S RANKING SURVEY!
Aoharu 0.5
Some days later...
SO, THE SURVEY RESULTS!! THEY'RE TERRIBLE!!
GAAAN
IT WOULD BE ANOTHER SIX MONTHS UNTIL THE CREATION OF UMARU-CHAN.
To be continued!!

How will Umaru-chan be born from this?! In the next volume, Sensei is assaulted by a new trouble!!

Special Thanks

My editor, Okuma-san; my assistants, Kitagawa-san, Nishioka-san, Jairo-san, and Kagetsu Suzu-san; my mom; Abara Heiki-san; and M Yuu-san, who made a dog figure for me.

SEVEN SEAS ENTERTAINMENT PRESENTS

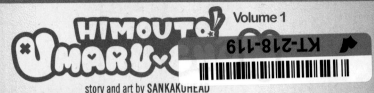

Volume 1

story and art by SANKAKUHEAD

TRANSLATION
Amanda Haley

ADAPTATION
Shanti Whitesides

LETTERING AND RETOUCH
Carolina Hernández Mendoza

COVER DESIGN
Nicky Lim

PROOFREADER
Janet Houck

EDITOR
Jenn Grunigen

PRODUCTION ASSISTANT
CK Russell

PRODUCTION MANAGER
Lissa Pattillo

EDITOR-IN-CHIEF
Adam Arnold

PUBLISHER
Jason DeAngelis

Seven Seas books may be purchased in bulk for promotional, educational, or
business use. Please contact your local bookseller or the Macmillan Corporate
and Premium Sales Department at 1-800-221-7945, extension 5442, or by
e-mail at MacmillanSpecialMarkets@macmillan.com.

Seven Seas and the Seven Seas logo are trademarks of
Seven Seas Entertainment, LLC. All rights reserved.

ISBN: 978-1-626928-81-7

Printed in Canada

First Printing: May 2018

10 9 8 7 6 5 4 3 2

FOLLOW US ONLINE: www.sevenseasentertainment.com

READING DIRECTIONS

This book reads from *right to left*, Japanese style.
If this is your first time reading manga, you start
reading from the top right panel on each page and
take it from there. If you get lost, just follow the
numbered diagram here. It may seem backwards at
first, but you'll get the hang of it! Have fun!!

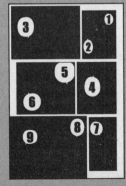